On Becoming a
Woman Leader

JOSSEY-BASS
A Wiley Imprint
www.josseybass.com

On Becoming a Woman Leader

Learning from the Experiences of University Presidents

Susan R. Madsen

Foreword by Reba Keele

BICENTENNIAL
1807
WILEY
2007
BICENTENNIAL

Published by Jossey-Bass
A Wiley Imprint
989 Market Street, San Francisco, CA 94103-1741
www.josseybass.com

Jossey-Bass books and products are available through most bookstores. To contact Jossey-Bass directly call our Customer Care Department within the U.S. at 800-956-7739, outside the U.S. at 317-572-3986, or fax 317-572-4002.

Jossey-Bass also publishes its books in a variety of electronic formats. Some content that appears in print may not be available in electronic books.

Library of Congress Cataloging-in-Publication Data

Madsen, Susan R.
  On becoming a woman leader : learning from the experiences of university presidents / Susan R. Madsen ; foreword by Reba Keele. – 1st ed.
      p.   cm. – (The Jossey-Bass higher and adult education series)
  Includes bibliographical references and index.
  ISBN 978-0-470-19762-2 (cloth)
1. Women college presidents–Case studies.   2. Women college administrators–Case studies.   3. Educational leadership–Case studies.
  I. Title.
  LB2341.M257 2008
  378.1′11082–dc22   2007034026

Printed in the United States of America

FIRST EDITION

HB Printing 10 9 8 7 6 5 4 3 2 1

The Jossey-Bass
Higher and Adult Education Series

Contents

This book is dedicated to my mother (Helen Willden) and my mother-in-law (Peggy Madsen); they have been incredible examples of leadership throughout the years as they have led faithfully in their homes, churches, and communities.

Credits

Parts of Chapter Two were adapted from the following two articles and are printed with permission:

Madsen, S. R. (in-press). Learning to lead in higher education: Insights into the family backgrounds of women university presidents. *The Journal of Women in Educational Leadership*.

Madsen, S. R. (2007). Developing leadership: Exploring the childhoods of women university presidents. *Journal of Educational Administration, 45*(1), 99–118.

Parts of Chapter Five were adapted from the following article and are reprinted with permission:

Madsen, S. R. (2007). Women university presidents: Career paths and educational backgrounds. *Academic Leadership: The Online Journal, 5*(1). Retrieved from http://www.academicleadership.org/emprical_research/.

Parts of the Leadership Training Program section in Chapter Seven were adapted from the following article and are reprinted with permission:

Madsen, S. R., & Turnbull, O. (2006, July). The role of leadership training in the development of women university presidents. *Women in Higher Education, 15*(7), 15–16.

Parts of Chapter Nine were adapted from the following article and are reprinted with permission:

Madsen, S. R. (in-press). Leadership philosophies and styles of women university presidents. *Advancing Women in Leadership Journal.*

Foreword

This book is a groundbreaking, scholarly analysis of the influences and opinions of ten women either currently serving as president or chancellor or who have recently retired. The women are presidents or chancellors of systems, Research I universities, regional comprehensive colleges and universities, teaching institutions, and Historically Black Colleges and Universities (HBCU), both public and private. Dr. Madsen has painstakingly analyzed the data gathered from extensive interviews in order to find themes of differences and similarities.

This may be the definitive work describing the leadership of the generation of women college presidents now between the ages of fifty to mid-sixties. Since they are the leading age of the baby boomers, I expect that this research will be the baseline for studies of women's leadership in postsecondary education as new generations move into place. Because these leaders were greatly affected by societal issues (most were pre-Title IX, for instance), the changing styles of leadership for women should reflect the changes for generations and in society.

Not only does the book explore the leadership principles that guide these ten women's adult lives, but it also documents their lives from childhood on. This allowed Dr. Madsen to explore both the influence of life experiences and the characteristics of individuals that moderated their circumstances. Leadership lessons from diverse college activities, for instance, allow me—as a leadership coach, faculty member, and administrator—to speak more clearly about how to learn from different activities and acknowledge that no single path is essential.

One of the surprises for me in the data is the similarities among such a diverse group, not just in the kinds of learning they drew from different experiences as young people, but also in their leadership styles and philosophies as adults. These women all used their experiences, success or failure, to reflect upon, to learn, and to change their behavior. Relentless self-examination about good and bad experiences was and is the norm for these leaders. Becoming and remaining leaders for these women has demanded honesty about themselves.

As a Regent for the Utah System of Higher Education, I participated in nearly a dozen presidential searches. I have also worked in various settings with many presidents. The leadership differences are both subtle and highly visible. For example, David Pierpont Gardner (former president of the University of California), Gordon Gee (presently leading Vanderbilt University) and Blenda Wilson (former president of California State University at Northridge and founding director of the Nellie Mae Foundation) all faced critical issues and met them in profoundly different ways. The research presented here allows analysts and scholars to discover the core issues of postsecondary leadership and to see the many different situations in which those core issues create success.

One cannot read this book without seeing the theme that some skill sets can be learned in various leadership programs, but many come from very different lifelong learning opportunities. One of the most important learning experiences for these women occurred when they met together with other women presidents in settings where they could speak openly. Male presidents, of course, have always been able to create a support subset of other presidents. Most of these women presidents had male coaches, supporters, and sponsors as they prepared for their positions as president, and they always continued to talk with all of their peers, regardless of gender. However, reaching a critical mass of female presidents has allowed broader discussions, identification of gendered issues, and opportunities for coaching their female peers as well as younger women.

Recently I heard a workshop leader guiding a reflection exercise encouraging women to "plan their legacy." I reflected on how much that sounded like teaching an "edifice complex," in which individuals assume their leadership is judged by buildings, sports, programs to which they put their names, and how much they can dismantle existing successful programs to put their name on them.

The legacy of the presidents studied here is one of realizing that they had the skills to do the job and searching for an organization with a mission they supported where their gifts could advance that mission. They see themselves as good at what they do, and what they do is use their skills to make their institution and higher education better. They did not "plan their legacies." They recognized and seized opportunities, choosing institutions they cared about. Anyone involved in leadership programs should read this book carefully to understand what can be taught and what cannot, as well as what is personal and what is not.

In a world of entitlement, postsecondary education is rivaled only by health care with its focus on rank and its privileges. The "planning of legacies" has become more common, and more postsecondary leaders are plotting career paths in much the same way that CEO's of large businesses do. Opinions differ about the consequences to the quality of postsecondary institutions. The women in this research model a different path, one that needs to be emulated by future leaders.

These women knew they had leadership abilities. They learned to persist, to welcome success, and to learn from failure. Most important to me was that they knew from their early years that service to honorable goals was the highest good. Their paths were very different, and they ended up leading very different kinds of institutions. Yet their end goal grew from their search for the best place from which they could serve.

This research comes at a crossroad for postsecondary education in the United States. Fewer students are attending and finishing college, especially young men. The ways in which postsecondary education has evaluated its outcomes, accredited itself, and used government funds is being questioned. Many faculty, staff, and administrators contribute to the worsening of our problems in society by insisting upon entitlement, resisting accountability, and forgetting the purposes originally articulated for higher education. I was heartened to read this book and to better understand how different experiences and very different people can contribute to society in very important ways when their search is for using their gifts and skills to make a positive difference. May the studies of the next set of women leaders continue to give us hope.

Reba Keele, Ph.D.
Emerita Professor of Management and Organizational
Behavior, University of Utah
Former Utah System of Higher Education Regent
Senior Faculty Member in the HERS leadership program

Preface

A number of years ago I was asked to speak on the development of high-level women leaders in higher education. As I started to look for related resources (articles and books) I discovered that there was very little written on this topic. I expanded my search to include the development of high-level women leaders in any setting and still did not find much in-depth, helpful information. In fact, most of what I found was not based on scholarly research. Yet the topic of leadership development is in high demand in higher education, government, and business. There seems to be a fascination regarding the development of leaders who have attained some of the highest leadership positions, such as that of a university president. Because we know that the development of leadership skills and abilities takes place throughout one's life, the lifetime development of high-level leaders is of particular interest. And since there are so few women in these positions, their development (until now) has remained a mystery.

After reviewing the literature, it became clear that there is a need for published work (based on scholarly research) that explores the experiences of high-level women leaders in developing the knowledge, skills, and competencies that have helped them obtain and maintain positions of influence in higher education. In response to this need, I designed a qualitative study and obtained the funding needed to conduct this kind of research. In the spring and summer of 2005 I traveled to the offices of ten U.S. women university presidents for two- to three-hour in-depth interviews. This book will share the findings of this study.

Chapter One introduces the topic and research study this book is based upon. I first discuss the purpose of the book and the audiences that have already shown interest in the results of the study. I talk about the applicability of this research in a variety of settings and for various segments of the population. Readers are challenged to study and reflect on the contents of this book not only for their personal growth but also to obtain ideas that will help others develop into the kind of leaders that will truly make a difference for communities and society. I then share a glimpse into my own personal interest and journey related to this topic and research study. Next I provide some details regarding the research background and methods used in the study, and then introduce the anonymous presidents by providing some basic collective demographic information. The chapter concludes with a short discussion of the need for this work in the higher educational arena.

Chapter Two brings to light the notion that childhood is an important time to analyze and understand in any individual's development. During the interviews I asked the women to talk about their family influences, such as home environments, siblings, and parents. I also wanted to understand their childhood personalities, school activities, extracurricular activities, influential individuals, significant events, and even the challenges and opportunities that they believed may have influenced the development of leadership skills and abilities. This chapter uncovers and discusses some interesting insights about the women university presidents' families and childhoods. I was able to identify some striking similarities and unexpected differences in the data.

Chapter Three discusses the adolescent years of the presidents, which are notably an incredibly important developmental time for all individuals. This is a vital time for young women to develop confidence and self-esteem, learn new skills and competencies, discover strengths and weaknesses, and increase their understanding of self and environment. During my interviews with the ten university presidents, each woman spoke in detail about her adolescent personality, schooling, activities, leadership positions, employment, influential individuals, significant events, opportunities, awards, recognitions, college plans, and goals. The women described how these experiences influenced their own development of leadership skills and competencies. It became clear that this stage in the presidents' lives was a dynamic time full of positive and negative experiences, challenges, and opportunities that all seem to have had a significant impact on their future development and decisions.

Chapter Four covers discussions I had with these women university presidents about the development of leadership during their college years. The chapter shows that some of the same themes that emerged during childhood and adolescence continued to surface during young adulthood. It addresses the influential individuals and valuable developmental experiences these women had during these years and shares the president's insights into what may have influenced their leadership development, decisions, and perspectives. The women were driven to develop leadership skills and were continually putting themselves in situations where they could learn to overcome the natural fear of new experiences and challenges. The ten presidents' college years were also a significant time in taking critical steps forward in learning to know and understand themselves.

Chapters Five, Six, Seven, and Eight focus on adulthood experiences of the women leaders. Each chapter spans their full adulthood, from their first professional jobs to their current positions, and focuses on one major category of their leadership development. Chapter Five traces and discusses the presidents' career paths and barriers, and offers their responses relating to how each position helped them develop leadership skills and competencies. Also discussed are the barriers or obstacles they faced throughout their professional career, with particular attention to obtaining and securing new positions and promotions. Chapter Six provides details about a wide range of individuals who influenced these women throughout their careers. This chapter focuses on influential individuals specifically in the presidents' own work environments by discussing general influences and issues followed by sections on faculty colleagues, peers, superiors, and others. Chapter Seven highlights a variety of development activities that the presidents believed were particularly beneficial for them. More specifically it discusses the development they received from work-related professional positions and assignments, leadership training programs, professional organization involvement, and work-related challenges. Chapter Eight provides insight into how these women were able to strengthen leadership competencies from the non-work-related aspects of their lives. These include their experiences and insights related to marriage, family, friends, motherhood, personal difficulties, and community involvement.

Chapter Nine presents information on the presidents' leadership motivations, styles, and philosophies. I asked the women at various times throughout the interviews why they accepted or sought out informal and formal leadership roles. I analyzed each woman's responses to discover the themes and then compared the multiple responses among all ten participants. The top nine motivations for leading are presented in this chapter. I also highlight their responses with descriptions and examples to my inquiry about their leadership styles. Finally, to look deeper into these presidents' ideas of leadership, I asked them to respond to questions about their own leadership philosophies. An analysis of their responses resulted in the generation of six primary themes: (1) hiring the right people and firing the wrong, (2) power and empowerment, (3) ethics, honesty, and openness, (4) developing and supporting others, (5) collaboration and teamwork, and (6) creating a vision and making a difference. Each of these themes is discussed in this chapter.

Finally, at the conclusion of each research interview, I asked the presidents what leadership development advice they would offer to other girls and women. Chapter Ten presents the information I obtained from this inquiry and conveys their advice and perspective. The chapter also shares their personal feelings and experience regarding the position of a university president or chancellor in higher education. Therefore this concluding chapter focuses on two broad areas: presidential advice and presidential perspectives.

The development of effective leaders is a critical topic within higher education. In fact, developing leaders is one of the top challenges in higher education today. The importance of and interest in this topic continues to increase. Efforts in all arenas are now being made (often mandated) to help women develop the competencies necessary to move into upper-level management and leadership positions. Therefore, to help prepare future leaders it is important that a variety of constituencies have a deeper understanding of the types of things that were most helpful in the development of past women leaders throughout various stages of their lives. Possible constituencies may include K–12 leaders and educators, postsecondary leaders and educators, parents, immediate and extended family members, high school and college/university counselors, human resource leaders and staff, corporate leaders and employees, government leaders and employees, nonprofit leaders and employees, community members, junior high and high school students, and college students. This book provides some important insights into this "deeper understanding" of which I speak.

Acknowledgments

I am grateful for the support and encouragement of many colleagues. Reba Keele has been a wonderful friend and colleague. Her experience in the area of women's leadership in higher education has been invaluable and her insights priceless. Shauna Peterson and Janice Gygi have provided critical perspectives and practical implications. I would also like to acknowledge Scott Hammond, Doug Miller, and Jim Fenton for their continuous support and encouragement. Their confidence in my ability and potential has been humbling.

I would also like to recognize my husband and children for their support, encouragement, and enduring patience.

And to the presidents who willingly participated in this study, reviewed manuscripts, and provided feedback and encouragement—thank you.

And finally I would like to acknowledge those who provided travel funding and support for the interviews: Utah Valley State College Presidential Scholarship fund, C. Charles Jackson Foundation, School of Business Dean's Office at Utah Valley State College, and the Woodbury Family Endowment.

The Author

Susan R. Madsen is a leadership and change researcher, scholar, educator, and practitioner. She is currently an associate professor of management and has also been an independent management consultant for over sixteen years. She has done both research and consulting in a multitude of settings, including higher education, government, nonprofit, and corporate. Her work is widely published in academic journals, and she presents nationally and internationally at academic and nonacademic conferences, workshops, lectures, and seminars. She holds a doctorate degree in work, community, and family education with a specialization in human resource development from the University of Minnesota; an M.S. from Portland State University in exercise science/wellness, and a B.A. in speech communication education (secondary) from Brigham Young University. She has taught in higher educational institutions since 1991, including Utah Valley University, Brigham Young University, University of Minnesota, and various community colleges.

Through the years Susan Madsen's research has focused on leadership, work-life issues, individual and organizational change, academic service learning, and strategic faculty development. She has received numerous teaching and research awards at her institution, within her state, and within her academic professional organizations. She serves on the editorial board of a Sage journal (*Advances in Developing Human Resources)* and is a guest editor for a 2007 issue on work-life integration. She is also currently serving as the chair and administrator of her campus IRB and is a special assistant to the dean for strategic initiatives. Other roles include various appointments within her academic professional organizations and within her community.

Susan lives in Highland, Utah with her husband and four teenage children. She enjoys playing racquetball and soccer and has been a coach for many years. She loves the western mountains and is actively involved in her community and church.

On Becoming a Woman Leader

Part I
Youth

1

Introduction

Blessed is the leader who seeks the best for those he serves.

Unknown

This book is about the lifetime development of ten strong, interesting, and competent women leaders. It shares experiences, stories, and insights into how they developed the knowledge, skills, and abilities throughout their lives to become the university presidents they are today. It describes commonalities and differences among these women. It is intended to help you (the reader) reflect upon your own life and consider possible meanings and implications.

I have shared the results of this research with many audiences, old and young, women and men, in higher education and in business. The interest of so many individuals with such varied backgrounds, positions, and current responsibilities reflects the broad application of this research. These have included

- College students

- Community members

- Corporate leaders and employees

- Family members (aunts, uncles, siblings, grandparents)

- Government leaders and employees

- High school and college/university counselors

- Human resource leaders and staff (business, government, nonprofit, and education)

- Junior high and high school students

- K–12 leaders and educators

- Nonprofit leaders and employees

- Parents

- Postsecondary leaders and educators

Not only has each group acknowledged these leadership attributes across organizational boundaries, but each has contributed important insights.

Leadership is no longer simple. It is a "partnership between the leader and his or her followers where together you discover the best of all of you" (university president participant). As one of the ten presidents in this study explained, "Leadership today must address greater complexities at multiple levels than in past generations." Leaders must listen more than ever before. One woman stated, "You have to hear the people, and you can only do that if you are quiet enough to listen to what they are saying." Leadership challenges now, as one participant explained, "intertwine and reach beyond a single community to touch communities across the entire planet." Preparing for this type of leadership is a critical endeavor for all who are up to the challenge. In today's society, we cannot be comfortable with preparing only a selected few for leadership. We need individuals who can lead in every facet of life (home, church, schools, nonprofits, government, business, and community). We should encourage all individuals to develop effective leadership skills.

Reading leadership books and attending leadership seminars and conferences has become a favorite pastime for millions of students, parents, workers, entrepreneurs, supervisors, managers, executives, administrators, board members, and academics throughout the world. In fact, there are now thousands of books available on the topic of leadership. Yet only a small percentage of *these* contributions are based on scholarly research. Of *these* books, a lesser portion focuses on the development of leadership. And among *these* books, a much smaller segment actually centers on the development of leaders in higher education, and only a few are written about women. This book is one of a kind. It not only shares exciting and intriguing information (based on a scholarly research study), but it also is about the lifetime development of leadership knowledge, skills, and competencies in women university presidents. It shares the commonalities and perspectives of ten women on their own personal journeys in developing leadership throughout childhood, youth, young adulthood, and adulthood. These ten women reflect a journey shared, in part, by all leaders.

Your Interest

Many readers care deeply about their own lifelong learning, development, and growth. If this is you, this book will help you reframe—in more detail and depth than you may have done before—influential individuals, activities, and experiences in your own lives that have helped you develop leadership. Warren Bennis (1989) once said that leadership is a function of knowing yourself, that "becoming a leader is synonymous with becoming yourself" (p. 9). My hope is that the journeys of these university presidents will be helpful for your own personal exploration and understanding.

Many readers will also care about assisting others in their personal and professional development. Again, if this is you, you will identify with some of the presidents in this book in finding great satisfaction in providing and facilitating opportunities and experiences for others. You most certainly have the desire to help others in becoming "all that they can become," and this is probably very rewarding for you. You may also have a deep passion for supporting and assisting girls and young women in a variety of ways. You may desire to help them develop the knowledge and skills to eventually become the strong, capable leaders we need throughout the world in higher education, government, business, communities, and homes. If this is you, then I applaud you. I encourage you to ponder on your selfless desires when reading this book. As you reflect, you will have ideas that will help you know how to make the difference you seek for others. This research will provide you with ideas about how to guide girls and women toward beneficial leadership experiences, some of which may actually be momentary interventions.

My Interest

People have asked me why I am interested and willing to commit so much time and energy to this research project. I have thought about this question for many years and have determined that there are two primary reasons. First, the topic of developing leaders has been a passion and near obsession with me for many years. And second, this study really matters. It matters to me personally as I continue to learn and reflect upon my own life. I have always yearned for continuous development and growth and love leading efforts, projects, organizations, and causes. I also have a teenage daughter and three teenage sons. I want to help them develop into the most conscientious, competent, and confident beings they can become. I yearn to help instill in them (in some small way) the desire to work hard and make a difference in whatever realm they choose.

I am interested in this research because it matters to everyone interested in having strong, ethical, effective, and competent leaders today and tomorrow. I have seen this in the faces of so many with this deep-rooted passion and desire. For you, this information can be helpful in counseling and designing efforts to assist those who are interested in developing the knowledge and competencies necessary for effective leadership throughout their lives. For these reasons and countless others this research really matters.

The Study

With a fascination regarding the development of prominent women leaders, I was curious about how specific high-level women leaders arrived where they are today. How did they develop what they needed to become leaders of reputable universities? For years I have been reading and reviewing related books, scholarly articles, and magazine and newspaper articles looking for specific information about the development of high-level women leaders. There is little written when it comes to scholarly research reports or application-centered writings. I discussed this lack of available information and research with a number of leadership scholars and scholar-practitioners and mentioned that I was considering embarking on a research study adventure that would not only fill the research gap but, because of the journey, also possibly change my life in some way. These scholars strongly encouraged me forward; however, they cautioned me about the credibility challenges of such an endeavor.

After pondering this project and its challenges for months, I designed a research study that would use a rigorous qualitative research methodology called "phenomenology." This method would help me

- Explore each of these president's "lived experiences"

- Gain a deeper understanding of their lives, experiences, and perceptions

- Get beyond just what they "did" or currently "do"

- Investigate the underlying meanings and influences of their experiences

My desire was to *hear* the women's own voices as they described their journeys and reflected upon their own beliefs and interpretations. I wanted them to tell stories (which ended up being essential in gathering information that was relevant and meaningful). Edgar H. Schein (2004) said that stories can assist in providing an understanding of culture, and that culture defines leadership. My hope was that the emerging data could provide insights into the development of the leadership competencies that are essential for effective leadership in higher education today. It did.

In spring 2005 I traveled to the campuses of ten women university presidents for two- to three-hour in-depth interviews (see Appendix A for more detail regarding the research methods). I asked these women a detailed set of open-ended, probing questions to explore their past experiences and perceptions (see Appendix B for the question categories). Analyses first included creating transcriptions of all the interviews. The transcripts were then reviewed by the presidents for accuracy and completeness. Other steps included a preliminary analysis, combined categorization, in-depth analysis, and finally theme generation. I maintained a continuous relationship with the presidents so that they could review the analysis, manuscripts, and chapters for accuracy. Accuracy was attested. Throughout the process many presidents shared additional insights, which is important in this type of research methodology. It is essential that the analysis and writing accurately represent the presidents' true perceptions and experiences. Because of the interactive relationship I maintained with the presidents, this book reflects their experiences. In fact, one president wrote the following:

> When I read the chapter on our leadership styles and philosophies, I was surprised. Every quotation could have been mine. They all sound like something I would say and believe. Your analysis makes sense and seems

accurate from my perspective. Your findings and discussion represent what I have believed for years.

Another president stated:

> I just finished the chapter on childhoods and was deeply touched. It is amazing to see my experiences and insights alongside nine other presidents. It is so interesting to see the commonalities and to read the other women's stories. You are doing important work that will benefit many to come.

The Presidents

I interviewed ten impressive, energetic, and distinguished women university presidents or chancellors. At the request of some of the presidents, they will not be identified in this book. However, here is a summary of some basic collective demographic information about these women and their institutions:

- Nine were or are presidents of public universities, and one led a private postsecondary institution.

- Eight served as presidents or chancellors of reputable research focused institutions or university systems; two were presidents of highly regarded teaching-focused comprehensive institutions with strong scholarship expectations.

- One teaching institution was what is termed "a historically black institution."

- Nine were the first women presidents at their current institutions.

- Eight were institutional presidents (overseeing between one and eight campuses) with student populations ranging from 2,000 to nearly 60,000 students.

- Two were higher education system-wide presidents or chancellors (overseeing six to sixteen campuses) with over 150,000 students attending the largest of the two.

- Eight of the universities were established in the 1800s and two in the early 1900s.

- Eight of the women were Caucasian, and two were African American.

- Four presidents were in their fifties and six were in their sixties, with the ages ranging from fifty-three to sixty-seven at the time of the interviews (two mid-fifties, two late fifties, two early sixties, and four mid-sixties).

- The presidents had been at their current institutions from three to fourteen years (with a mean of 6.7) at the time of the interviews.

- The presidents were raised in a variety of places: Northeast, Southeast, Midwest, South, and Mountain West.

A Few Highlights

The findings in this study support the seminal works of Bennis (1989) and Drucker (2001). Importantly, their past research and writings were primarily based on male leaders or mixed gender samples. Although many of the emerging themes in their work are similar to mine, I would argue that certain findings are even more pronounced in my all-female group of prominent leaders. I will introduce four such examples so that you can look for these themes throughout the book.

- First, the women in my study paid almost meticulous attention to the task of knowing and understanding themselves. There are examples throughout this book of experiences where these women discovered something new about themselves that helped them change their behaviors and choices appropriately. For example, one president said, "Through participation in a number of efforts during my secondary education years, I learned that I needed to either be in charge or else be working with certain people to accomplish things." She made future choices based on this information.

- Second, they were particularly self-reflective. For example, one woman explained, "Reflection has been an absolute lifesaver." Another stated, "Reflection can be the most enriching experience if you are willing to deeply acknowledge your own frailties . . ." Chapters Two, Three, and Four will provided detailed examples of how they began to develop this skill early in life.

- Third, they became passionate about learning from failures and mistakes. For example, one president explained, "I learned that if you are not failing, you are not learning. I didn't realize how important that was until later. It was amazing how much I learn from difficult things." Struggles and difficulties provide a rich resource for personal growth.

- Fourth, they loved learning and developed the ability and desire to learn from everything. For example, one president spoke of the intense learning experience that difficulties had provided her: "I have had some terribly difficult moments in my life that have been among the most important growth experiences that I have had."

Another spoke of accepting challenging assignments as a means to learn: "You can obtain challenging tasks, assignments, or positions by developing your own unique talents so that you can become the very best that you can be." Others spoke of learning from individuals and training opportunities. They looked for learning in everything they experienced.

The Higher Education Need

I have already spoken to the need of this type of book in general terms. However, it is important to say a few words about why it is important for higher education. According to Brent D. Ruben (2003), author of the book *Pursuing Excellence in Higher Education: Eight Fundamental Challenges*, "Extraordinary challenges face higher education nationally, and leaders with exceptional capabilities are needed to help institutions meet these challenges" (p. 288). In fact, leadership development has now become a critical topic in higher education. Diane Chapman Walsh (2006), in *Trustworthy Leadership*, discussed the "urgency of our need for better leadership" (p. 4). She wrote of what it was in leaders that allows them to address some of the most pressing problems in higher education and beyond:

> It is our ability as leaders to discover our solid ground, to truly hear the quiet prayers that are building to war cries, to sense that time is short, and to trust that our lives can matter. It is summoning the discipline to focus attention in directions that cause discomfort, facing moral dilemmas in all their complexity. It is seeing past the self-interest of short-term electoral and business cycles and cultivating the imagination and the generosity of spirit—in ourselves and those we touch—to focus on wrenching problems and yet not to lose heart, to open

our hearts to sorrow without being paralyzed, to find in
the world's suffering our bonds of humanity. (p. 3)

In today's constantly changing environment, higher educational institutions must have leaders who are capable, strong, smart,
strategic, ethical, honest, motivating, inspirational, competent, innovative, creative, networked, organized, empowering, perceptive,
reflective, collaborative, and insightful. Discovering such leaders is
no small task, and developing such leaders is no small challenge.
Yet developing yourself and others for leadership responsibilities
and positions is a fascinating and rewarding opportunity and experience. It happens, and it happens successfully.

The Book

Instead of highlighting each of the presidents in different chapters and asking readers to attempt to draw their own comparisons
and conclusions, the analysis of all of the data creates chapters that
summarize findings on that topic across all of the interviews. It is important to note that both similarities and differences are interesting.
Often what is *not* found can be as enlightening as what *is* found.
The chapters are organized (generally) in chronological order in
three parts. Part One: Youth deals with family background and
childhood, adolescence, and college years. Part Two: Adulthood
focuses on themes: career paths and issues, influential individuals,
developmental activities and other life roles. Part Three: Leadership discusses leadership motivation, styles, and philosophies, as
well as advice and implications.

This book is dedicated to teaching you what I've learned from
this research. And yet, it is also dedicated to providing thought-
provoking information so you can reflect on the things "in the
margins" (things not said) and teach yourselves. In my experience,
this can be the most powerful type of learning there is. Enjoy.

2

Family Background and Childhood

Leaders grow, they are not made.

Peter F. Drucker

Leadership and learning are indispensable to each other.

John F. Kennedy

W hen I began this project I hoped to uncover some interesting things about the women university presidents' families and childhoods, and I did in fact find some striking similarities and unexpected differences. During the interviews I asked the women to talk about their family influences, such as home environments, siblings, and parents. I also wanted to understand their childhood personalities, school activities, extracurricular activities, influential individuals, significant events, and even the challenges and opportunities that they believed may have influenced (at least in some way) the development of leadership skills and abilities. It was important to understand this background so as to learn about the starting points of the presidents' journeys.

Childhood is an important time to analyze and understand. It is clear, as Lorenzen (1996) stated, that "a person's inner sense of authority will be developed during childhood in the system of family relations, when the parents express their expectations, ideas, and emotions to their child" (pp. 25–26). Another researcher believes that women leaders have drives that "spring from childhood patterns and experiences that have carried into adulthood" (Coutu, 2004, p. 67). And even others (for example, Hartman, 1999; Wells, 1998) argue that relationships within the immediate family circle are central to effective development during this stage of life in terms of feelings of success, competence, and confidence. This warrants a deeper description and discussion of the presidents' homes and families. However, before doing so I would like to highlight a few points. First, it is important to keep in mind that these findings may be somewhat generational. The women in this study were generally members of intact families with supportive parents. This appears to be common for many women leaders of this and previous generations. Of course, young women today can also attain leadership positions, but some may need to overcome family issues or lack of support that may not always have been present with women leaders in past generations. Some may have to master those leadership competencies, which were previously gained through enriching family environments, in different ways.

Home and Family

All ten university presidents in this study were raised in two-parent homes. Nine of the ten were raised with their biological parents, who were married before having children. One president lost both parents early in life (her mother died at her birth, her father was murdered when she was seven) but was raised by relatives (great aunt and uncle) whom she called her parents.

The women all described their families as being *modest middle-income* families. A few of them talked about even being poor sometimes. Two others said that when they started attending college they met others who had a lot more (financially) and then determined they were probably poorer than they had thought during childhood. The presidents made statements like:

> We were okay, financially. We lived modestly. Honestly, however, I didn't know how modestly we lived until I met rich people.

My needs were met. We were always well cared for and had good food. My mother and grandmother made most of my clothes. I didn't know that everyone didn't do that until I got to college. It was a good, loving, supportive, steady, wonderful childhood.

When talking about their family's economic conditions, seven women described their modest family vacations as children, which included either camping or trips to stay with and visit relatives. Now, it is clear that although most women described their families' financial situations as modest, they were possibly influenced by school or church in developing a middle-class value system. They believed in the American dream, that if they worked hard they would have viable opportunities for success. They somehow had instilled a real sense of possibility when thinking about future opportunities, with education being central to gaining access to these possibilities. All ten presidents valued education.

The women presidents described their homes as being generally stable, safe, supportive, and loving environments. One mentioned some turmoil and struggles at times but still felt it was an enriching environment. All of the presidents described their parents as loving. One said,

I was raised by loving parents who encouraged and inspired me. They instilled in me a lifelong love of learning.

Prior research has found that children raised in intact families generally feel protected, safe, and loved. This stability is often linked to the development of positive confidence and self-esteem. Other leadership development studies (Hennig & Jardim, 1977; Keown & Keown, 1982; Woo, 1985) with women samples in business, government, and public education have found the same to be true—that successful women leaders (at least for past generations) have been primarily raised in two-parent homes. However, the findings related to African American women leaders in higher education are mixed (Robinson, 1996; Waring, 2003). Some strong African American women were raised in single-parent homes and had fathers who were not present in their lives. Some were raised in unstable home environments. Obviously certain events and situations were beyond the control of a child. Yet it is important to note that some leaders in these studies, as children, found ways (or were provided opportunities) to develop the confidence and leadership skills that others may have developed and enhanced through a stable and supportive family and home.

Most of the women in my study felt that their religious beliefs and church participation were important and influential elements of their personal development and overall upbringing. For many, their church activity was a central part of their lives and sense of who they were.

Siblings

Six of the ten presidents were first or only children in their families. Interestingly, although three were only children, two of these women felt that they did not have all of the "characteristics of only children" for different reasons. The first was the only child of biological parents who died early in her life, after which she was raised by relatives who had other children living in the home during much of her upbringing. The second was raised in a small town and grew up with a group of close-knit peers who were "much more like siblings than friends and peers." Another three presidents were the first-born in families with multiple children; three were second siblings in their families and one was third. All presidents who had siblings (seven) were raised with at least one brother, two women with older brothers and five with younger. It is important to note that no presidents were born into all female families. Three presidents had no siblings; three had one sibling; one had two siblings; two had three siblings; and one was born into a family whose parents eventually had five children.

At this point I believe it is important to describe a few of the general results of one of the few studies that have researched the lifetime development of women leaders. In the 1970s, Hennig and Jardim (1977) interviewed twenty-five successful U.S. women CEOs who were born between 1910 and 1915. These women were in the first wave of female leaders in the United States. They discovered that all twenty-five of these women were first-born children in their homes. Some were only children whereas others were the eldest in all-girl families with no more than three children. These researchers wrote a great deal about how being the only or first child of all-girl families was beneficial for them to learn and experience the skills needed for corporate leadership. Times have changed. Even in the early 1980s, Keown and Keown (1982) said that being an only child or in families with only female siblings was no longer a crucial factor for success. The women in my study were born primarily in the 1940s and 1950s. Their mothers and grandmothers were actually the ages of the women in Hennig and Jardim's sample. My research provides evidence that brothers can be a good thing. My participants spoke of positive (and sometimes negative) relationships with their brothers and what they learned from them. Speaking from someone who knows (I was raised with six brothers and no sisters), brothers can teach us a great deal (of course we can probably teach them more). Still, it is important to remember that over half (six) of the presidents in my study were first or only children. And, on an earlier point, Hennig and Jardim's CEOs also talked of their happy childhood times with close and warm relationships with their parents.

Mothers

Nine of the ten mothers of these university presidents attended college (probably during the 1930s and 1940s) for at least a few years after high school. This compares to only six of the fathers. One mother earned a master's degree, and seven completed college programs (bachelor, associate, or certificate). The types of degrees varied; two acquired teaching degrees and the others completed programs in areas such as dietetics, political science, English, museum studies, nursing, home economics, and medical technology. These college emphases and programs were very traditional for women at that time. Clearly their mothers' higher educational backgrounds provided strong influences or models for these women. Many expressed extreme pride when speaking of their mothers' college degrees and experiences. The importance of at least some college education for both parents is discussed in other studies (Hojaard, 2002; Keown & Keown, 1982; Walton & McDade, 2001). Interestingly, in the Hennig and Jardim (1977) study ten of the mothers had equal educational levels with the fathers, and thirteen mothers actually had superior education.

Most of these women came from very traditional homes; eight of the ten mothers (at least when their children were young) were full-time homemakers. At least six of the mothers were working either part-time or full-time by the time their children were in elementary or secondary school. Interestingly, one of the two presidents, whose mother worked full-time throughout her life, saw this as a possible advantage in her development because her mother worked in the evenings, and she was able to learn "a fair amount of independence and self-directedness."

The mothers' employment was very traditional for that period, but interestingly, most worked in professional positions. As I analyzed data regarding the mothers' positions (whether before or after the births of their children), most mothers had idealistic employment positions generally focused on the future, making a difference, serving others, and influencing. As for the mother's occupational areas, three were school teachers at some point in their adult lives, two were employed in nonadministrative positions in for-profit businesses, two worked in the social work or welfare arena, two were employed in the nursing or medical field, and one mother never worked (full-time or part-time) outside the home.

The presidents made statements and used descriptive words to describe their mothers. The findings show a different type of relationship and respect when compared to earlier studies. For example, Hennig and Jardim (1977) stated that CEOs' recollections of their mothers were "vague and generalized" but the father-daughter relationship descriptions were rich in detail and energy. It was clear that the CEOs not only had more respect for their fathers, but their fathers played a much bigger role in influencing their leadership development throughout childhood and youth. My findings were different. The presidents vividly and with detail remembered and described their mothers. The women not only viewed their mothers as loving, committed, and dedicated, but most also saw them as influential, competent, strong, intelligent, and fun. My study found a profound influence by both parents but a richer description (from most presidents) of their mothers and their influence. It is difficult to determine, however, whether the mothers were credited with a stronger influence than the fathers. A few presidents connected more with their fathers whereas others seemed to be more influenced by their mothers. However, many spoke equally about the influence of both parents. It is important to note that some of the more recent research does support a stronger influence of leaders' mothers (Coutu, 2004; Matz, 2002).

The majority of comments the presidents made about their mothers were positive, loving, and understanding. Some of their short statements are telling:

- My mother felt fortunate to have me.

- My mother had high expectations for us.

- My mother instilled in me a love for learning.

- My mother loved being with me.

- My mother made happy times.

- My mother taught me things and taught me well.

These statements demonstrate the presidents' feelings of acceptance from their mothers. One president told stories throughout the interview to describe the friendship she had with her mother. She explained:

> My mother was my best friend. She was wonderful. If I didn't want to go to school, she would call the school and tell them that I was needed for some kind of appointment. She would come and pick me up, and we would go shopping. We had fun; it was a great time.

The presidents described the types of things about their mothers that were influential and memorable to them. One woman stated:

> My mother was very dedicated and skillful. She made all my clothes through high school including smock dresses. She did my hair and went with us on hikes, picnics, and huckleberry picking expeditions. She made happy times. She was always very busy, but I never had the sense she was overwhelmed. She had an amazing capacity to adjust and adapt and had a wonderful sense of humor.

Another described two important characteristics of her mother (education and resourcefulness) that became particularly influential throughout this president's childhood and adolescence:

> My mother was influential in my life. She was the only woman I knew, except for my school teachers, who had graduated from college. I was proud of that. I was proud that she expected me to graduate from college. She worked hard to make ends meet with very limited income. As I got older, I began to see how limited the resources were. I was surprised to see how invisible that was. I think people thought we had more than we did because of what she was able to do.

Her mother's college attendance and graduation also made an impact on another president who said:

> My mother graduated from college because her brothers worked to send her. They did not get to go, but she was identified out of six children of a very modest income family as the one who should go to college, and she was a woman. I always had a sense of pride that my mother had gone to college.

Finally, one president talked about a powerful unspoken expectation that she felt throughout her childhood and youth:

> The women in my family were expected to make a contribution to the world; nobody spelled it out but I just knew it.

Two of the women did make some negative statements (related to short-term emotional instability or irrationality regarding certain issues) about their mothers, but interestingly, in all cases, they explained what they learned from the experience or behavior and how they now understand (at least in part) their mothers' struggles.

When comparing the words used to describe their mothers with the ones used to describe their fathers (presented next), more of the words describing mothers focus on personal characteristics and relationships, whereas the words describing their fathers highlight respect (possibly from a distance), strength, high expectations, and being a protector. Although not with all words, the common themes continue to emphasize two kinds of caretaking: a mother who is affectionate and relationship-focused, and a father who is the traditional provider (for example, food, shelter). Yet there is a nontraditional characteristic about these fathers that will be discussed later.

Fathers

Six of the ten fathers went to college, and two of them received master's degrees. Their college degrees included physics, engineering, chemistry, agriculture, secondary education, and physical education and recreation. Five of the six college-educated fathers were employed in the fields of their specific degrees. Of the ten fathers, two were employed as school teachers; two worked in managing family businesses; and the others had careers in sales, the postal service, engineering, entrepreneurship, construction, farming, and manufacturing.

The presidents also described their fathers in some detail. As with the statements about their mothers, the majority of comments were positive, appreciative, and loving. Many of these statements began with "My father..." and finished with comments like the following:

- Believed in training my mind

- Cared for me

- Encouraged me to achieve

- Felt education was important

- Focused on the importance of education

- Had a strong sense of responsibility to his family

- Had high expectations

- Helped make sure we had a good time

- Loved politics and debate

- Provided helpful feedback

- Turned inward because of the war

- Was flexible with roles

- Yearned for more education

These women also shared stories and perspectives related to relationships with their fathers and how their fathers helped them develop beneficial knowledge and skills. One president who described a particularly close relationship with her father said the following:

> It was a very formative time. He was teaching us all of the time. His space was a sacred space of inventing and doing important things. We learned. He encouraged creativity and hands-on doing. We could pursue anything we were interested in. It didn't matter what it was; if we were interested in it, my father made sure we did it. I think that was a really wonderful thing . . . I practiced problem solving all of the time with my father. He would say, "The worst thing that could happen is the prototype works the first time, so you don't learn anything from it." He was always talking; he would be verbalizing what he was doing, thinking, and why it was so. If it worked, "okay"; if it didn't work "good." We would figure it out . . . My father was really a big cheerleader of mine my entire life.

Another president described the things she learned from her father at the dinner table each evening:

> At the dinner table he talked about the politics of the day, all kinds of topics. It was an interesting conversation at dinner every evening. I loved to learn the argument. I had different opinions than my father about people's needs, welfare, and discrimination. We both loved the argument. That taught me to live in that world. I think it is so important to a child to be able to talk and discuss and be treated almost like an adult . . . to have that conversation.

Another participant told a story about her father teaching her to love learning:

> He would sit me on his lap and would say, "The only thing black people have are our minds. You have to really be able to have your mind trained." He used to play little historical games with me. "Now do you remember when Roosevelt did this?" or "When did a certain event happen in history?" I didn't know anything about Roosevelt or many historical events at that time, but I would remember dates. He made learning fun.

One president talked about her father's flexibility with gender roles, which appeared to have influenced her role perspectives later in life. Her father had since passed on, but she spoke lovingly of his powerful influence and delightful personality:

> My father was influential in my life. He was the kind of guy who would grab a kid at a family reunion and change his or her diaper; he wasn't hung up on roles. He was sort of the "Macho cowboy who wasn't." He wore cowboy boots and bow ties with his suits. He was wonderful.

Some of the fathers also appeared to have a profound influence on their daughters' desire to excel in school and attend college. One described her father as follows:

> My father was a wonderful man and very smart, but he didn't get to go to college. It was a burden that he bore throughout his life. It was a theme in his life. Even as a child he knew he was plenty smart enough to go, but he didn't have the opportunity. The depression came, and he couldn't go, but he desperately wanted it. He instilled that yearning and desire in my brother and me.

Another explained:

> In high school my dad said, "When I give you a college education, no one can ever take that away from you, and I know you can take care of yourself." That had a real strong impact, but I think beyond that they believed that I could, if I wanted to work for it, do anything. Anything could be achieved through hard work.

One president learned from her father that

> . . . the inherent value system was that education was a great enabler; and that in order to have options, one wanted to be as well educated as possible. My father's basic mantra was that one had to work hard and aim high.

Another said that her father taught her that

> Education was always important. It is the great equalizer. The only thing others can't take away from you is a solid foundation and education.

As with the comments and stories about their mothers, some of the presidents did share some struggles or challenges they had seen with their fathers or that their fathers faced that made life difficult at times (for example, failed business ventures, war experiences, yearning for different direction in life). It was clear that these women had reflected on these issues, and they had a genuine sense of understanding. They spoke of what they personally learned from seeing their fathers' struggles, and the presidents felt that observing and living through some of these challenges helped them in their personal and professional development.

As mentioned previously, in the Hennig and Jardim (1977) study, women CEOs identified with their fathers more than their mothers. The authors argued that this father-daughter relation-ship was central in the development of skills, abilities, and per-spectives needed to be successful leaders, especially at that time. The fathers of these women had a stronger influence on the de-velopment, aspirations, and educational goals than their moth-ers. At least one other set of researchers (Astin & Leland, 1991) found some of the same findings in their sample of women leaders. My study suggests something different. Although fathers remained vital in the development of their daughters, in most cases the presidents' fathers did not play a more influential role than did the mothers.

Overall, the presidents described their fathers' occupations as relatively traditional for that period. Only six of the ten went to college; those who did majored in predominantly traditional male fields (although two became secondary school teachers). Interest-ingly, three of the four fathers who had not gone to college had almost stronger voices regarding the importance of higher educa-tion for their daughters. The nontraditional aspect of these fathers is that most of them believed that it was vital that they teach their daughters (as well as provide encouragement, opportunities, and education for them) to become self-sufficient. After analyzing the times, I believe there are a number of possible reasons for this emphasis. First, many of these fathers may have served in wars or had fathers, uncles, brothers, and friends who did. With the ex-tended leaves and possible deaths, these fathers may have seen and felt the need for women to be prepared to support themselves and their children. Second, many of their fathers' and grandfathers' oc-cupations may have been dangerous; a lot of occupations were at that time. It was not uncommon to have men die in the mines, in farming accidents, and so forth. Third, these fathers married more educated women who worked (at least at sometime during their lives) in professional jobs. The men may have had a convic-tion early on that education was as important for women as it was for men.

Childhood Personalities

I asked the presidents to describe their childhood personalities. One of the major themes that emerged is that, as a whole, these women were very obedient as children. They obeyed and respected their parents, teachers, religious leaders, neighbors, and adult relatives and friends. Most of the presidents had a strong desire to please others and to live up to others' positive expectations. A number of presidents gave examples of the *worst* things they did during childhood to show their tendency toward obedience. One president explained:

> The most rebellious thing I did was to take a flashlight to bed and read under the covers.

Another stated:

> The worst thing I ever did as a kid was when I was about five. We lived in a house that was just down the road and across a highway from a park. I was told never to go down there and cross that street. I took my little brother to the playground. My mother came to get us in a police car.

Only one of the presidents described herself as having a rebellious streak; yet, from her description, she was still generally obedient. In reflecting about this *obedient* theme I have come to conclude that some may have been doing things more out of respect—not just blind obedience. A number of them also noted that they also enjoyed responsibility. One stated:

> I assumed a lot of responsibility when I was a child. I naturally loved responsibility and learned that from my parents.

A second major theme revolved around the presidents' reflective and observant natures as children. They were concerned about understanding what types of behavior would bring the best results from others around them. One president explained:

> I'm a very observant person and learned this from an early age; I watch people carefully, and in watching, I sort of learned what to do and how to do it . . . I was reflective. I give the credit to the church. I grew up in the Methodist church and we had some very intelligent pastors who did a lot of sermons that weren't hell, fire, and brimstone. I grew up in more of a reflective environment. I thought about what people do, why they do it, and such.

Another said:

> Being prepared mentally, paying attention, being ready to trace the argument or the reasons and so forth was important. That's why I loved math so much. It was a heaven sent discipline because it was so logical. I loved it!

A president of a large university in the east mentioned:

> I stepped in the shadows of people I liked and trusted and followed their footsteps.

This notion of the presidents' reflective natures is powerful. The more I've studied about reflection, the more I have realized how essential it is in the learning process. These women, as children, appeared to have a gift that many children do not. This gift is the ability to observe, listen, and learn from many things, including mistakes. They had inquisitive minds, and they yearned to learn and be successful in all arenas or domains of their lives. They had a desire to improve their skills and abilities in a variety of areas and continuously reflected upon words, situations, opportunities, and challenges so they could (1) do things better than those they had watched, or (2) adjust or change themselves in ways that would bring more optimal results. Of course it is not clear how they acquired these observant and reflective natures, although there are some clues in some of the relationship descriptions. Importantly, many people who are raised in stable homes do not have these skills. As mentioned earlier, there are many events beyond the control of a child. The key appears to be in developing the ability to make learning opportunities from various situations and circumstances through being observant and reflective.

When asked whether they were shy or outgoing, the presidents differed in their responses. One woman stated:

> I'm not painfully shy, but as a young person growing up I always liked to watch what was going on around me and figure out what's happening before I jumped in.

Another explained:

> I was not shy or outgoing; I was probably a pretty reticent person, but I wasn't shy. I could do public speaking and so forth, but I definitely was not a social butterfly . . . I had confidence in my ability to do the work. I knew I was smart.

A third reflected:

> I was shy in some social situations that were undefined, but I was never shy in school when I knew the boundaries.

Another said:

> I was always comfortable by myself for long periods of time; it was not punishment to be sent to my room to read all day.

Overall, these women had a variety of childhood personality traits. For example, whereas some were outgoing and "bossy," others were bashful and reserved. And although some described themselves as extroverts, others described themselves as introverts. However, as children the presidents were obedient, respectful, reflective, smart, self-directed, helpful, and concerned about pleasing and meeting the expectations of respected adults. Although some talked about areas of possible insecurity or lack of confidence, all described themselves as confident (or as having high self-esteem) with regard to many situations and environments. It was also clear that these young girls had high expectations for themselves and liked to be respected for their abilities. A few of the presidents spoke of a period of loss of self-esteem as other studies (Sills, 1994) report, and many spoke of their sixth-grade years (during eleven to thirteen years of age) as important and empowering years. All expressed achievement-oriented tendencies and a sense of competency. Other studies (Baraka-Love, 1986; Hennig & Jardim, 1977; Stephens, 2003; Wells, 1998) found some of these same findings.

My research differs somewhat from the finding of Hennig and Jardim (1977) that the twenty-five CEOs thought of themselves as very successful and able, and they admitted they were arrogant toward peers. The presidents in my research didn't report this arrogance toward peers or others. They did not spend their childhoods in the spotlight. The presidents in my study had rather humble and moderate beginnings. It is important to note that the variations could be, in part, because of generational differences, as well as the natural dissimilarities between those individuals who choose corporate versus higher education paths.

The women university presidents were at least moderately competitive. Of course a few were more highly competitive, but overall they had healthy but moderately competitive demeanors. This is a bit different from the findings of Hennig and Jardim (1977), who reported highly competitive natures among their CEOs. It also differs from the research of Stephens (2003), who examined leadership through a rhetorical lens. She reported that she "didn't see a strong sense of competition" in any of the thirty women leaders she interviewed (church, business, and higher education). Some presidents described their competitiveness in other realms, including academics, music performance, speech contests, card and board games, plays, and dance recitals. A number of women said they were competitive with themselves, meaning that they set high goals and worked to achieve them. It was clear that these women enjoyed (many actually thrived on) challenging themselves and others. They had a deep need to be as good as they could be. This drive requires self-reflection and, at least in part, may have been what allowed the women to progress and develop their skills, confidence, and self-esteem.

Some research (Robinson, 1996) reports that women leaders had strong desires for leadership responsibilities in childhood, but the presidents in my sample did not describe being a "leader" when they were young. Some mentioned having some "influence" but not formal leadership positions or desires. It is important to note, however, that these young girls may not have sought formal leadership positions during childhood because such opportunities were rare. Yet I did not find a driving need for leadership titles and power during their childhoods. It is possible, however, that they may have been informally "leading" during this time. Many may have been confident enough not to need titles to lead, which seems to be a critical skill for presidents. Their leadership tasks may have been defined as service, such as one president who was asked to read to other students in her combined second- and third-grade class. The limited leadership opportunities they did have clearly helped build their feelings of competence and confidence (Cohen et al., 1996). Unlike experiences some have reported in research (Fels, 2004), these presidents did not speak of feeling that they received less attention and recognition than boys in their school classes.

School and Other Activities

I was interested in discovering more about the presidents' childhood experiences by exploring their perceptions of school and other activities. My hope was that it would be helpful in figuring out what may have influenced the development of leadership in these women.

The first theme that became clear was the presidents' positive feelings about school and learning. All ten presidents said they enjoyed school, and most of them described themselves as model students. One explained that she "found joy from thinking, reading, and learning," while another stated, "I loved school and absolutely yearned for learning." All embodied a strong commitment to education and understood (as young children) the importance of education in life. Six specifically mentioned the benefit of having wonderful, caring teachers. Eight explained that their teachers liked or appreciated them for their abilities and contributions. Seven explained that doing well in school came fairly easily for them, and that they "flourished in school." Four spoke of specific recognition or awards that were meaningful and provided support for understanding as well as acknowledging their intellectual and social competence and abilities. Three presidents stated that it was in elementary school that they began learning that "*women could do anything.*" Interestingly, this last statement (or one similar) was made exclusively by the presidents who attended all-female schools led by women.

Other researchers (Cubillo & Brown, 2003; Klenke, 1996) have found that a majority of women presidents also spoke of their involvement in school activities as children (plays, clubs, service, and such) as important in their personal and leadership development. It is interesting to note that one researcher (Wells, 1998) who studied women entrepreneurs stated that they did not like school and its related experiences. There are clearly some differences between this generation of women who become university presidents and those who become business leaders. This one is particularly no-table. One study (Rayburn, Goetz, & Osman, 2001) also reported (and my study confirmed this finding) that school and home were the most important arenas for learning leadership skills throughout childhood and youth. Lesser but important arenas also included work, community, and religious settings.

The presidents specifically mentioned an intense love of reading. One said:

> I loved reading. I was a huge user of the library. I would ride my bike to the library and come home with a mountain of books and devour them. I have very strong images of not wanting to come to dinner and walking around with a book in my hand, fiction mostly, the Nancy Drew, classic stuff that kids read.

Other studies support this finding (for example, Robinson, 1996). These women leaders as children were avid readers and sought education in their various experiences.

When asked about their involvement in sports, most presidents reminisced about the lack of organized team sports that were available at that time. A number of presidents talked about the historical emphasis of girls' participation in individual (not team) sports. As one president in her mid-sixties explained:

> Girls were expected to excel in individual ways because it was before the advent of sports. My father was adamant about girls not doing things that made them sweat. He was very opposed to this. I think this was one of the problems of early women leaders. We didn't have a lot of experiences with teams, a lot of early women had trouble understanding victory and getting any satisfaction from it. In fact, we saw some real grandstanding and in some cases disastrous women presidents in the very beginning. They needed some feedback that was satisfying and it

only came if *they* did it. At that time you only played solos, sang solos, and had the "one" part, because these were the roles open to women.

Only three described sports team involvement during childhood, but eight described themselves as being physically active in general. Again, when asked whether they were competitive, eight said they were moderately to highly competitive and the other two said they were somewhat competitive during childhood. Notably, the women who participated in organized sports felt they were very competitive.

The women were members of many organizations and clubs and participated in all types of other activities, such as music lessons, sports activities, and dramatic productions. The women believed that each activity provided them with opportunities for growth in speaking, organization, interpersonal skills, teamwork, networking, responsibility, delegation, motivation of others, internal strength, persistence, and more. It is interesting that the participants in Hennig and Jardim's study voiced dissatisfaction over restrictions placed upon them during childhood, whereas my participants felt they had many opportunities for growth and development in a variety of arenas. As children, eight of the women were involved in musical activities (piano, choir, band, and orchestra) and half were involved in Girl Scouts. One explained:

> I lived in a small town so everyone got lots of opportunities, even in early grades, to be in school plays, church pageants, piano recitals, choir concerts, and such. As a result I got pushed into doing the kinds of things that helped me grow up to develop confidence and public presence without ever being aware of it. However, I was not different from other children in my small town. Everybody did the same things. We just assumed everybody had those kinds of experiences. It was much later that I realized this was a blessing.

Four of the presidents mentioned that their experiences with dramatic productions were also helpful. One stated:

> In sixth grade the local state college was putting on a play and needed some young girls. They selected a group of us and we went a few nights a week for practice over a long period of time. I had my own speaking roles in the play. It was a big deal. It allowed me to connect to that environment but also made me feel like I was accomplishing something, being able to do that in front of a group. It was a good experience for me.

The presidents made other statements that might be interesting to consider:

> I was good enough on the violin to be considered really good but not superb. I learned that if I practiced I could be really good. I was first or second chair all of the time. If I practiced—I was first; I knew that. It gave me a confidence that when I worked very hard, excellence was achievable. I loved music, and it was a wonderful opportunity to just know other people and enjoy doing something.

> I went to camp all summer, and I loved it. I would be packed in March and was eager to go. We did sports, swimming, rowing, anything with a ball, hiking, and camping. Being with other people, who were not your own family, was good for me. We made little teams in our cabins which was also good. In fact, if you want to blame anything on me being able to lead—it's camp!

> I had so many opportunities as a child to develop public presence, to assume responsibility among peers, to participate and to interface within a group.

When asked whether they believed these childhood activities in general were helpful in developing important skills and abilities necessary for effective leadership, all generally agreed. These women felt many of the activities helped them develop a variety of competencies, including confidence, dependability, responsibility, organization, and teamwork, as well as interpersonal, intellectual, social, and communication skills. These findings support the notion that high involvement in school and other activities may be helpful for the initial development of future leaders.

Influential Individuals

The presidents also talked about individuals, other than their own parents and siblings, who were a positive influence on their development during their childhood, such as teachers and extended family members.

Seven presidents spoke of the influence of some elementary school teachers, particularly in fifth and sixth grades. One stated, "In my life I certainly have had the great benefit of wonderful teachers." Another president said:

> My sixth grade teacher was a woman who was passionate about education. She conveyed her own personal joy and passion in the way she taught us. In some ways I think these times made up special moments for me in (what we now call) the life of the mind. This includes being able to gain shared joy out of thinking, reading, and learning. I saw that in her, and I felt it in myself—the sheer joy that she felt was the joy that she ignited in me. I don't think I ever had the chance to tell her that. I was much older before I realized it. It makes me want to be sure that teachers know of their potential impact.

Another president also spoke of her Catholic school sixth-grade teacher. She had previously (in fourth and fifth grades) had nun teachers who were taskmasters, and she felt negatively influenced by them. She said:

> I remember a sixth grade teacher who was a breath of fresh air. Learning became fun. The classroom was no longer a place of punishment and rote learning. It was a much more open and interesting experience.

One president talked about a sixth-grade teacher who was single and older. Every year she picked a small group of children to provide special opportunities and attention. This teacher took her and a few other children to plays in the city. After the productions she would take them to get a special treat. According to this president:

> She opened up to me a new world that I didn't know existed. I was pretty provincial in my little neighborhood. I think that was really important to me, to reach beyond my little world. I really discovered for the first time there were people who dressed better and who lived in a different world than I did. I loved it.

One president said she liked all her teachers; however, she decided that her Hebrew school teachers were the most influential. When asked why, she stated:

> Both of my Hebrew teachers were very influential because they were real scholars. They appreciated having kids like my brother and me in their classes. We were seriously interested in learning, and they would teach extra to be sure we learned.

One president spoke of her fifth- and sixth-grade teacher as having great strength. She explained:

> My teacher taught in a room not much larger than my office and had the strength to keep 20 little kids quiet in the fifth grade while she taught something to the

sixth graders in the same room. I always admired her. I remember her style and how she would look at me to make me shut up, rather than having to do anything really rough.

Finally, one president spoke of the profound influence of a split second- and third-grade class, where she was always asked to read to the younger grade while the teacher worked with the older grade. She stated:

> I was given a lot of responsibility to do different things. I was like a teacher's aide. She would ask me to do things that, looking back, were quite unusual for my age. With this responsibility I believe I moved into a leading-type role at a very early age. It certainly built my self-confidence.

Extended family members were also positive influences on these women. Seven presidents were very close to their extended families. These family members seemed important in their development by being role models, providing feedback, interacting with them, and influencing them in subtle ways. Four specifically spoke of influential aunts. One president spoke of an aunt who had a "put together" and business-like demeanor. "I remember that I liked that. I remember admiring her brightly colored scarves." Another was deeply influenced by an unmarried aunt who was a camp director. She was a very independent, business-type person. She explained:

> We bonded; she would come over on Friday evenings for dinner. When I got big enough I would take a bus to her house. She was a big influence on my life. I loved camp.

A third president had an aunt who was "a true role model" for her. She owned a very prestigious kindergarten. At that time in the south, education in the kindergarten was really stressed. President explained that her aunt was "a very powerful woman" in this large southern city.

> She was the principal and ran the school which had 400 children. They had great progress and kids started reading at four. I enjoyed seeing her do all that. The women teachers at her school had not graduated from college, but they believed in education and wanted to learn her methods. There was no nonsense allowed.

Another president spoke of the strong women on her mother's side of the family. She spoke of one aunt being very strong and particular. Everything had to be done right. She explained:

> I was absolutely scared to death of her because we had to iron our napkins perfectly. Another aunt was a first grade teacher for 50 years, while another owned a flower/gift shop and we would spend summers with her to learn how to be proper. I saw all of these women as very strong and independent, wonderful women. My mindset was that women had to be strong and competent and the backbone of the family, yet it was clear that they couldn't do anything they wanted occupationally.

Others spoke of the strong influence of a grandmother, and they reminisced about their personalities, thoughtfulness, listening ears, and love of learning and thinking. A few women also briefly mentioned the subtle positive influences (primarily through acknowledgment and encouragement) of church members, neighbors, friends' parents, and others.

A few presidents had a difficult time thinking of specific influential individuals during their childhood. One stated, "My memories are fairly devoid of stars." Another explained:

> I have learned something from almost everybody that I have interacted with, even as a youth. I watched what people did. When they did things really well I thought

about what they did and why it worked. I pondered about whether there was something that I would incorporate and I could learn from that observation. If there is anything for me that was life changing, it was watching, thinking, and implementing.

These examples demonstrate how these young girls observed everything around them, thought about what they saw, and arrived at personal conclusions.

The women presidents in this study spoke highly and often of the positive influence of their school teachers, particularly in fifth and sixth grades. Outside their immediate families, the most influential individuals included female teachers, aunts, and grandmothers. Based on their descriptions, many of these individuals were single and living models of service, a model that was somewhat counter to traditional roles at that time. So, in spite of their obedience they may have witnessed some contrast to the "rule." Some of the past research (Hennig & Jardim, 1977) reports that female leaders may have seen women as inferior to men in most ways. However, in my research the positive influence of women in the presidents' lives was very clear. Women were not generally seen as inferior. These presidents had examples (role models, mentors) who were strong and competent women. These women also drew their strength from a wide variety of individuals (families, friends, teachers, peers, and community) as opposed to one particular individual.

Significant Events, Challenges, and Opportunities

During the interviews, I also asked the presidents about any childhood significant events, challenges, or opportunities that may have had an impact on the development of specific competencies related to leadership. A few spoke of issues related to serious illnesses of siblings or close relatives. They described developing sensitivity and awareness of others' circumstances and perspectives, finding internal strength in times of difficulty, improving responsibility and dependability, and learning to change and adjust their own behaviors and expectations when situations merited such. One president spoke in detail of a sister's critical lifetime health problems. Her sister was only eighteen months older, and this president had vivid memories of stressful times when she was only four or five years of age. She spoke of understanding the importance of taking care of herself and staying out of the way. She said:

> I was okay with that. I remember adults moving around, hovering, and worrying. I was too young to be helpful in other ways, but I remember that I knew that if I stayed out of the way then it would be helpful to my family. When I got older I understood the importance of finding my internal strength during times of difficulty for my family. During my older childhood years and into my teenage years I would often go places with my sister. My parents had taught me to recite symptoms and treatments. If something happened when I was with her I could tell people all of the important information they needed to take care of her. It was a heavy responsibility, and on top of that—she was not to know.

A number of presidents spoke of moving to new towns and schools as significant events and challenges. From these experiences they developed, at least in part, the ability and confidence to adjust to new people, places, and situations. The presidents learned they could reach out and develop new friendships and fit into different environments and cultures. One president explained:

> Moving was hard for me. I was pretty involved in different kinds of activities. It was a tough time for a young girl to move. It took me a year to create a place for myself in a new environment, but it happened. It just took a little while. At the time I didn't think it was good for me, but in retrospect I think I understood that there were a lot more opportunities for me there. Yet, I did have to

go through that transition period. It probably taught me some important things and enlarged my thinking. So, in the end it probably was good for me. I learned that I could adjust to new places and find friends wherever I went. I have used those skills in many different ways throughout the years.

The presidents spoke of a variety of difficulties but realized that they had learned from each of these challenges. Three presidents mentioned that difficult times helped them develop leadership qualities even more than the easier times. Interestingly, the most influential and memorable developmental childhood events for most presidents were challenging, difficult, or traumatic times.

Overall, the presidents sought out opportunities for growth and development in all kinds of experiences. I believe that, although these ten women may not represent all leaders, the finding that one can "learn to learn" in every situation can be generalized to all. No matter your "lot in life," the ability to use challenging situations and circumstances as learning experiences—instead of excuses—is truly a remarkable ability. In fact, this may be a particularly important ability to develop in future women leaders who have not come from stable childhood environments.

Five presidents (two African American; three Caucasian) shared specific experiences related to moments in their childhood when they were profoundly affected in learning about segregation and other racial issues. The detail they used in describing specific moments was rich and interesting. It was clear that these experiences played a role in decisions they have made (and continue to make) with regard to the importance of diversity issues on their campuses. For example, one Caucasian president shared the following story:

> One specific incident really shaped me with regard to racial challenges. Even though we were of modest means, like most families in the south we had a black maid. Her

name was Ophelia. She was in our home most days from the time I was crawling until I was seven. In many ways she raised me. I still remember so many things about household chores and cooking that she taught me. I loved her dearly.

Usually Ophelia took the streetcar home, but for some reason one day my father decided to take her home, and he asked me if I would like to go. I was terribly excited and jumped into the back seat of the car. My father said, "No, you have to sit in the front seat. Ophelia will sit in the back seat." That did not make sense to me as a child because the adult should be sitting in the front. Well I sat in the front and was pretty upset about it. I cried easily, and I think I cried all of the way. I was in the front seat, Ophelia was in the back, and it was just not right. When she got out of the car, my father turned to me and said something unforgettable: "If she had ridden in the front seat with me, she would be dead by morning." It hit me to my very core in a way of understanding the injustice of the world that I lived in, where race was such an important issue. That had a huge impact on me, and it's a story I will never forget.

This story was of a child without race filters. She learned why her father did what he did and deeply reflected upon this for many years. From the context she then chose to eventually fight the system, not her father.

Final Thoughts

In summary, as children these women developed the ability to learn from all types of experiences. This development stemmed from the reflective and observant natures of these women as children. Some attributed the development of this ability to their parents, religious leaders, teachers, relatives, and others. All presidents agreed that the ability (and possibly the passion) to learn and grow from all types of experiences is extremely helpful in developing the kinds of skills most beneficial for effective and successful leadership throughout life.

Takeaways

1. Assisting children in developing observation and reflection skills and abilities can benefit them throughout their lives.

2. The passion and desire for learning should be developed early in life.

3. A child can benefit from the support and encouragement of many influential adults.

4. An essential competency to develop during childhood is the ability to recognize one's mistakes, failures, and deficiencies and then have the desire and fervor to improve and change.

5. Involvement in various types of activities can provide a favorable environment for children to develop leadership skills.

6. Providing opportunities for children to participate in competitive activities or events can help (particularly children who are competitive) continuously develop and enhance leadership knowledge and skills.

3

Adolescence

Leadership is not so much about technique and methods as it is about opening the heart. Leadership is about inspiration—of oneself and of others. Great leadership is about human experiences, not processes. Leadership is not a formula or a program, it is a human activity that comes from the heart and considers the hearts of others. It is an attitude, not a routine.

Lance Secretan

The quality of a person's life is in direct proportion to their commitment to excellence regardless of their chosen endeavor.

Vince Lombardi

The adolescent years are an incredibly important developmental time for all individuals. It is a vital time for young women to develop confidence and self-esteem, learn new skills and competencies, discover strengths and weaknesses, and increase their understanding of self and environment. Since leadership is also a network of relationships (Ahn, Adamson, & Dornbusch, 2004), experience and opportunity in building healthy relationships with a host of different people and organizations is critical during these years. Adolescence is a dynamic time full of positive and negative experiences, challenges, and opportunities that all seem to impact people in some way for the rest of their lives (Hartman, 1999). This proved true for these university presidents. During these years it seems they were taught by life itself.

Researchers have continued to voice support for the exploration of early histories in "shaping women's thinking and enabling them to aspire" (Cubillo & Brown, 2003, p. 289) to leadership positions. Looking at what has affected their growth and development is a vital piece in evaluating the leadership development of young girls and women. Understanding the "foundation of successful women and the early experiences that instilled self-confidence and leadership traits" (Matz, 2002, pp. 3–4) can assist parents, advisors, and leaders in providing programs and experiences that may be helpful in facilitating the development of important leadership competencies. This is particularly important, as one study (Anonymous, 2005) reported that girls consistently felt they couldn't be leaders and perceived being a leader as a negative image. As briefly discussed in Chapter Two, Sills (1994) and others (Erickson, 1978; Rotheram & Armstrong, 1980; Stiles, 1986) believe that adolescence (between seventh and twelfth grades) is the optimal time for teaching leadership skills to young girls because research findings show that girls become less confident, less ambitious, and less assertive during these years. These researchers found that girls between the ages of twelve to fourteen are on the "brink of making important decisions which will influence the direction of their futures" (Sills, 1994, p. 61). It is clear that girls who become leaders have somehow developed positive views of themselves as well as an understanding of how to transform obstacles into challenges that can be overcome (Cantor & Bernay, 1992). This chapter will explore these and other issues that will be helpful in understanding the development of the ten university presidents I interviewed. Again, it is important to keep in mind the possible generational limitations and implications of this study.

During the interviews of the university presidents, each woman spoke in detail about her personality, schooling, activities, leadership positions, employment, influential individuals, significant events, opportunities, awards, recognitions, college plans, and goals. The women described how these experiences may have influenced the development of their own leadership skills and competencies. The adolescent period in the presidents' lives was important to consider in the continued search for understanding the starting points of their journeys.

Personality

Each of the presidents described her personality during her junior high and high school years. Many spoke of the continuation of qualities or characteristics from their childhood as already discussed in the previous chapter. However, there were some particularly interesting themes that emerged from the interview data regarding the women's personalities during adolescence. The women continued to be generally respectful, reflective, smart, self-directed, and helpful. Many women also used the word *obedient*, but more in the sense of following the rules, not necessarily blindly conforming to them. A few presidents mentioned a continued insecurity or lack of confidence, particularly during seventh and eighth grades. However, during high school all of the presidents described themselves as having good self-esteem and a sense of competence, as well as being confident and generally comfortable with themselves. One president explained:

> I was still immature, bashful, and not very confident in seventh and eighth grades, but I was always a good student. In ninth grade I suddenly became more outgoing and confident. I'm not sure why, but there was definitely some kind of transformation.

It is clear that none of the presidents were confident in all areas of their lives, but each was undoubtedly confident in at least some of their abilities. One woman stated:

> I was very confident in my own abilities during this time in my life; however, I wasn't always confident in my position or place.

Four women specifically mentioned that they were not easily intimidated by others, particularly peers. One stated, "I was confident and never let anyone intimidate me." Most were generally outgoing as they entered their high school years. One president's experience was typical:

> I was active and involved in my youth. Some would probably say I was bossy. I liked leading things and was comfortable with it. I wanted things to happen, and I learned that if you want to do something then you have to take charge to make it happen.

It is important to note that, although confident, a few women did describe themselves as "soft spoken" during these years.

Some of the women spoke in detail about popularity. Being popular was certainly more important for about half of them than it was for the others. Some of the presidents were in popular groups; others were not. One explained: "I wanted to be in the right group. I wanted to date the right boys. I wanted to be accepted and to be popular." Although all of these leaders-in-training wanted to have friends and be accepted, many did not care as much about being in the "right crowd." One president made a particularly insightful statement regarding her high school status and her own self-esteem:

> I think I was more popular than I thought I was. I didn't think I was popular, but I always had a boyfriend and guys asking me out. I was never a cheerleader. I saw myself differently. Academics were my strength. I knew I had good critical thinking skills, and I could see issues, problems, and solutions. This was more important to me than popularity.

It is clear that they all needed a support system; in all cases they were seeking support.

The women continued to demonstrate their strong academic skills and also continued to develop a passion and love for learning. One explained, "I was attentive and wanted to learn; I loved to learn." They enjoyed their formal and informal educational experiences and often noted the joy they found in developing themselves by participation in activities or serving in leadership roles. Sills (1994) reported that in general, female youth during that time often acted naïvely and hid their intelligence and abilities. This was not the case with these university presidents. Besides being confident in their abilities, they also continued to develop their self-awareness and self-reflection skills. For example, one president commented:

> I learned to keep my mouth shut about how well I did. I discovered people didn't want to hear about it. I continued to be reflective as I viewed the world around me and tried to find my place in it.

As Katira (2003) explained, it must have taken self-reflection and conscientious decision making to learn behavior and "new ways of being in and with the world" (p. 254). Researchers (Van Velsor & Hughes, 1990) have noted that there is a remarkable difference between genders with regard to the use of reflective learning about self and about self in relation to others. Women report a much higher rate of lessons learned from this type of activity. This was the case for these presidents. Researchers (Atwater & Yammarino, 1992; Van Velsor, Taylor, & Leslie, 1993) also argue that self-aware individuals will have more accurate self-assessments. Accurate self-reports are linked to effective leadership, self-esteem, intelligence, achievement status, and locus of control.

The combination of being self-confident and dependable, working hard, and having a good mind (being smart) seems to be at the crux of comments such as "I was bright," "I got good grades," "I kept on top of my homework and did well in school," and "I was a good student and always did beyond what was required." One president stated that she was confident in her ability to do any kind of work. Another explained, "I was a hard worker, determined, and competent." Interestingly, all of the presidents spoke about their desire and ability to work hard during these years. Like most teenagers, these presidents also wanted to enjoy life and have fun.

All of the presidents continued to have high expectations for themselves, and they also seemed to thrive on the expectations of others regarding rigor and excellence. Similar to the findings of Hennig and Jardim (1977), these women set for themselves an ideal in achievement. They were self-motivated, independent, goal-oriented, competitive, and self-directed. I found that my participants had "strong voices and a keen sense of competency," as did Stephens (2003, p. 51). As youth, the presidents continued to have a strong need to achieve. All of these women were active and involved during their high school years. They seemed to enjoy having multiple responsibilities, duties, and roles. They liked to do well, and they liked to get things done. One president explained, "I loved doing things really big and important!" Another stated:

> I was self-motivated and liked to get things done. I was always interested in figuring out how to make things better.

A third president explained:

> I had strong accomplishment needs as a teenager. I was a bit compulsive, but I had a lot of fun. I was driven in many things in my life and was excited to succeed or help others succeed.

These ten presidents displayed little fear of success, which was somewhat different for young women of that generation. Similar to Woo's (1985) findings, these presidents also "seemed strongly focused on professional goals and perfectly comfortable with their achievements" (p. 286). They were also beginning to be comfortable with power and influence in small ways.

Three of the presidents told stories about their sensitivity to criticism. These women listened to feedback from many sources and "sometimes took too much to heart." One explained, "I took things very personally, because I thought I should have been able to do better." It seems that most (if not all) of the women had some sensitivity to negative feedback. In fact a number of presidents spoke about sensitivity being an issue even into their current positions. The ability to self-reflect seems to have been an imperative element to assist these youth in being able to separate criticism from their identity and confidence and then still be able, in some way, to use at least a portion of the criticism to effectively improve and develop.

The presidents were certainly practicing many behaviors in their youth that would make them leaders. Based on observing the results of experiences and listening to feedback, they were learning which behaviors worked and which ones did not. They were getting practice in reading their environment and learning to adapt. They were developing the ability to learn from their mistakes, which they and others (Katira, 2003) argue is invaluable. Astin and Leland (1991) also found that effective leaders have a willingness and capacity to learn from any experience—even mistakes and failures. In fact, during this time they were beginning to hone the ability to look at failure as an opportunity to learn (Pankake, Schroth, & Funk, 2000a). Bennis (1989) stated that good leaders learn from their experiences. He showed that "mistakes contain potent lessons but only if we think them through calmly, see where we went wrong, mentally revise what we're doing, and then act on the revisions" (p. 117). A host of other writers (e.g., Bass, 1990; Hoy & Miskel, 2005; Pankake, Schroth, & Funk, 2000b) have also cited examples and research about high-performing leaders learning from mistakes and failures better than low-performing leaders.

As others (Hennig & Jardim, 1977) have reported, the women were also clarifying and developing their values and concepts of self at this stage. They were beginning to search for and find their voices. As Lyman (1995) argued, "developing voice is key to developing women's sense of themselves as leaders" (p. 211). By the end of high school the presidents were beginning to value their own voices. They had a strong need to influence. In fact, they were also exhibiting control. They wanted a sense of control over their environment. They didn't like being acted upon but wanted to understand how to influence their environment. They were managing their environment through their choices (for example, activities, network, goals, and reactions). They were setting boundaries for themselves. For example, they would choose places to excel, and they weren't interested in doing things when they couldn't excel. They were also starting to recognize and work within a systemic perspective. Some began to consider going against the societal norms (for example, college interests) and a few were going against their family norms (such as in choosing to obtain a college education). They started looking ahead at roles available later in life and wanted to prepare. In many ways they were already practicing leadership.

Youth Activities

Instead of focusing only on the activities that the presidents perceived as directly affecting their development of leadership skills, I chose to have the presidents reminisce about all of the activities in which they were involved during their youth. It has been said that "leadership development is an unintended consequence of many activities" (Sagaria, 1988, p. 9). Researchers (Guido-DiBrito & Batchelor, 1988) have found that all student activities and organizations "play an especially critical role as a laboratory for leadership development in which students learn, are tested, succeed, and sometimes fail" (p. 51). Hence, I analyzed all emerging themes related to their activities during adolescence. Most of the presidents explained that they continued many of the activities they had begun during childhood. The presidents spoke of the types of activities they enjoyed during their youth. For example, three presidents made the following comments:

> I loved to make things with my hands; I was always doing crafts. I sold the things I made door to door. It didn't scare me. It was actually fun. The more I sold the more excited I got. I saved the money and then probably spent it on clothes. I loved buying clothes!

> Band was important, so from seventh through twelfth grades I played in every football game. It was a small town. I loved band. It was an organization with a purpose. You had a job and could see how everything fit together. We marched, we played instruments, we went to the games, and we made a lot of noise.

> I was the class treasurer and was in charge of a magazine sale. I did great. I had opportunities to motivate and influence people. It was exciting, and I enjoyed that. I liked getting things done. Sometimes others volunteered, but I did a lot myself because I just wanted to get it done. I was beginning to have real accomplishment needs as opposed to power needs. I think they've turned out to be very useful personality traits.

It seemed that many of the presidents were not as interested in titles as being in places or positions to influence and make a difference. Although many of the presidents were involved in student government, some were not. A few presidents said that there seemed to be no benefit to taking "all kinds of time and energy to run for office in high school." They fulfilled their accomplishment and achievement needs in other, less structured forums.

All of these presidents enjoyed being involved and engaged in a variety of activities from sports to music to school leadership. One president commented, "I was very engaged in the things that were very much a part of high school life at that time." One explained: "I was involved in so many things and got positive feedback." They were busy by choice and learning to lead in areas they enjoyed. They were finding places in which they could excel or at least be good enough to enjoy. They were also seemingly seeking out supportive groups as they were developing competence, which is not purely an internal process, but rather a multidimensional interaction between an individual and her environment (Loeffler, 2000). A sense of competence can actually become an "ever-increasing force in women's lives as it dictates what activities women will or will not attempt" (Loeffler, 2000, p. 5).

Because of the presidents' self-reflective natures and abilities, they were also continuously learning about their own interests, circumstances, and selves. For example, one president reflected:

> Through participation in a number of efforts during my secondary education years, I learned that I needed to either be in charge or else be working with certain people to accomplish things. I didn't want to be involved just to be involved. I wanted to get things done. I needed to get things done.

Another discovered a weakness:

> I learned in high school that I wasn't good at delegating. It was good to learn this early. I've decided that it is a terrific learned skill. If you can do things well it is hard to have others do it. It took me many years after high school to do something about this. I've had to change. You can't do everything, and you also demoralize people when you do that.

The notion of learning from mistakes and failures is again a threaded theme through many of the presidents' comments regarding their adolescent activities.

> I ran for a visible office in our high school student government and lost. I did a lot of reflecting on what I might have done differently and why I didn't have the support I thought I had. I learned early that the practice of studying your mistakes and failures is a very important learning experience. This has been an important part of my leadership development. Maybe some of it is actually from taking on responsibility that I don't mean to take on and then analyzing failures and learning from them. I believe this is an important part of what defines me today. My failures may have been more useful in my growth and development than my successes.

One president told me a story of a particularly visible failure in leading one high school event and made the following conclusive comment:

> I had a difficult experience in high school that taught me that everything doesn't always turn out right. I got used to that, and it didn't frighten me after that. When people would worry I would say, "Well it will go wrong, and what if it does?"

Interestingly it appears that most of these women would move on to something else when the activity or experience no longer provided learning and developmental opportunities. They lost interest and motivation when they believed there was nothing left for them to learn. They seemed to thrive on challenge.

There was also a sense that these women wanted to influence (possibly even control) their environment through some of their adolescent activities. It also appears that nearly every activity they chose to participate in was social-oriented. Membership, leadership, and even just basic involvement in their activities meant that they were continually interacting, connecting, and building relationships with others, particularly adults and peers. This notion of the importance of relationship building during their youth was particularly powerful.

Competitive activities, including getting good grades, continued to be a theme throughout the presidents' youths. Although there were not competitive sports available for young women in many parts of the country (pre-Title IX) when the presidents were growing up, a few did have the opportunity to participate on organized sports teams. There seemed to be some resentment regarding some of the rules for women during these years. Those interested in competition began to see some injustice. A number of presidents commented on the stupidity of half-court basketball. Some were beginning to feel a sense of injustice because of their experiences with selected activities such as sports. One president was fortunate enough to be in a high school that offered the "real" (full-court) basketball team experience. She said:

> I absolutely adored the whole experience of being part of a team. It was a very enriching experience. I enjoyed sports. I was not the best person, but I was pretty good and loved it. I won the free throw city-wide shooting contest, and that is my great claim to fame. The whole notion of sports, of excelling physically and being a part of a team, was important to me.

When asked what competencies and skills one president developed from participation in sports, she explained:

> Sports are about a sense of team, of interchangeable parts. My leadership now is about building organizational capacity behind a vision. Our team is focused on building organizational capacity. It may not be as much about a team as it is about the way players adapt to one another

to advance toward that larger goal of winning the game. This could have very well been an important part of my own evolution that began during my youth.

Other researchers have also found leadership development opportunities with sports participation (Astin & Leland, 1991; Cornwall, 1993; Hennig & Jardim, 1977; Kelinske, Mayer, & Chen, 2001; Rayburn et al., 2001). In addition to learning competitiveness, sports provided women the opportunity to develop and learn goal setting, fair play, networking, teamwork, prowess, rules, principles, and values.

Sports participation is just one realm of competitive activities in which these women participated. Others are discussed below. However, it is important to note that, whatever the activity, these women seemed to seek out learning experiences that provided them with three things: competition, cooperation, and autonomy. They loved competition (even if it was only with themselves). They thrived on developing relationships and participating in activities that housed cooperative opportunities and challenges. And finally, they flourished when they had independence, decision-making authority, and problem-solving responsibilities and opportunities.

All ten of the women spoke of activities related to writing and speaking and the development of these related competencies throughout junior high and high school. Three were editors of their school papers. The one president who admitted she had somewhat of a rebellious streak told of a related experience:

> I liked being the editor of the newspaper. I remember one experience when we had to take the newspaper to the printer. We had to take the bus and go to another part of town. The printer was located on a big street in the busy downtown area with all of the shops. We did not go back to school that day. We ran around all afternoon. My friends remind me to this day that I led and they followed. I guess I learned political skills early.

A few of the presidents participated on high school debate teams. During that period, young women in general were rarely included on such competitive teams with young men. One woman spoke of her experience in the following paragraph:

> I didn't want to be on the debate team because I had too many other things going on. The debate coach said, "We need one more person, and we've decided on you." I told them I didn't know how to debate. They told me I had to get up and the topic was free trade, and I'd have to give a speech on why it was a bad thing. They said, "If someone objects then get up and deal with them." I remember the first time I debated. I wrote a speech, read it, and sat down. The judge was so troubled because I had time left. I told him I didn't have anything else to say. We won the debate, which was what the coach and my teammates had counted on. They knew I would be able to analyze the issue and take anyone's argument and "deal with it." I was the first girl on the team, and we took state that year.

Another explained:

> I learned early that I could think on my feet and speak well. Many of my activities during high school—school, church, and community—including debate, helped me practice and strengthen this talent. A variety of activities were helpful in providing me with opportunities to speak, convince, and argue my points, thoughts, and passions.

Two presidents reminisced about the opportunities they had to speak in church settings during adolescence. Both were asked to serve in leadership positions in their church organizations and were even asked to speak to the full congregations from childhood.

By the time they were in high school these leaders-in-training were fairly comfortable with giving speeches and presentations to children, youth, and adults. Overall, the presidents enjoyed being heavily involved in activities:

> Involvement in a lot of different activities and experience during my youth helped me develop a number of characteristics or competencies that have continued to be helpful in my leadership roles today. These include dependability, responsibility, organization, motivating others, networking, leading change, people skills, viewing barriers as opportunities, learning from my mistakes, and understanding roles.

As other researchers (such as Robinson, 1996) also found in their samples of women leaders, these presidents sought education in virtually all their experiences. There are also some new themes that seem to span much of the youth activities data. First, in addition to thriving on a sense of accomplishment, as already discussed, these women liked finishing things. They enjoyed projects with specific conclusions. They were very task-oriented and enjoyed the completion of events, projects, and assignments. Second, the data show that during adolescence the presidents began to understand there could be different ways to accomplish the same objectives. When they encountered roadblocks, they would figure out other options. These young women began to see that there was rarely one path to achieving any goal. And third, they were rewarded in different ways for their involvement in various activities. More directly, they were being rewarded for their gifts. These rewards came in various forms, such as positive feedback from peers and adults, invitations to participate or lead other groups or activities, awards and recognitions, and internal feelings of pride and accomplishment. It was clear that other people had confidence in them, and this also served as a type of reward. Interestingly, what seemed to serve as one of the greatest rewards for these women was the confidence, encouragement, and support that came from those individuals (often teachers) who held them to rigorous standards.

Leadership Positions and Experiences

Next I explored the presidents' perceptions of formal leadership positions and experiences during adolescence. First, I asked the presidents when they first remembered being in a leadership role. One said:

> I started taking leadership roles early on. However, I'm not a politician so I did not run for student government offices. My roles were based on discipline and academics.

Another explained that she organized neighbors and kids on the block to clean and sweep the streets and sidewalks. She said, "We got the block looking pretty neat." One president explained:

> I don't remember there being "leaders," but I was involved in the decision making. We created lots of things. I was active and engaged in deciding dates of dances, the name of yearbook, the school colors, and things like that. My ideas were valued. I enjoyed having many balls in the air at the same time. From these experiences I think I developed more confidence, and I improved my skills in speaking, expressing ideas/opinions, and definitely multitasking.

One president said that she had often been asked when she began leading in her life. Her first memorable leadership experience was with a valentine's box in first grade. She explained, "I wanted it done right. Others could help but I clearly had to direct." Another woman spoke of her early interest in leadership as well:

> People would talk about doing something, and I would say "Why don't we do it this way? This is faster."

These leaders-in-training seemed to be aware (consciously or unconsciously) of their leadership choices. They sometimes seemed to pick venues that provided opportunities for them to lead or manage in some way or at least offered the opportunity for them to control or influence their surroundings through their choices. Although informal leadership can be helpful for young women's development, it seemed that leading in formal settings also provided growth opportunities for these women. Their leadership choices were generally service-oriented, confidence building, and competency developing and strengthening. They were learning leadership by doing—not just theorizing about it. They showed the ability to self-start and seek out situations that would be beneficial for them. They were beginning to find the power within themselves to make a difference.

The presidents mentioned a variety of formal leadership positions during adolescence:

- Club (president, vice president, or secretary) (9)

- Student government (4)

- Girl Scouts, Brownies (3)

- School paper editor (3)

- Community service (3)

- Church youth (3)

- Sorority (2)

- Band quartermaster (1)

- Children's music director (1)

- Future homemakers (1)

Club leadership was the most common form of leadership for these women at that time. One president spoke of her experiences:

I became the president of everything I joined. People saw me as strong and capable. I was very organized and worked hard. People want you involved if you open your mouth and talk about how things could be done better. For example, I went to the first Latin club meeting, and I saw that they were floundering. I gave them ideas about how to improve and ended up in leadership. I ended up being in pretty responsible positions and loved doing that.

Another reflected on why she felt she ended up in club leadership positions and what she learned:

I was involved in so many things. I was the president of a bunch of organizations. I think if you are a worker bee, people always want to give you more work to do, and I was always willing to take it. That is a very good way to find yourself eventually in decision making positions because if you have done the work then people will want you to do something more with it. I ended up doing a lot of the work before I figured out I didn't need to do *all* of it to be *part* of it.

After serving for a number of years in club leadership positions, one president figured out something that then guided her future leadership decisions. Again, this is an example of the presidents' unique abilities to learn and reflect at this age. She said:

When I was a senior somebody wanted me to be the VP of something, and I said, "No, I don't want to do that because you never get anything done as a vice president. I'll be the president." I understood that the president was the position I needed to be in to really influence.

The previous list of leadership positions also mentions a band quartermaster. The president who had this position spoke of the enjoyment she found from the responsibility and autonomy that the position offered:

> One of my responsibilities in high school was taking care of the uniforms, which I thought was great. I was the quartermaster in the band. For one thing they had a uniform room, and I would go in and work instead of going to study hall. I would always make up work to do in the uniform room even if there wasn't anything. I loved the responsibility and thought it was fun.

One research study (Rayburn et al., 2001) reported that women learned more leadership in school than at home, work, community, or in a religious or spiritual setting. I found similar results. However, the presidents also found opportunities to lead in venues outside the formal school environment such as Girl Scouts or Brownies, sororities, church youth groups, politics, and community service. The presidents stated that most of these leadership opportunities were also helpful in a variety of ways for their development.

Two presidents stated that they "didn't seek leadership positions as a youth." Of course this does not mean that these women did not *lead*. They did not seem to care about formal leadership titles, at least during their teenage years. Yet many of the examples they cited included informal leadership within the framework of some kind of organization.

The women made similar comments regarding how they stepped into leadership positions. Most did not remember particular people telling them that they had leadership skills and encouraging them to become leaders. The presidents either became involved by going to meetings and voicing their opinions or someone would ask them to serve in certain positions or to accomplish certain tasks. One president said that she probably positioned herself so that she would be asked. Years ago one researcher (Ernst, 1982) explained that most women in this era waited for professional development opportunities to be handed to them. This was not the case for these presidents. Most mentioned that teachers or administrators would request their involvement in leading efforts or serving in formal leadership positions. Many of these requests included working on small tasks, not necessarily large visible work. It was clear that people around these women seemed to know that they had the skills and abilities to make things happen.

Employment

The presidents mentioned that they held a number of paid jobs during high school. Three of them were waitresses and seemed to have fond memories of the experiences and the competencies gained. These presidents spoke of the various skills acquired from being a waitress: multitasking, interpersonal relations, and political competencies (for example, being courteous and attentive to get more tips). One mentioned:

> I started out being a busgirl and soda jerk. I enjoyed the experience of being a waitress. I learned multitasking. I loved the challenge. My dad would help me count my tips at night. I become the cashier and then ran the office. I continued this into college and during the summers.

Three presidents worked in retail. One found it very boring saying, "It was a lot of standing around, and I don't like to stand around." Yet another one loved retail because it was challenging, explaining:

> I was good at sales. I was a service-oriented person. I remembered client's names. I was willing to work later hours. I enjoyed the opportunity to buy at a discount. I was a good producer. I strengthened my skills in networking and persuasion through this job. I was the one who could be counted on.

At a glance these two quotations might seem opposite; however, there is an underlying theme that should be considered. The first quotation came from a president who worked in a low- to middle-end retail store. She was paid the same rate per hour no matter her performance. It was a fairly reactive and passive environment. She wanted to keep busy, but she didn't have enough to do. The other woman worked in a high-end retail store that was busy and challenging. She was paid commission for her sales and was rewarded for putting forth increased effort. She liked being held accountable for her performance. There was clearly a difference in motivation for these presidents. I expect that if the first president worked in the same environment as the second, she would have enjoyed her job.

Three of the university presidents were instructors with supervisory responsibilities of some kind during their youth. One taught ice skating and had management responsibilities that came with it. She enjoyed the organizational and leadership opportunities this gave her. Another taught swimming lessons and was also a lifeguard. She explained:

> I loved teaching swim lessons. I liked the different levels and watching my students grow and develop. I taught in the mornings and lifeguarded in the afternoons. I became the head lifeguard the second year and learned the work and operations. I wanted to be able to do everything. Do it all. Do it by myself.

Again, the themes of autonomy, influence, and control seem to surface in many of these and other quotations. As discussed previously, the women's choices were generally service oriented, confidence building, and competency developing. Another president had been a camp counselor for many years. She not only helped supervise and organize the children, but she also had opportunities to teach and educate them. She said:

> I was a full-time camp counselor during the summer with
> about 60 kids. They were always getting into fights so I
> had a lot of practice with conflict management. I thought
> of it as helping people get along and be okay together.
> Working as a camp counselor helped me learn to work
> with different types of people and motivate them. I paid
> attention to who was there and figured out how to get
> things done. I practiced my problem-solving skills.

This quotation highlights a few important themes that span various
sections of this chapter. First, this president was able to practice new
skills—something all the presidents enjoyed doing. Second, she was
able to work, interact, and build relationships with different types
of people. And third, she was given the opportunity to problem
solve. All of the presidents thrived on opportunities to problem
solve in any kind of situation, including employment.

Many presidents mentioned they did odd jobs such as cleaning
house and babysitting. One of the presidents was a secretary in her
father's business. She learned to type well, which she thought was
a very helpful skill in life; yet she saw the dark side of a family
business and knew that she did not want to be involved in similar
businesses when she got older. Another president had a job working
in a political campaign:

> It was a great job. It was the best job in town for kids.
> The Happy Channer was running a romp campaign on
> the democratic ticket and everybody in the state of
> Kentucky was supporting him. He was an old gover-
> nor who had been passed over by the new party big wigs,
> and he actually won. We stuffed envelopes and all those
> wonderful things. We had a very good time. Sometimes
> we went to rallies, and we carried these nifty little signs

that said, "Be Like Your Pappy and Cast Your Vote for Happy." Later I learned that I was the "bag lady." Everybody knew every kid in town, and we were trustworthy. On Friday evenings I went up to [name] Law Offices. He gave me an envelope of money, and then I went to others who gave me envelopes of money, and I took it back. I had no idea what I was doing until I was in a college political science class.

Of course I had to chuckle as this particular president was telling me this story. She smiled and laughed as well. Through this job she learned that she did enjoy some of the elements of the political environment. By reflecting on this experience during college, she also learned how people can sometimes be used by others to unknowingly participate in unethical or dishonest activities.

Interestingly, three of the women had families who did not allow them to work regular jobs. Two of them were the African American women interviewed. One explained:

The kinds of jobs that were available to an African American woman at a high school level in the summer were not jobs that my parents wanted us to take.

This president continued to learn lessons of injustice, discrimination, and class issues through experiences and situations such as this. The other woman stated:

My family didn't believe in paid employment for youth. Your school was your work. I had lots of chores. In my large southern city the children and men were taken care of. The children were kind of cherished and not allowed to work. We weren't allowed to be involved in the things in the society. We were kept very insular. I did help my mother's cousin (who lived next door) with her catering business as a volunteer. We couldn't run around outside. We had to be in the house under our mother's sleeve. We lived in a very hard neighborhood so we were kind of protected.

The Caucasian president said that her mother would not let her work during high school because she had too many other things to do. During the summer they traveled and did things as a family. Although she wanted to work, her mother would say, "You need to spend your summer having a good time." Her mother had a lot of responsibility when she was a child and wanted to make sure her two children had the opportunity to "enjoy their childhoods." She was reacting to her own experiences.

Based on the presidents' responses, employment experiences taught them a variety of leadership skills and competencies. As other researchers (Rayburn et al., 2001) have found, employment opportunities during adolescence can teach skills such as multitasking, responsibility, negotiating, communicating, planning, organizing, and dependability.

Influential Individuals

When I asked each of the presidents to speak about the individuals who influenced them during their adolescence, most of them smiled. They had fond memories of a variety of individuals who they felt had made some kind of impact on their lives. The presidents used a variety of words to describe all of the individuals who had influenced them in some memorable way. These terms included *role model*, *mentor*, *coach*, *advisor*, *supporter*, *sponsor*, *friend*, and *example*. The women mentioned the following individuals:

- Parents (10)

- English teachers (7)

- Peers (5)

- Math teachers (4)

- Latin teachers (3)

- Relatives (3)

- Church teachers and neighbors (3)

- Family friends or nanny (2)

- Chemistry, biology, economics, Hebrew, history teachers (1 each)

- Camp counselors (1)

- Principal (1)

All ten presidents spoke of the continued strong influence of their parents during adolescence. The importance of parental relationships and influence during these years is well documented (Astin & Leland, 1991; Cubillo & Brown, 2003; Hennig & Jardim, 1977). Most of the presidents mentioned that their parents continued to encourage them to learn, be educated, use their minds, and aspire for college. Similar to what other researchers (Cubillo & Brown, 2003; Hennig & Jardim, 1977) have also found, the presidents' homes continued to be generally stable and enriching.

Before addressing the specific quotations, it is important to address some broad themes that emerged from these interviews. First, it was clear that all of the presidents had authority figures that saw their gifts and talents and demanded quality and rigor. Although many of the parents of the presidents fit this criteria, all of the women had a least one (most had more) other adult who did this. Their self-confidence increased when other individuals demonstrated trust and confidence in them and their opinions (Dunlap & Schmuck, 1995). As Fels (2004) explained, "Without earned affirmation, long-term learning and performance are rarely achieved" (p. 54). Second, as already noted (Wells, 1998), the women in this study learned a great deal from relationships and connections with others. Van Velsor and Hughes (1990) found that women have a remarkable capacity to learn from other people. Wells (1998) noted that the foundation of what shaped women entrepreneurs' self-images was in their relationships with others. Images of themselves were formed as they were reinforced and rewarded by people they respected. They were also exposed to authenticity and were changed by it. Third, partly through the positive influences of others, each participant began finding her own voice, realizing a sense of empowerment, and discovering a power within. Other researchers (De la Rey & Suffla, 2003; Green & King, 2001; Wells, 1998) also found this to be the case with future women leaders. Outside the presidents' immediate families, the individuals who had the greatest influence were teachers, peers, and other adult figures.

Teachers

All of the university presidents had teachers in high school that made a profound influence in their lives in some way. One said:

> I had great teachers in high school, some of which I wanted to be like and some of which I did not want to be like. Interesting, I learned from both types.

Sometimes it was the one-on-one attention given by a teacher:

> I had many great teachers in high school. They continually worked with me and would often pull me aside and work with me individually.

Other times the presidents were influenced just by being one of many students in a particular teacher's classroom: "Teachers were influential but none really gave me personal encouragement." These women spoke most highly about teachers who had passion about their subject areas. The word *passion* emerged over and over in the interview data. The presidents described themselves as being passionate during high school, and they appeared to be strongly influenced by teachers who were passionate about their own subjects and lives.

One of the most interesting similarities among these women was that seven of the ten spoke of the strong influence of at least one high school English teacher. One explained:

> She was an amazingly challenging teacher who really pulled out things that I think most of us never thought about. We had lots of writing assignments and lots of challenges around things like vocabulary development. She wrote the most provocative thing in my yearbook: "No lesser lights for you . . ." It has stayed with me forever. She was really challenging me to be all I could be. She was very important in my life.

This president loved being challenged and appreciated this teacher because of her rigor and encouragement. She clearly remembered this yearbook inscription over forty years later. Another president reflected on the following incredibly powerful experience:

> Ms. Wyman was our high school principal and also the English teacher. She was strong, powerful, and impressive. She was a force to be reckoned with. The day the Brown v. Ferguson ruling came out of the Supreme Court, I met her in the hallway. I had been at the school for play practice. She uncharacteristically looked troubled and upset. She said that the Supreme Court had just ruled, and the day would come when there would be blood in the hallways. She was so troubled. That was all she said. At first I thought she was a bigot, but she wasn't. She understood the cultural clash that was coming and was ahead for schools in the south. She knew the

> impact that it was going to have. She was looking ahead
> with a kind of grief that it couldn't happen some other
> way . . . that it had to come to force to make it happen. I
> was in a totally segregated school.
>
> Years later I understood things. I met a person of color
> at a professional meeting who asked if I knew a black
> individual in my small hometown. I did not. We then
> realized that I never had a way to know her. The isolation
> of the two worlds was absolutely complete, and none of
> us noticed it.

This experience gave a young girl a profound look at the issue of
discrimination during those years and in years to come. In fact,
this woman's current institutional priorities centering on the issues
of diversity speak to the possible impact of this initial experience.
This event also served as feedback to this president by giving her
a vote of confidence that she would be able to think through what
was said. In fact, this single experience may have forced her into
a reflection that was far beyond her years and experience. It very
possibly helped her with an increased realization that the injustice
in the world was now in her own life and hometown.

Two other presidents made particularly insightful statements
about their English teachers:

> She was really tough and harsh, requirement-wise. She
> was feisty and had high expectations for her students.
> She probably helped steady me a lot in terms of goals and
> working towards them, staying on the path, being less
> reactive to things, and by just being able to kind of take
> things in stride. I think this was through her example as
> a role model. She challenged me individually, but she
> somehow did it in group settings.
>
> My English teacher was very influential. She also worked
> with the newspaper, and I was the editor so I worked

closely with her. She was a very strong, demanding teacher. She pushed very hard. She loved literature, and she loved writing. She would sit and read poems, and it would just be wonderful. She had that passion. She would handpick the best students coming in and put them in her English classes. She would then sort of nurture them through high school and then help them get their applications submitted to college. I was one she mentored. She had a strong positive influence on me during those years.

There are some interesting characteristics that emerge from these stories and statements. The English teachers had passion, they respected these young women enough to demand rigor, and they made it possible for the presidents to succeed.

Four of the presidents stated that their math teachers were influential as well. One explained:

He made math come alive for me. He was a pretty significant influence in my life at that time. When I went to college, my intention was to major in math. That is the kind of influence he had on me. He saw potential, and he pushed and jostled me. He would ask me how to solve problems. He put me on the spot because he thought I could do it, not because he was trying to embarrass me. I always knew that.

The comments from the other three presidents highlighted the competence and commitment of the instructor, the joy they had from interactions with these teachers, the one-on-one attention (one called it a unique relationship), the way the teachers challenged them, and the specific methods they used to teach. All four of these women (and others) spoke of the importance of learning math and how that kind of logical thinking is an important leadership competency.

The presidents also mentioned Latin, biology, Hebrew, orchestra, chemistry, economics, and history teachers. Many of these teachers did not necessarily "pull" them aside. The presidents said they "just really enjoyed the classes." They acknowledged that some of these teachers even sent them in the direction they eventually took in college. The women also spoke of the teacher's passion, support, and encouragement.

The two African American presidents spoke of attending high schools with all women teachers. One explained:

> I went to a black high school. There were strong women all around me that showed me women could do or be anything. This made me believe I had choices and options for my future.

It seemed important to both of these women that they saw strong, competent women working in professional jobs and making an impact on those around them. However, one president spoke of a continued understanding during high school of injustice, race, and gender:

> The teachers were all African American women. They were looking to encourage and push young African Americans who had talent. My teachers were very encouraging to me. In another time and place these women could have been anything. They would have been economists instead of economic teachers. They would have been classics professors or scholars instead of Latin teachers. They were very intelligent and capable women in the sense that they knew their subject matter very deeply. They were committed to teaching and did a great job. They were very motivating. They were focused on students who had certain capabilities and were motivated at moving us along.

The message that this president received was that she needed to make a difference in her life. She needed to do more. The future college plans and career paths of this woman and others (Olsson & Pringle, 2004) seemed to focus on openings and opportunities instead of dwelling on injustice and barriers. It was clear, however, that the ten university presidents did begin gaining an understanding of discrimination and injustice during their youth.

In sum, the influential educational authority figures had a number of common characteristics. These individuals had confidence in the presidents, challenged them, and gave them appropriate and accurate feedback (appraisal support). They held them to rigorous and demanding standards while making it possible for these leaders-in-training to succeed if they worked hard and were engaged in the learning process. The teachers were passionate about their topics and about the education of youth. They enjoyed teaching and made it an interactive and uplifting experience for the presidents. And finally, they provided encouragement and support.

Peers

Although all presidents spoke of their peers during their adolescent years, five of the women felt that their peers were particularly influential and important in helping them develop leadership skills and competencies. One said she "learned from friends who were more experienced." Another explained that "I planned to go to college because they planned to go to college." Some researchers (Rayburn et al., 2001) argue that peers were often seen as more influential during adolescence than were teachers or parents. Although important, I didn't get the sense from the ten presidents that peers were necessarily more influential for their development of leadership skills than were adult figures. It is clear, however, that friendships were vital for effective human development during these years. One research team (King & Bauer, 1988) stated, "Peers who are willing to commit themselves to giving individual and group support for commonly shared situations are an invaluable source of friendship"

(p. 83). I found this to be the case in my research. Although all of the women mentioned friendships during these years, the five that stated their peers were very influential seemed to do so for one reason. These friends were those who gave them candid and accurate feedback. One president explained:

> I had really close friends that became my base of support from which I operated. They were the sounding board to tell me what I was doing wrong. We were very open. We didn't think too highly of ourselves and talked about everything. We would tell it like it was. It was so important that you have people who do that, to tell you when you are being silly.

These were friends who the presidents believed were rational, compassionate, smart, sensible, and honest. They were stable peers the presidents could trust.

Other Adult Figures

The presidents mentioned others who also made an impact on their development. Similar to their childhood experiences, a number also mentioned aunts (and uncles in one case). Their comments focused on the examples, encouragement, talents, attitudes, and values of these individuals. One president said:

> My aunt was an absolutely marvelous woman. She was a great role model. Her husband was an invalid, and she had four children. She also took in two of her younger brothers during the Depression. She worked a regular job, and for extra money she took in foster children when their parents went on vacations. She was strong, and she was competent.

They also mentioned others: nanny, godfather, church members, camp counselors, neighbors, school administrators. The presidents were influenced by them because of their competence, strength, abilities, talents, rationality, and openness. The presidents were also influenced because they trusted these influential individuals. They believed that these people had their (the presidents) best interest in mind. The presidents chose adults who would give them feedback and who they could talk to them as though they were adults. The presidents' reflective natures and abilities emerged in some of these data. One president stated:

> I watched and learned from a lot of different people. I would think about what they were doing that made them successful at something. I've always done this, I think. I had a wide variety of people who had an impact on me because I was able to do that. I always got lots of encouragement, because I was a good student. I received reinforcements. People had expectations for me (teachers, people in church, scouting advisors, club advisors, and others). Those expectations helped me in having goals and in developing confidence.

All of the presidents made general statements regarding their interest and ability to observe and learn from others. During these years it appears that the presidents had the ability to observe systems in which they could see fairness and rigidity. They had the ability to step back and discover meanings. The influential individuals around them helped them understand (through openness and discussion) issues and events. Somewhere in these women's childhoods and youth they had adults who let them speak openly and freely. They knew adults who provided examples of rational and accurate discussions in which two or more sides of issues could surface. I wonder if some of this came in their dinner table conversations during childhood and youth, as mentioned in Chapter Two. Somewhere during their youth they were able to express their opinions in a rational forum in which the conversations (sometimes arguments) were enjoyable and enriching. Their voices were not hushed (at least in some settings) by adults who weren't worried about being viewed as the "authority." They were allowed and encouraged to think critically. They were encouraged to find their own voices.

Significant Events, Challenges, and Opportunities

Throughout the entire set of interview questions, the women spoke of memorable events focused on their adolescent years, and they shared what they learned from each of them. Some of these have been discussed in previous sections of this chapter. The events and challenges not yet covered revolved primarily around such issues as health, financial struggles, and relocation. Besides the information already presented in this chapter on opportunities, the presidents also mentioned receiving recognitions and awards.

It is important to note that although discrimination and injustice have already been addressed, four Caucasian presidents told of situations where they first discovered discrimination existed. They seemed to struggle with these issues and situations even though they were not the ones discriminated against. Some events focused on seeing race discrimination around them. A number of presidents also mentioned the type of discrimination that comes from the issue of popularity versus unpopularity during these years. The African American women also spoke briefly of race issues and the types of challenges and opportunities that came with those.

Three presidents talked of health issues in their families. One spoke of continued challenges with her diabetic sister, as already described in Chapter Two. One spoke of a personal injury that took years of physical therapy. She remembered thinking "I'll be darned if this knee isn't going to bend, and I'll be darned if I'm ever limping." She worked hard and fully recovered. Two spoke of their fathers' health issues. One father had an accident when his daughter was in tenth grade. This president spoke of the strength of her mother during this time as she took charge of the family. She explained:

> This taught me not to expect life to be predictable, to just not think that things are just going to be wonderful all of the time—that hard times are going to come. This was an important lesson to learn. I have used it throughout my life and have been better for having learned that.

One president spoke of what she learned from a failed family business:

> When I was in high school my Dad's business failed. There were lots of emotions and issues that had a major impact on my parents and our family. Because of this experience I became very aware of financial fragility. I learned that I was never going to be financially vulnerable again as long as I lived. I learned that I couldn't depend on anybody but myself. I wanted to make sure that was the case. I learned that you are in a very different position with an education if you have a bachelor's degree before you worry about a career. After that happened my mother went back to school and worked for years on getting her degree. I could see the value of having a degree early in life to be prepared.

Family moves were other challenging events for these women. One spoke of the types of activities she was planning to participate in before her parents announced that she would be moving. She had been very involved in school and was traumatized by the move. She said:

> It took me a year to kind of get into creating a place for myself in a new environment. I can say now, looking back, that it was good for me and taught me a lot.

Another remarked:

> Through enduring a family move during my teenage
> years, I developed resiliency. I learned to adapt. I had to
> figure out how to reach out and make new friends and
> become part of a new group. This was helpful. I've had
> to do similar things throughout my life and continue to
> do so in my current role.

Many of the presidents had opportunities to discover that they
could overcome difficult events and situations, and then exercise
or gain some control over the next steps. As one researcher (Katira,
2003) explained, "The way leaders embrace the struggles and strife
that life throws at them is a telling tale of their strength of character . . . To me, this ability to transform moments of struggle into
constructive, positive and transforming learning situations is a sign
of a true leader" (p. 254). Some character traits that surfaced as the
presidents spoke about these events include tenacity, sense of obligation, caretaking desires, and capacity to overcome challenges.
They seemed to learn these things from life itself. The ability and
desire to learn from things around them seemed to serve these presidents well during adolescence. It definitely helped prepare them
for college and professional lives.

I asked the women about any recognitions or awards they received during this time. Some mentioned being prom queens or
winning speaking or other types of contests. Such recognition did
not seem to mean a great deal to these women. In fact, they weren't
even sure there was a link in any way to developing leadership.
Two women did share experiences of awards that made a difference
in their lives. The reason was because the awards came with enriching opportunities for experiences and growth. Two presidents
explained:

> In junior high I won the Ford Motor Company award
> for school editors. I won a trip to Detroit to be in the
> national competition. It was a wonderful experience. I

met people from all over the country. It was great, it was fun. I loved writing. It made a difference in my life in many ways.

I won the speech contest and had the Odd Fellows send me on a sixty-five-day bus tour of the eastern U.S. and a week at the United Nations. I actually met Eleanor Roosevelt. It was a wonderful trip. I met some interesting people and there is no question that all of those experiences put together contributed to my self-confidence, my knowledge of the world, and my ability to function in the world.

An interesting theme emerges from these comments. The awards or honors that had long-term meaning or value for these presidents were the ones that came with opportunities for growth and development. As mentioned previously, the women thrived on experiences and rewards that provided them with opportunities to learn, including the exposure to the broader world.

College Plans

Nine of the ten presidents said that throughout their childhood and youth they always planned to go to college. One president was the first in her family to attend college. She explained that although there were no college discussions or expectations, she was always expected to get straight A's in school. Some of the presidents mentioned that educational goals after high school were a topic of discussion at home, whereas others said that the expectation of college was unspoken. For example, one woman explained:

There was a quiet expectation that I would attend college after high school. I didn't feel any pushing on the issue from my parents, but I always knew that is what I needed to do.

As expected, each president had a different plan for college. Some of the presidents conformed somewhat to the wishes of their families. One president noted:

> I knew I would go to college. I majored in English because my grandmother insisted "I had to know something." I minored in economics because my dad insisted "I know something." They had different definitions of what it meant to "know something." I loved the writing and reading. I knew that education was going to make me a better person and be well rounded.

Some of the presidents' plans were different from those of their parents. For example, one president said:

> Without expressing or planning it, there was this un-stated expectation that I would go to the state teachers college and become a teacher. Yet I wanted to go to another college. I got a scholarship so I could go to this other college. I wanted to major in math.

In a number of cases the presidents had to create ways to do what they wanted to do. They used their problem-solving skills by thinking of different options to be able to achieve their goals. They began understanding that there were different ways to get to a specific goal. They made some plans and decisions and then moved forward.

I compiled a list of what the presidents (during high school) thought they would major in when they attended college (some women gave more than one response):

1. Math (3)
2. Chemistry (3)
3. English (2)

4. Science (2)

5. Biology (1)

6. Latin (1)

7. Economics (1)

These are difficult subjects, and many were not traditional at that time for women.

Four of the women spoke of negative experiences with institutional counseling and advising during high school. One president stated:

> The high school counselor didn't do a great job with me. I had the most minimal kinds of support. She had a devotion to the kids who were clearly going to college. I was sort of left to fend for myself. I had no family sense of what I was doing. My parents were not overly enthusiastic; they thought I could figure it out. They weren't resistant but kind of neutral. I had to pay for it, so I started working early. My friends came from circumstances where they were expected to go to college. However, I did not and had to find my own way.

Another explained:

> I didn't have a counselor to give me good advice. I would have probably gone a different route if I had been counseled differently. Going into medicine just didn't occur to me. I majored in zoology.

The women were able to learn from both positive and negative experiences. They were aware of gender injustice issues but didn't dwell on them. When they faced obstacles they did not give up. Most did not push the obstacle down. These women made mindful choices—sometimes they chose different routes to accomplishing a larger goal. They also demonstrated the ability to let things go and move on. They didn't hold on to resentment and anger. Much of the time they were able to make rational and logical decisions even in the face of injustice and other obstacles. It is important to note, however, that they remained true to themselves, and they did what they loved. Interestingly, today these particular presidents have a strong belief (backed by action) that good solid high school advising leads to better choices in education and careers.

Seven of these women did not think they had a lot of career options. Many of the presidents reflected on societal norms about women's roles. Some thought they needed to be school teachers. Their definition of success was somewhat limited in the sense that nobody "had to go to college." Some did not think they would work full-time after having children. Their expectations revolved around the notion that women's primary responsibility was to raise families. Higher education was important, but raising a family came first. In contrast, others planned to go to college and then work. Three of the women felt they had lots of choices, and education was the means to get them there. One stated:

> It didn't occur to me that I couldn't do something. I just always assumed I would do something that was worth doing. It was never a question as to whether I would or not. I assumed I would. I saw women do that and it was helpful.

Another explained:

> I understood priorities, but I knew women could do any-thing. We always thought we could do anything.

One concluded:

> I felt external barriers, but my parents had the expec-tation that I could do anything I wanted to do, and I believed it.

Final Thoughts

The results of my study are supported by the work of Kaminski (2003), who outlined the following four stages of leadership development. During adolescence the presidents had a melting pot of experiences that provided them the opportunities to begin learning how to do the following:

1. *Find their own voices.* They learned to speak out and continued to realize that their opinions mattered. They focused on basic self-esteem.

2. *Develop basic skills.* Through schooling, activities, and influential individuals, they improved their written and oral communication skills and learned to work under the direction of others. Their focus was on developing skills and confidence.

3. *Figure out the politics.* They were learning how to get things done in the existing political context. Their focus was at an organizational level, and they were developing an understanding of political and institutional factors.

4. *Mobilize others.* They were developing and directing projects that they chose and they stayed committed to them. Their focus was on having a long-term impact.

By the time these women entered college they had thus already built a solid foundation for competency in leadership. Although young women may have different developmental preferences and processes for various activities and skills, it is clear that competency development during adolescence is imperative for the development of leadership skills and abilities.

Takeaways

1. Adults who are demanding and hold youth to high standards—yet provide a way for them to succeed—can facilitate substantial growth in youth who have desires to learn and grow.

2. Providing youth with experiences that help them discover that there can be different paths to accomplishing goals is important. Obstacles and challenges do not mean that one should quit. They provide opportunities to use creativity and problem-solving skills.

3. Supporting an adolescent's desire to participate in a wide variety of activities and experiences, particularly those that provide new opportunities for them to stretch beyond their current comfort zones, can assist youth in developing a wide range of leadership skills.

4. Engaging conversation at the family dinner table can provide powerful developmental experiences for children and adolescents if they are allowed to voice their own opinions and ideas and also feel they are heard, respected, and valued.

5. Adolescents benefit later in life by developing the ability to hear criticism, separate it from their own identity and confidence, and then use at least a portion of it to effectively improve and change.

6. To strengthen skills in teamwork, networking, and interpersonal communication, adolescents benefit from involvement in a wide variety of experiences that allow them to interact, connect, and build relationships with others.

7. Through school, church, community, and family opportunities, young women have leadership opportunities (if they chose to take them) that are typically service oriented, confidence building, and competency developing and strengthening.

4

College Years

People who are making an effort to embrace the future are a happier lot than those who are clinging to the past . . . People who are attempting to grow, to become more comfortable with change, to develop leadership skills—these men and women are typically driven by a sense that they are doing what is right for themselves, their families, and their organizations . . . [Those] who encourage others to leap into the future, who help them overcome natural fears, and who thus expand the leadership capacity . . . these people provide a profoundly important service for the entire human community.

John P. Kotter

Knowing others well enough to lead them successfully can only be as powerful and as concrete as how well we truly know and understand ourselves.

Parker Palmer

The women university presidents continued to learn and develop important leadership skills and competencies during their college years. Interestingly, the same themes that emerged during childhood and adolescence continued to surface during adulthood. As Coutu (2004) notes, the drives that have sprung from childhood and adolescent patterns and experiences carry over into adulthood. These women were still attempting to grow and to become more comfortable with change (see Kotter, quoted at the beginning of the chapter). They were driven to develop leadership skills and were continually putting themselves in situations in which they could learn to overcome the natural fear of new experiences and challenges. During adolescence and young adulthood, when the presidents began encouraging others to develop, they found enjoyment in others' accomplishments, and thus, as Kotter (1996) stated, they "provided a profoundly important service for the entire human community" (p. 186). College years were significant times for these ten university presidents. They took critical steps forward in learning to know and understand themselves. Each took a different educational path that was enriched with a variety of educative experiences in and out of classrooms.

Researchers (Boatwright & Egidio, 2003) have not yet identified the "factors that influence women to have an interest in seeking leadership aspirations prior to entering the work world and experiencing competing external pressures" (p. 654). Yet Astin and Leland (1991) explained, "leaders emerge from the critical interplay of personal values and commitments, special circumstances or historical influences, and personal events that motivate and mobilize people's actions" (p. 66). And Galambos and Hughes (2000) contend that all types of lifetime activities and interactions contribute to leadership development, including family, school, social, and community. This appeared to be the case for these ten presidents, as they continued in their distinctive voices (Walton, 1996) to describe their personal journeys to top leadership positions in higher education. The commonalities in their experiences may provide insight for other women about their own lives and situations. As Cooke (2004) also confirmed in her own research, these university presidents' life experiences and opportunities have come together to create their unique hearts and minds.

During the interviews, each woman spoke in detail about her college-related background, activities, employment, influential people, leadership positions and experiences, awards and recognitions, plans and goals, and significant events. These stories provided insight into what may have influenced their leadership development, decisions, and perspectives.

Backgrounds and Personality Characteristics

Bennett and Shayner (1988) once wrote:

> To effectively educate women and encourage women to be leaders, we must establish an educational environment that is simultaneously supportive and challenging, demands the intellectual rigor necessary to develop the capacity for value formation and commitment, and provides the structures that encourage independence, strength, self-confidence, and autonomy, as well as caring and interdependence. (p. 33)

In different ways each president's educational environments provided this foundation. Clearly, these women had the ability to create their own support and experiences from their surroundings, which is not necessarily common for most female college-aged students. Particularly in previous generations, women who had the ability to see opportunities (sometimes in unobvious places), create opportunities, and then take those opportunities were those who developed strong leadership competencies.

All of the women presidents went immediately to college after completing high school. Two were seventeen years old and eight were eighteen years old when they started college. Within a few months of high school graduation, eight of the women had moved into the on-campus dorms (now called residency halls) at their universities or colleges. One lived at home for the first year and then changed colleges and lived in a boarding house and then a sorority. Until she married, the remaining president lived at home while attending college. Half of the presidents spoke of receiving scholarships of different amounts. Some had parents who provided much of the financial support during these years, yet a few presidents were required to support themselves.

Most of the women passionately immersed themselves in having the "full college experience." One president exclaimed, "I loved it! I had a wonderful time in college!" Another explained:

> I liked what I was doing. I was away at college, and I was in a strong academic program. That was my dream fulfilled! I had good experiences and lots of friends. I did lots of socializing. Overall, it was an enriching experience.

Although all presidents loved their college experiences, there were difficult moments for each of them. One president made the following insightful statement:

> I was so thrilled to be there. College was great, and college was terrible. It was all of the things it was supposed to be.

They continued to love and thrive on learning and education. One president explained, "I was very much oriented to learning and to following my intellectual interests." Another stated, "I enjoyed everything I took." College deepened the skills and competencies they had begun to develop earlier in their lives. Now they were developing in different ways and exploring diverse areas.

Each woman had a wide variety of first experiences, and college was an exciting place to be. One described her experience:

> It was exciting, a rich array of sources and different ideas, different people, and beautiful buildings that I could contemplate in. My campus had wonderful huge libraries, museums, and music. There was a lot of things that I had not yet experienced in my life that all came rushing in.

> I loved higher education—the complexity. It was absolutely fabulous; it was a rich experience. I am absolutely confident that the quality of the studies at the university I attended is the reason I made higher education my life's work.

It seems that many presidents had profound experiences or realizations during college, consciously or unconsciously, that may have eventually brought them back to higher education as their life's work.

Seven presidents completed their bachelors' degrees in four years; the other three were awarded their degrees after only three years. One participant noted:

> I went straight to college after high school and was done in three years. It just seemed like I should be done early. I always pushed myself. Nobody told me I needed to hurry. I guess I just liked the challenge of doing so.

Although the women loved learning and the overall college experience, they were somehow driven to graduate in four years or less. A few were driven by impending marriages and wanted to make sure they were able to graduate. Others made statements regarding their drive or achievement needs. Some had work-related dreams, as one president stated:

> I wanted to graduate quickly and become a school teacher. I did it in three years even though I also had to work my way through college.

These women were driven, self-directed, disciplined, and goal-oriented during their college years. It is evident that they pushed themselves to succeed. They also became more astute at seeing opportunities and devising strategies to obtain them. Table 4.1 lists how the presidents described themselves during their college years.

Five presidents eventually obtained education-related bachelor degrees, four received degrees in the math and science area, and one

Table 4.1. Personality Traits

As a college student I was described as . . .	
A critical thinker	Having a good mind
Accomplishment-focused	Having a good orientation toward needs
Achievement-focused	Intelligent
Adaptable	Innovative
A good decision maker	Learning-oriented
Always doing my best	Logical
Aware of opportunities	Motivated
Aware of others	Not an extrovert
Competent	Open to development
Competitive	Optimistic
Confident	Passionate
Curious	Rational
Determined	Reflective
Disciplined	Self-aware
Driven to excel	Self-directed
Enjoying challenges	Self-driven
Focused	Self-improvement-focused
Fun and enjoyable	Setting the curve on the exam
Goal-oriented	Strategic
Going the extra mile	Successful
Hardworking	Task-oriented

acquired a social science degree. These women attended a variety of undergraduate schools that included public and private, large and small, all-women and mixed gender, liberal arts and comprehensive, teaching-centered and research-centered, and renowned and less recognized institutions. All but two (Midwest, mountain-west) institutions were located in the east (north and south) generally within the same state or adjoining state of the presidents' upbringings.

All of these presidents either majored or stated that they would have majored—if the counseling or opportunities were "different" or "better"—in math or science. For example, one president said that her high school counselor didn't give her the support she needed, and she felt that she had to fend for herself. Her parents were not overly involved, and she knew she had to pay for her own college. She started out in a male-dominated science program and eventually had to change majors. She stated:

> I was a good science student and loved it. Had I had better counseling maybe I would have tried a different kind of science first that may have been more acceptable for women. The only fields that were acceptable for women at that time were nursing and teaching.

Another woman recalled:

> Chemistry was my favorite subject in high school, but I ruled it out. I had to work to pay for my education, and my schedule and the required labs didn't appear that they would work. I decided to go into a different direction because of my schedule. I did not really seek counseling but dismissed it before I even tried.

Another explained that chemistry was always her favorite subject as well, and she excelled in it. She wanted to major in chemistry, but she was "afraid of one professor" and didn't feel she could talk to anyone about it, so she went into humanities instead. Finally, one president stated that as a freshman she tested very high in hard science and medical fields, but the counselor said it was not good for girls to major in these areas. She took this advice and majored in education. This president explained:

> I went through some specialized testing as a freshman in college. My advisor said that I had VERY interesting test results. She said, *"If you were not a girl I would put you immediately into a premed or heavy science program. It's just*

> *VERY clear*. Yet, the reality is that if your father is not in a position to endow the medical school then you are just not going to get in. *I just think that it is a bad direction for a woman."* I remember that conversation well. Counseling was not good at that time. I wasn't intimidated. I just thought that was the way it was. Women just didn't get into med school in those days. It was reality.

These self-confident women had the ability to accept what they couldn't change. They chose to adjust, as needed, and didn't spend time on the things they could not influence or control. They were able to confront reality, including sexism, and then chose to move on. They made pragmatic adaptations. They acknowledged others' perceptions but were interested in accomplishing their own goals, as well as the goals of the efforts or organizations they led. If needed, they looked for different pathways to achieve these objectives. The presidents were practicing rationality in the face of obstacles.

Most of the women felt their degrees and at least some of their courses were helpful in the development of specific leadership skills. For example, one president stated:

> One of my favorite classes was philosophy. Thinking through philosophy and having it make sense was one of the hardest things I ever had to do. It was a challenge—to be able to take it from the place where the philosopher began to the end. I would try to think through how the philosopher went from here to here to there. That is the way I could hold on to it and remember it. I use the same thinking skills often as a university president. I began learning this skill in philosophy.

A number of women loved math and spoke of its helpfulness in leadership. One said:

> I've always thought that math skills were one of the most important things that I had. You break things down, put

them together, and proceed in a logical fashion. It's a real discipline, that discipline of thinking logically and sequentially. When something pops up that doesn't make sense, we figure out how it fits. I think my liberal arts education was enormously important in giving me a breadth of mind exercise. I had lots of philosophy and math, and I know now that it was beneficial in my development.

These courses helped strengthen thinking and processing skills. All presidents seemed to enjoy logical, sequential, developmental topics and courses. Half of the women majored in education. The presidents explained that increasing teaching and curriculum development skills was immensely helpful. One explained that she has become a lifelong teacher. In fact, she continues to teach each day although now she teaches staff, vice presidents, and boards of trustees rather than students.

Although the presidents were driven to complete their college educations, many did not have a definite plan of what they were going to do after obtaining degrees. They were interested in education for life, not just for a job. Some saw themselves primarily as mothers and homemakers, at least while their children were young. Four wanted to obtain degrees before marriage and children. Some knew they would go directly into the workforce after college but did not know what specific work they would be doing. Many of the education majors did plan to teach after college, at least until they had children. Only two said they had plans to continue their education immediately after graduation. A few outright stated that they had no idea what they would be doing with their degrees once they graduated. These women practiced flexibility and adaptability in planning and setting goals during these college years. During their undergraduate years, the presidents did not know that their lifelong careers would be in higher education administration.

Activities and Employment

Klenke (1996) wrote that leadership development should include opportunities to learn and practice technical and task-relevant skills, a variety of interpersonal and social skills, and various conceptual and cognitive skills. She explained that these are critical leadership skills, as they are important in working effectively with team members or followers and they help facilitate the establishment of vision and effective decision making. The ten presidents in my study had opportunities to develop these attributes. Boatwright and Egidio (2003) explained that competent women with needs for positive relationships often seek leadership. These university presidents had those needs, as will be evidenced by the activities discussed in this section.

One president had plans to marry early, because she had met her husband during high school. She had to pay for her own schooling and didn't have time to be involved on campus. The other nine were very engaged in college activities and experiences outside their general course load and college requirements. One noted:

> I was immediately elected as a class representative on our campus, which was a big deal. I loved being involved on campus and trying to lead change for the good.

Another stated:

> I immediately became involved in leading clubs and efforts on campus. I never planned to run things. It just kind of happened to me. I couldn't keep my mouth shut. I tend to say something and was always willing to speak out. In fact, I don't remember ever saying nothing. I'm not the silent type. I just *have* to speak my mind.

It is important to note, however, that leadership opportunities for women outside of women's clubs, groups, dorms, and sororities were rare on most co-educational campuses. One president also discussed the added limitations that the combination of gender and race played on available leadership opportunities. However, it is clear that these leaders-in-training took advantage of the opportunities available to them. They often created these opportunities instead of passively waiting for them.

The presidents mentioned that they participated in the following activities as leaders, followers, or participants:

- Campus activities (for example, sporting events, dances, parties)

- Community volunteer (YWCA, hospitals, political and community activism, voter registration, Girl Scouts/Brownies, other)

- Dorm or residency hall leadership or work

- Honor societies

- Projects and research with faculty and administrators

- Royalty (homecoming court, queen of parade)

- Socializing, partying, and dating

- Sorority

- Student government

- Student organizations, clubs, or projects (traditions commission, theater production, event planning, national women's chapter-president)

- Yearbook editor

Student activities and organizations in college play, according to Guido-DiBrito and Batchelor (1988), a "particularly critical role as a laboratory for leadership development in which students learn, are tested, succeed, and sometimes fail" (p. 51). The activities and responsibilities of the presidents provided occasions to strengthen their abilities and competencies, feel a sense of service, claim recognitions and honors, and expand their experiences and understandings. For example, one president explained:

> I learned about tea on Friday and where you wear gloves and hats; this sounds silly now but it was a very empowering experience, not just academically.

The sorority experience was particularly influential for some of these women. Although most of them lived in dorms, six were members of sororities. A few said that they joined a sorority because it provided a "social and community service outlet," and they enjoyed it. The presidents who became sorority leaders had a stronger sense of the significance of sorority life. One stated:

> I was in a sorority with a great group of friends. It was good. Just getting in was a huge deal. I didn't realize at the time how important it was. It felt right to me, and that was where I wanted to be. I became very active in sorority things. I became an officer in the sorority, and it was interesting. It was just a local sorority but there was great pride in the fact that the major nationals were always after us. We were considered the best. We were always winning the contests, and we were always at the top. These are good memories for me.

Another sorority leader spoke of profound experiences that this leadership provided her specifically in developing competencies that she would use in her later positions:

> I was the president of a chapter of a black sorority for two years during college. We had to manage across a broad geographic area. We could not be chartered on

our own campus, so we could not have our functions at the colleges we were attending. We had to rent space for our functions, arrange security, charge people to join or attend, take care of the finances and budget, plan themes and activities, interface with other organizations (such as law enforcement and the fire department), recruit, figure out transportation, and generally bring people together.

One of the important skills this president learned was managing without support and outside the system. This was a particularly powerful experience for an African American female college student during the turbulent decades of the 1960s and 1970s.

These presidents had a strong desire to continuously learn and develop. When they did not believe that experiences or activities could provide them with growth opportunities, they often discontinued their involvement. One president explained:

> I joined a sorority my first year of college, and I did a lot in that. I remember that it was a big deal to get in. However, I wasn't crazy about sorority life. I thought a lot of it was kind of silly, so I wasn't real keen on it. I actually dropped out my senior year because it wasn't a big deal to me any longer. I found that I was more interested in my academics and, when that was jeopardized by something in the house, I just didn't bother staying with it. I never lived in the house. I wanted to live in the dorm because I worked there.

The women who became leaders of the sororities stayed involved and enthusiastic about the value of sororities. These women had continued opportunities to develop and practice leadership in at least some of its complexity (leading female college students is definitely complex!). For the others, once they learned what they felt they could learn from involvement, they lost interest.

Reports on the benefits of sororities on the leadership development of female college students are mixed. For many years sororities provided the only leadership experiences for women on college campuses (Fisher, 1991). Some researchers (Fisher, 1991; Robinson, 1996) contend that sororities can increase the self-confidence of members, help students identify with something of worth, and provide a support system and resource for networking and mentoring. Yet others argue that they do more harm than good by "promoting superficial interpersonal relationships, attitudes of social elitism, excessive alcohol consumption" (Fisher, 1991, p. 65); endorsing "anti-intellectual, conservative, pragmatic, and unduly social emphasis to student life" (Wilder, Hoyt, Surbeck, Wilder, & Carney, 1986 as cited in Fisher, 1991, p. 65); and restricting the development of autonomy, and encouraging homogeneity. Hennig and Jardim's (1977) study of twenty-five CEOs reported that all of the women rejected sorority life and chose to live in the dorms. Six of the presidents in my study did join sororities but then chose to live elsewhere.

The presidents also spoke of employment experiences during these years. As expected they all wanted to make money. Many of them spoke of the "fun" that they had with particular positions. Most highlighted a few areas or skills in each of their jobs that were helpful in developing leadership. For example, over half of the presidents (during high school or college) were employed as waitresses. The presidents felt they learned many important leadership skills from this work experience, such as multitasking, conflict management, customer service, dependability and responsibility, motivation, political skills, and interpersonal skills. All of the former waitresses believed the experience provided them with helpful leadership training. Learning responsibility and dependability was common to all employment experiences. Learning to work hard, even when they did not "feel" like it, was also an important lesson for some presidents. Overall the presidents had a general optimism and awareness of what they could learn from various jobs. They continued honing their skills and competencies through the following employment opportunities:

- Cashier

- Dorm receptionist

- Instructor

- Lab worker (dishwasher; assistant)

- Library worker

- Odd jobs

- Registrar's assistant

- Research assistant

- Secretary

- Summer jobs (camp, lab worker, state park, waitress)

- Teacher's aide—children

- Waitress

A few presidents made some interesting comments about their employment experiences. One wanted to work in a science lab and there were not often openings for research assistants. She took a job as a lab dishwasher so she could spend time in the lab. She said:

> Sometimes he would ask me to look in microscopes and give my opinions. I was so thrilled. I loved being there—being around the people who worked in the labs. I loved seeing what was going on and talking to them about their work.

She felt that by being in the lab she could learn about her field. She learned about management and leadership by observing others during this time. Her persistence, ingenuity, and fortitude led to enriched opportunities later in her college years. Another president spoke fondly of her lab positions and experiences. She also enjoyed the work because it gave her the opportunity to use her existing knowledge and to learn new things. Another president spoke in detail regarding a secretarial position she had in an attorney's office:

> I worked for an attorney as an intern. He took us under his wing. Often the women who interned for him would work for him after college. It was a great and valuable experience. I learned to type well. I worked in an office building in a big city. It was a real growing up experience for me. Yet it became more drudgery than exciting. It wasn't challenging after awhile. It certainly convinced me that I never wanted to have to do that for a living. I remembered that lesson for years in making career choices.

This was a useful lesson for this president in planning her future career. A number of presidents said that managers or supervisors gave them additional responsibility because of their skills and ability to step up and adapt. For example:

> In the summers I worked in a state park. That was fine, but when the hostess was sick I always had to do her job. I didn't want to be the hostess because it was not my favorite thing to do. I was the only other one who got the numbers down and understood what was happening. I knew that I was the rational choice to be the interim hostess.

The last few quotations are examples of women in positions that could no longer teach them new concepts or skills. The presidents wanted challenge in the various arenas of their lives and, if they didn't have that challenge to help them continue growing, they no longer enjoyed the experience and preferred to move on to something else. Many noted that their experiences have created who they have become and how they continue to learn.

Overall, through participation in activities, organizations, and employment opportunities, the presidents realized—as did those in the research study of Fels (2004)—that doing something well could be a reward in and of itself. As other researchers (Galambos & Hughes, 2000) have also reported, the women in my study also discovered that college provided them opportunities to expand their understanding of themselves as empowered members of a community. It helped them learn that they had abilities in the areas of leadership, influence, use of power, and collaboration. These women continued to find their "voices" by being true to themselves (Lyman, 1995). Voice is a means for manifesting internal truth (Helgesen, 1995). Similar to what Wells (1998) found, the presidents continued to learn about themselves, and to define their self-image and identity. In part, this takes a self-monitoring personality. Day, Schleicher, Unckless, and Hiller (2002) argue that self-monitoring personalities are linked to leadership emergence. Cooke (2004) believes that only when self-identity and integrity blend does an individual have both the heart and mind to lead well. Finally, Boatwright and Egidio (2003) stated that "glass ceilings are broken by opportunity accompanied by desire" (p. 654). In all these ways the presidents began to discover that individuals with ability, desire, drive, *and* opportunities are those who can be successful in life and leadership.

Influential Individuals

The lives of these university presidents focused on relationships and trust. Sagaria (1988) explained that the "concerns and values of women are embedded in the interdependence of human relationships" (p. 7). As Wells (1998) also found with her business entrepreneurs, women learn through relationships and connections with others whom they trust. It was other people who, in a way, gave them permission to be themselves, act, aspire to reach their full potential, and transcend traditional gender roles (Astin & Leland, 1991). Astin and Leland's (1991) work confirms my research that the women presidents often admitted they would not have accomplished their goals and desires without the influence, encouragement, and guidance of other influential individuals.

Half of the presidents mentioned that they really didn't have any notable formal mentors or role models during college. One explained:

> There were no women on the faculty. I had very formal relationships with professors. I never felt particularly influenced by them. There were lots of things that influenced me, but I don't think there were role models or particular people that influenced me during these years in terms of my attitudes and values.

Many presidents spoke of the lack of female mentors available during those years because of the shortage of women faculty. As one president noted:

> There were so many more males than females in faculty and administrative positions on college campuses. That was just the nature of it.

Some would argue that female mentors are best suited to prepare protégés for leadership (Noe, Greenberger, & Wang, 2002), and that women must have female leadership models to encourage them to aspire to these positions (Wood, 2006). Yet most of the university presidents in this study did not have female mentors or role models in their college environments, and they were still able to succeed.

Despite these issues, all of the women did provide examples of individuals who made an impact on their lives in some way during these years. In addition to the continued permanent positive influence of their parents and families during these years as other researchers (Hartman, 1999; Wells, 1998) have found, these presidents' responses fit into three primary categories: (1) faculty members, (2) academic leaders, and (3) friends and peers.

Faculty Members

The presidents mentioned influential professors in a variety of disciplines: economics, education, classics, zoology, physics, philosophy, history, speech and drama, and sociology. Some presidents spoke of one-on-one connections with faculty members, in which they received appraisal support, as the primary reason for the influence. For example, as a freshman one woman was summoned by an economics professor after an exam. She explained:

> I didn't know what economics was until this course with 300 other students. After the first exam the professor called out two names and asked us to come by his office. I went to see him and he said, "You have a gift for economics, and I think you should consider majoring in economics." He didn't know who I was before this meeting. He explained that there were not many women in economics, and he would be pleased to serve as my faculty advisor. I was surprised. I didn't switch immediately, but I did the next year. He served as my advisor until I graduated. He was one of the most important people in my development in many different ways. He looked after me but didn't hover. He was a coach. He would say, "Have you thought about graduate school? Why don't you come in and talk about it when you are ready." He was very important in shaping my life.

This male faculty member encouraged this president to go against the norm with regard to traditional female majors. He became her advisor, coach, and mentor.

One president spoke of the powerful learning experience she had in working one-on-one with a professor on a theater production. Another president told of an influential speech-drama professor who provided feedback that was helpful in increasing her self-esteem:

> When I was young I had bad teeth, and I had always been afraid to get in front of people or smile. My speech and drama teacher loved my speaking voice and encouraged me to speak. She would say, "Your speech is so well organized." She made me feel so good, and I became confident that I could speak well. I remember her still today. She taught me not to be afraid of teaching. She would say, "When you speak you lose all of your inhibitions. You have a beautiful smile." She helped raise my self-esteem.

Fels (2004) confirmed that in the "overwhelming majority of cases, the acquisition of expertise requires recognition" (pp. 53–54). She explained that long-term learning and performance are rarely achieved without this earned affirmation, and that an important source of affirmation is ambition. These presidents received affirmation for their strengths.

Other women were not specifically influenced by one-on-one interactions and encouragement from faculty but felt an impact from the overall classroom teaching-learning experience. One president simply stated "I loved my classes. I was impressed with the faculty." A second noted, "I loved to learn so lots of my professors influenced me." Another noted:

> I liked a lot of professors in zoology. I just liked the classes and the lectures. They didn't really advise me or even serve as role models or mentors.

A common theme throughout their upbringings is that they were most profoundly influenced by educators with a passion for teaching and their subject matter. Stories are an important way for individuals to learn and develop. One president who was majoring in the sciences explained:

> My favorite was a classics professor who taught Greek and Latin medical terms at 7:30 in the morning. I never missed a class. He had stories about how each one of those words in the little dictionary came about. When you take the word and break it down into the different parts, it came from Greek or Latin roots. I absolutely loved it. He never pulled me aside. It was a big lecture class, yet I learned and developed through classes and stories.

One president explained that education faculty members had high expectations and standards. Although she didn't remember specific situations, she recalled:

> They were very direct and engaged with their students. In education we had a lot of day-to-day coaching. There was probably a lot of mentoring going on there that I didn't even realize at the time.

These presidents didn't necessarily need individual contact and encouragement from academic mentors to move forward in their scholastic goals; yet being in classes and feeling a professor's passion was influence enough. The presidents provided examples of certain instructors or classes that influenced their choices in college majors. For example, one president explained:

> My freshman physics professor was uniquely interesting and taught a special way. That was exciting and was probably what got me interested in physics in the first place. I never particularly developed a personal relationship with him during my undergraduate years.

Another stated:

> We had a very young, energetic, cool—probably not
> quite Ph.D.-type—instructor. We did Plato and Aristo-
> tle. He was a great teacher. I thought this was the most
> wonderful stuff I had ever run into in my entire life. This
> experience convinced me early that I wanted to become
> a philosopher.

My final point is this: the presidents provided examples of
types of comments faculty members would make (often in the moment) that would help them understand their own strengths and
weaknesses—a vital skill in self-discovery. One president said:

> When I graduated from college my advisor said I had one
> problem. He said, "You assume the rest of the world is as
> smart as you are. A lot of the world is not rational, and
> a lot of the world is not smart. That will bother you." It
> still does. That has been said by others since. I did not
> know this but I think it was helpful that he pointed that
> out to me. It was insightful. I do assume a rationality
> that is not always there. People don't always behave in
> rational ways. The academy tends to accept and assume
> that, and often that is not the case.

Academic Leaders

Four presidents mentioned academic leaders as individuals who had
made an impact in their development during college. One president
spoke of the opportunity she had to work with an associate dean
on a long-term project:

> The associate dean asked me to work on a research
> project with her. It was a very valuable developmen-
> tal experience. I had just a modest role, but I went to her

office and home over an extended period of time. It was a great experience for me and opened up yet another part of what I think that connects me so deeply with what universities are and what universities do to the students that go through their portal.

Sometimes it was just a short incident that would cause reflection and change—even in some small way—in the hearts and minds of these women. One president shared an example of a seemingly small gesture by a school administrator:

> From a distance I admired the dean of the graduate school. He was kind of a role model, and I knew he was a remarkable human being. I was working in the academic office, and I remember that my paycheck had gotten lost when I moved from one job to the other. I was poor and couldn't literally buy food if I didn't have it. I remember overhearing a quiet conversation between the male dean to his office manager. It was getting late in the afternoon and nobody could find my check. She came out and informed me that the dean would give me a personal check if they couldn't find my check. He didn't know me at the time and was very distinguished. I was profoundly touched by this. I couldn't imagine anybody like him doing something like this. I had never known anyone like him in the first place. He worried enough about me to be willing to give me a personal check. I learned about the importance of compassion, even in the workplace and even with individuals who may have insignificant positions.

The dean was taking care of an employee, someone he didn't even know. He was an example of an individual in authority who was interested in developing and caring for others. This president, as a college student, had the ability to understand the pivotal nature of these types of moments. The presidents showed a type of humility that comes with the openness to listen, learn, and be influenced. Although they were confident, they did not exhibit a sense of entitlement. They appeared to stay grounded in reality and rationality.

The presidents were also influenced by other academic leaders. The dean of women at universities was the most powerful women's position on campuses at that time. These deans were known to be empowered and had major influence with other administrators, faculty, and students. One president stated:

> The dean of women at my university was a very strong woman. She was an all powerful creature. Today that position just runs the dorms and passes out the contraceptive policies, but in those days she had an office just about as big as the president's. She ran the women students. She was powerful and very good. We all knew her pretty well because we interfaced with her all the time. She was a real presence in the minds of the women. I admired that she was absolutely rational. I respected that quality and learned it was an important trait in leadership.

The women respected positive female examples of rational thinking and behavior. Rationality was viewed as a strength and logicality as an asset. Many of the presidents admitted they were not the most patient individuals. The importance of learning patience was not particularly important to them until they had positive examples. One president explained:

> During my undergraduate education I worked with a female registrar. I learned a lot from her. I learned to regard patience as a virtue, something I had never considered before. She was an extraordinarily patient person. She gave people time to learn and grow. During that time I also saw, for the first time, some real examples of

discrimination. Until this point in my life, being a woman had been nothing but an advantage. I saw her work devalued when it should not have been. Although we kind of knew that women didn't always get a fair shake, it hadn't touched me personally until now.

Peers

Finally, three presidents spoke of the influence of good friends and peers during their college years. One spoke of a close-knit group of friends in high school who continued on to college. Her friends were sounding boards to tell her what she was doing wrong or what she was doing right. They were open and honest. They would "say it how it was." She recalled:

> Open feedback from friends was critical for me to gain insight and strength as I went through college. I learned to be open to feedback from people I trusted. This has helped me through the years. It is so important that you have people who will do that for you.

Women don't always know their greatest gifts until someone tells them. They often believe that all people are good at the types of things they've excelled in. These women were not arrogant college students. Although they were confident, they did not understand the powerfulness of their skills and abilities during these years. Influential people helped them understand themselves.

Recognition of Leadership Ability

After discussing the most influential people around them during college, I asked the presidents who, if anyone, recognized their leadership skills during those years. A few had people single them out, as already discussed. One president said, "They saw things in me I could not see in myself." Although influential individuals saw competence and ability, the presidents did not believe that most saw or looked specifically for leadership talent during college. One president explained:

> I don't think anyone recognized my leadership ability when I was a student, but I think they knew I could be an effective part of a team.

A second stated:

> They didn't see leadership ability, but a lot of faculty affirmed the strong characteristics, good mind, and that I always went the extra mile.

People did ask these leaders-in-training to be involved, do tasks, or serve in leadership positions. Others knew these young women were responsible, dependable, could figure out how improvements could be made, and liked to get things done. People naturally asked them to be involved.

Significant Events, Challenges, and Opportunities

The women shared insights regarding the events, challenges, and opportunities that they believe had an impact on them during their college years; about half were positive situations and the other half were difficult and challenging. These college experiences can be placed into five categories: (1) involvement, (2) influential individuals or relationships, (3) family and partner issues, (4) roommate or friend issues, and (5) academic experiences. The first two categories were discussed earlier in this chapter. First, the presidents' involvement in specific groups (as a leader or member) and participation in other activities were important experiences, and gave them profound experiences in the complexity and influence of leadership. Their decisions to join or quit groups or organizations (for example, sororities, student government) changed the course of their experiences. Second, the influence and opportunities provided by specific people were important in the women's development.

The third category many presidents mentioned was family and partner issues, which facilitated a need for reflection and decisions, thus providing a growth opportunity. Three participants spoke of the death or serious illness of a father during their undergraduate college years. These experiences caused, for the first time, "deep grieving and traumatic moments." All spoke of the incredible strength of their mothers during these years. One president spoke of her mother moving to a new town after her husband's health deteriorated quickly. She wanted to be close to a family support system while she moved into a house where she could care for her husband and also care for two additional patients so that she could provide for her family. This president said:

> My mother needed a continuing income so she could care for my father. There were a lot of struggles my parents didn't talk much about. I knew money was a real issue.

A few presidents also noted some serious struggles they had with parents regarding the choice of colleges and of degrees. Some of these women could have been swallowed up in their various challenges, but they saw themselves as worth fighting for.

Some of the women were married and spoke of the opportunities and challenges those circumstances provided them, including a husband on active duty during these years. One president spoke of falling in love with a young man, dealing with his draft, and then coping with his death. Two women spoke of pregnancies before graduation and the joy and challenges they provided. One spoke of a husband who was not supportive of her finishing school, causing difficult and reflective times. Two spoke of high school boyfriends attending different colleges and how growing apart and changing priorities during those years caused pain and difficulty in decisions that needed to be made. One president explained:

> I realized that I didn't want to go home. He still wanted to go back to our hometown. We'd live in a house on a hill and have a station wagon full of kids. I didn't think that would be enough.

Some of these women had hard choices to make early in their lives. They had the self-realization that they should fight for themselves, although often in quiet yet firm ways.

A few presidents shared stories about roommates and friends related to broken confidences, drug or drinking issues, pressure to be involved with things they did not believe were right or helpful, boyfriend problems or pressures, and a few minor altercations with law enforcement (fourth category). The women learned a great deal from these experiences regarding conflict management, enduring through hard times, courage, standing alone when necessary, keeping a vision in mind, and remaining logical and rational when emotional issues surrounded them.

Finally, additional college experiences (fifth category) included curriculum struggles, switching majors because of gender issues, an accusation of cheating, challenging programs or instructors, and problems because of lack of counseling and encouragement. Three presidents spoke about the profound impact of their student teaching experiences. One explained:

> My student teaching was a real eye opener for me. I had never been in a public school. I experienced teaching at an all-white junior high while it was being integrated. It was a very interesting time. I learned a lot.

Another president discussed a particularly influential internship that demanded that she reflect on life and death.

> I spent time in the morgue during my internship. That had a real impact on me. I had a chance to do a few autopsies but the concept of bodies coming down within minutes of death wrapped in sheets and tied was strange. I had to tie the neck up and tie things down. Seeing them wrapped in sheets, tied with a toe tag, and put in the refrigerator impacted me in a different kind of way. I saw them come in and go out. It's a life, and now it's gone. I thought about how fast life can go. I wondered once you had died if you were really gone. After death it seemed that people just became objects like a sack of potatoes or something. I struggled with that. It was hard. I thought about how important life is to live. It is one of those things that I really remember.

Such experiences offered the young women opportunities for profound realizations.

So many *moments* were particularly influential in these presidents' lives. There were many situations in which these women were influenced by watching, observing, studying, and listening to others around them. They were even influenced by one-time statements, encouragement, or feedback given by someone who may not have been a mentor, coach, or even role model. Insightful moments came in a variety of ways. For example, one president stated:

> I remember walking into a school building and seeing something etched in the wall. It was the Athenian Code. It talked about our role being to leave a place better, stronger, and more beautiful than when you entered it. It spoke of honesty, courage, reverence, respect,

and civic duty. I loved this. I read it from the first day, and I thought "Isn't that a wonderful, wonderful set of ideas and a way of thinking." I have it in my office area now.

This president had an open-mindedness that seems to be important in growth and development. She was forward thinking and carried with her critical learning from her life thus far. She loved being reminded about the nobleness that life could be.

Overall, I was struck by the presidents' awareness and ability to learn from ordinary and extraordinary experiences. Even in the face of difficulties, these women focused on openings and opportunities (Olsson & Pringle, 2004). As Cooke (2004) found, from times of chaos and uncertainty extraordinary leaders grow to "know and recognize their inner selves as well as the outer reflection in the mirror." Katira (2003) stated that the ability to "transform moments of struggle into constructive, positive, and transforming learning situations is a sign of a true leader" (p. 254).

Graduate School

Wisker (1996) once said, "The knitting of life and study are essential in many women students' lives. The cohesion and coherence of the two helps produce a framework for learning and development" (p. 43). The connection of these two spheres begins to take center stage particularly during graduate school. All but one (who went immediately into a Ph.D. program) received various types of master's degrees (M.A., M.S., M.Ed., Sc.M.) in areas related to their bachelor's degrees. However, one did receive a master's of education administration with goals of obtaining a leadership position in a K–12 environment. Degrees ranged from philosophy to social work and also included special education, economics, secondary education, and a variety of science-related emphases. Seven presidents pursued these degrees immediately (or within a year or so) after graduating with undergraduate degrees. Two started working on master's degrees two to four years later, and one took a longer break to bear and raise children. The presidents explained that they decided to pursue graduate education for a variety of reasons: desire for more education, encouragement from others (undergraduate professors, employers, spouses, and family members), opportunities, boredom, need for challenges, drive to do more in life, need for career progression, or problems and questions that needed more education to understand. A president described her experience as she sought answers to questions through education and wanted to be part of a solution:

> I taught for two years in the public school system. I had students who were not learning. I was intrigued with their problems and what I might do to better work with them. I started going to night classes at the university. I discovered they had a strong program in the psychology of learning. This was a brand new field at that time. Psychologists didn't agree that learning was malleable back then, and they were beginning to change their views. It was an exciting time. This inquiry eventually led to starting a graduate program.

The following statement was made by one of the presidents about the challenge of boredom:

> I loved raising my kids, and I loved the time I spent at home. After I had had my last child I discovered that I was busy but bored out of my skull. That year the bookmobile stopped right in front of our house and had all kinds of wonderful things on American history and world philosophy. I was hungry for learning. I felt kind of brain dead. I hadn't planned on graduate school, but I started taking courses and one thing led to another.

Clearly, the presidents picked fights or causes that were critical to who they were becoming. They chose not to fight all injustices. One president provided some history and advice on how young women should determine where to focus their energies:

> I did not choose to do physics either knowing that I was the first or one of the first to do so. I just did it to do physics, because I loved it. I thought it was important. I've always felt that science and engineering are important. I wanted to do it, had the talent to do it, so I did it. When I speak to women now, I tell them not to get discouraged by talking so much about the treatment and struggles of women and minorities. I tell them to focus on why they want to do it. They need to understand that they may struggle at times, but they should focus on what it is that they really want to do.

Four presidents obtained doctorate degrees in higher education administration; two additional women had other types of educational doctorates. Hence, six of these women had doctorates in the educational field, and four majored in noneducational areas. Four received Ed.D. degrees (doctorates of education), five received Ph.D.s, and one remains a doctoral candidate because she had job opportunities and promotions that interfered with the completion of her dissertation. There is wide variation regarding the timing of doctoral degree completion. Some started the doctoral program immediately after the completion of previous degrees. However, some of them gave birth to children and stayed home with them for several years before deciding to pursue terminal degrees.

The women continued to develop discipline-specific skills during their graduate school employment positions and obtained part-time jobs that interested them. Many of these positions let them experiment with securing support and working in their fields of interest. The presidents listed their employment during the graduate school years.

- College and summer programs instructor

- Experiment evaluator

- Graduate assistant

- Higher education administrator

- Internships

- Teacher in K–12 school

- Odd jobs in science: cadaver dissector, note taker

- Ph.D. assistant

- Research associate

- Science fellow or grant recipient

- Special projects coordinator in higher education (curriculum, programs, administrative assistance)

- Statistical associate

A number of the presidents were working full-time when attending school, especially during their doctorate programs.

Professors and faculty advisors made up the core of the individuals who had a positive impact on the presidents during their graduate degree programs; some became mentors and role models and occasionally coached when there was an opportunity. A majority of the presidents were strongly encouraged by faculty members and researchers to continue into Ph.D. programs and to apply for specific discipline-related fellowships. In two cases, influential faculty members and advisors moved into powerful administrative positions and offered the women wonderful jobs. One

president commented about the relationship she had with her doctoral chairman:

> He was a powerful force for good in my life. He was a
> friend. He pushed me hard. He knew I had what it took,
> even when times were very difficult.

Another had a graduate professor who gave her one-on-one encouragement. She remembered well one day when he told her that
he knew she could do great things. Another had some one-on-one
guidance but appreciated her advisors for other reasons:

> They were good mentors because they left me alone.
> They knew what I was going to do or what I wanted to
> do. They kind of pushed me in the right direction and
> let me do it. They gave me feedback, but I was left alone.
> I liked it.

Most of the presidents seemed to have had good matches with
their advisors that were probably not accidental. The president
who made the previous statement thrived when she was left alone.
Others flourished by having closer guidance and direction.

Similar to previous educational experiences, the presidents were
still strongly influenced by classroom experiences. One president
explained:

> I had an elderly professor in my doctorate program. I
> didn't spend one-on-one time with him; it was just his
> classroom presence. It was the influence in class that
> made the difference. He was a role model. He told stories
> of his life, and I considered his influence. I looked at how
> he could walk into a classroom and calm things down in
> various ways. He had a strong presence. I read everything
> I could find that he had written. He had the ability to
> put the world and his faith together in a beautiful way.

Again, this president was influenced by a passionate educator who loved teaching and his subject area. As previously discussed, there were also powerful moments when someone would give these women one-time insight, encouragement, or ideas that they would then seriously reflect on and ponder. The powerfulness of "the moments" continues to become clear in the data. One president explained that nearing the completion of her Ph.D. she was place-bound. Her institution wanted her to teach part-time after she was done. A faculty member from another school on campus told her:

> Don't let them turn you into an adjunct professor. There are a lot of ways to be happy. Get a tenure-track job or go do something else. You can be active in research without being a researcher by profession. It will take a lot out of you. It will wear you out, but you can do it.

She remembered this statement well. It challenged her to really analyze her choices after graduation.

Most of the presidents mentioned the word *role model* as they spoke of those whom they watched and respected from afar. One woman spoke of an internationally known faculty member whom she enjoyed listening to and observing. Another president referred to these individuals as *indirect mentors*. She watched them and tried to learn from them, but she wasn't able to get direct mentoring or encouragement because of her gender and race. These mentors may never have known that they were indirectly mentoring through their words and actions. This same president was able to work directly with the president of her institution because of a student leadership position. She said:

> I watched how he dealt with controversy and pressure and finding solutions when people seemingly did not have common ground. He was very influential in that I had opportunities to observe him and reflect on things that had happened.

The presidents also told me about some of the memorable challenges during these years. One spoke of a serious situation regarding admission:

> When I applied for a master's degree, the university accepted me unconditionally in the administration and supervision program. The night that we had to register on campus was a teaching night. I spent the day teaching 140 fifteen- and sixteen-year-olds. Then I traveled to the university to stand in line. The dean was registering students. He looked at me and told me I couldn't major in administration. I pushed him about it. He told me that I had to major in secondary education. I was floored! He was really saying that blacks couldn't get the top jobs and being a woman was even worse. It was wrong, and I knew it. So, I had to major in secondary education. I took the hardest courses the first semester and got straight As. After that I petitioned the school and got admitted into the administration and supervision program. I was the first African American to get her master's in this degree. I liked that. I finished there and went back and taught in that same department.

This president showed tenacity in the face of closed doors, which is a common theme for all of the presidents. She learned from this experience that she could push against the system and succeed when she chose to do so.

The following comment was made by a woman who, although not happy about it at the time, felt injustice but chose to take another path:

> I applied for the Ph.D. program at Duke and got a letter back which said, "We do not accept married women into our doctoral program. We've found that married women

tend to get pregnant or not finish the program." I was
so mad. I tore it up. I was insulted. I felt horrible, but I
didn't think it was wrong in some way. I didn't think it
was fair, but I guess I felt they had the choice to do that.
I wish I had kept the letter.

She had early practice in picking her battles wisely. Ultimately she
was pleased with the alternate path she chose to take.

The presidents mentioned a variety of difficulties or challenges
during their graduate school years. A number of women bore and
raised children during their schooling, a situation that, although
rewarding, inherently brought work-life challenges. One president
shared the following experience:

My mentor had such high hopes for me. He secured a
full fellowship for me so I could begin my Ph.D. Then
I became pregnant again. When he saw me in mater-
nity clothes—the expression on his face said everything.
Words were not necessary. He thought that his investment was down the drain. I think it was just a momentary
lapse. Yet it made me more determined.

This woman became more determined in the face of obstacles.
Again, the presidents chose carefully when to fight battles head-
on and when to move aside and make other plans, having already
learned that there were multiple paths toward long-term goals.

Another president spoke of the profound learning and developmental experience of her graduate internship in social work. She
learned something about balancing life.

I had to stand up for clients in my graduate internship.
I would find myself frequently fighting the system on
behalf of these clients. It was the first time in my life I
had the opportunity to do this. I discovered that I had

the strength about me to do this. However, I couldn't sleep at night. It took everything out of me. It was hard to see people suffer. I learned that you had to concentrate on what you can do and not on what you can't do. This was a valuable lesson for me in my current position. I concentrate on helping people to the extent I can, and then I go home and sleep. I learned I couldn't do everything.

Another woman learned a similar lesson from the following powerful and life-changing experience:

I didn't know that I could fail. I had some family emergencies one afternoon and evening, and I stayed up the entire night before my qualifying exams at a hospital. I decided to take the qualifying exams anyway and failed one section. I passed the exams, but I was told I would need to prepare in the orals for intense questions on that portion. I knew people on campus were talking about this. It was a surprise to me and a lot of others. Yet it made me more determined. I learned a lot from it. I learned that everyone fails, and that we can't do everything. No one is infallible, not even me.

Other presidents mentioned experiences in which they had to learn to listen to undesired criticism. Two mentioned situations in which their writing was ethically challenged, and although accidental and fairly trivial, one president talked about the tremendous learning experience it became. Both said they would never forget the incident. As one explained:

I've gotten to the point where when I feel horribly bad about something, I remember that it won't feel as bad tomorrow, the next day, and the next week.

Finally, the presidents spoke about events and experiences that were positive in nature. They mentioned many of the situations discussed earlier in the chapter in the sections on activities and employment and influential individuals. Many women spoke of their leadership opportunities on campus as profound and memorable learning experiences. Others mentioned, again, their courses and the college learning experience as a whole, including the design of their graduate programs:

> I did my doctorate work during the summers, and I was working full-time. The program brought in cohorts of professionals who had work experience. We had learning groups—now called learning communities. We all came together during the summer to learn. We met new people and learned what each graduate student was doing in his or her position. We were able to apply what we learned from the program in interesting ways, and we discussed it using unique techniques. It was very good for helping me build a broader framework. The collection of people from different programs, different parts of the country, and different positions was a powerful learning experience for me.

Final Thoughts

Day and O'Connor (2003) state that "development is not a matter of mere experience; rather, it depends on how the experience is organized and interpreted in terms of underlying concepts of knowledge structures" (p. 15). It was interesting to listen to how these women interpreted their college experiences so that they could learn leadership abilities and competencies. Leadership development often emerged out of "ah-hah" or epiphany moments. These sometimes resulted in reflective times when connections were made between the experience and life. Yet some of the development came from long-term relationships, opportunities, and experiences. One president reflected:

> I learned that there is more to life than just being success-
> ful in school. College helped me broaden my perspec-
> tive on how life could be rich in areas beyond school
> and reading. College experiences helped me with or-
> ganizational skills, networking, teamwork, and building
> personal friendships with people that I admired. All of
> that was an important part of my collegiate experience.

College helped these women discover that they thrive on complexity: "the university gives you a rich array of complex opportunities." College helped them discover their gifts and strengths, as well
as their weaknesses. Some had experiences in leading during "tem-
pestuous times." One explained, "I learned to work with complexity
and pressure. I guess things haven't changed that much!" The presidents learned to "dig deeper, focus, study, and build and integrate
knowledge." One explained, "I learned all of the skills that I really
needed to learn to help me be successful." They learned from everything they did and from organizational influences around them.
They began to discover that closed doors should be viewed as challenges instead of obstacles. College helped them clarify their values
and find increased internal strength. These leaders-in-training had
"a host of very powerful learning experiences" during their college
years that helped them develop a wide array of leadership compe-
tences (see Table 4.2). Galambos and Hughes (2000) explained
that effective leaders need to have a variety of interpersonal skills
and individual strengths to draw from, and college provided the
enriching environment needed to do just that.

Jack Zenger and Dan Folkman (2002), in their book titled *The
Extraordinary Leader: Turning Good Managers into Great Leaders*, decided that the best way to understand leadership was to examine the
impact leaders had on the people they lead. They analyzed 200,000
questionnaires from subordinates, peers, and bosses regarding more

Table 4.2. Leadership Competencies Developed During College

I learned and developed the following leadership competencies in college:

Accountability	Listening
Analysis of motivations	Logic
Articulating positions	Management
Being candid without offending	Negotiation
Budgeting	Networking
Building a program	Organization
Building relationships	Overseeing and supervising people
Communication skills	Planning skills
Complexity	Political skills
Creating and moving forth a vision	Preparation and studying skills
Creating goals and objectives	Presentation skills
Critical thinking	Reflection
Dealing with difficult situations	Representational skills
Delegating and organizing people to get things done	Representing the institution to stakeholders
Dependability	Responsibility
Focus and concentration	Spirituality
Focusing on results	Strong work ethic
Handling complexity	Teamwork
Integrating knowledge	Time management
Knowledge of strengths and weaknesses	Voicing my views
	Writing

than 20,000 leaders. They then compared the top 10 percent of leaders to the bottom 10 percent. These researchers found five major leadership attributes in top performers: (1) character, (2) personal capability, (3) interpersonal skills, (4) focus on results, and (5) leading change. These major elements are clearly evident in this group of women leaders as well. Zenger and Folkman provide lists of attributes for each of the categories. For example, the interpersonal skills element includes attributes that were clearly found in the presidents as they spoke of their experiences during college and adulthood. These attributes include inspiring others to high performance, building positive relationships with others, developing the skills and talents of others, working in a collaborative manner with others, being open and receptive to new ideas, responding positively to feedback, effectively resolving conflicts, influencing others (including upward), and building the self-esteem of others. There are striking similarities between these attributes (and the rest listed with the other four elements) and those discovered in my research study.

Sullivan (2003) stated that "being a leader is about understanding how individuals work differently from one another, and how they can all work together with the most efficiency. At its highest point, leadership is understanding how you can teach another to see the same" (p. 51). These presidents had college experiences that helped them come to this understanding.

In developing upcoming women leaders "colleges and universities must create experiences that will foster the growth and development most relevant to the world women will experience" (Sagaria, 1988, p. 7). Bennett and Shayner (1988) found that leadership development in college requires "an intellectual environment that opens and reinforces the philosophical habits of mind" and "the teaching and nurturing of the skills and behaviors that move leadership from the abstract realm to the world of action and accomplishment" (p. 28). They wrote:

> [Educators] must see it as their duty to develop, within and outside the classroom, a learning environment that requires individuals to question, form values, and develop intellectual strengths—the philosophical approaches that lead to conviction, commitment, and moral and ethical strength. Educators must never lose sight of the fact that without providing for and encouraging this central and critical intellectual attainment—the ability to use knowledge to make

personal decisions, form commitments, and then trust one's own judgments—all the trappings of leadership that we might model or declaim are essentially meaningless. (p. 29)

During the time these presidents were in college, formal leadership programs and efforts were not in place to strategically develop women students into competent leaders. However, it is clear that these women had the influences and experiences, however random and incidental they may have been, that wove together the groundwork for a lifetime of continued leadership development and a love for work and service within higher education.

Takeaways

1. Individuals with ability, desire, drive, *and* opportunity are those who can be successful in developing and practicing leadership.

2. Relationships and trust are the foundation for effective leadership development.

3. The continuous exploration of understanding oneself can be the most empowering and rewarding experiences one can have.

4. Discovering and accepting support and opportunities can provide valuable developmental experiences. The ability and drive to create ones' own support and opportunities is even better.

5. Effective women leaders pick their battles carefully and don't force things they know can't be changed, at least at that time.

6. Learning that comes in the moment can be the most powerful kind there is.

7. Different paths can lead to the same ultimate desires and goals.

Part II

Adulthood

5

Career Paths and Barriers

There are always many choices, many paths to take.
One is easy. And its only reward is that it's easy.

Anonymous

There is no single formula for leadership, nor a single
path to leadership.

Mary S. Hartman

I n the previous chapters I have discussed various stages of the presidents' lives. These stages—childhood, youth, and college years—provided a foundation for the continued development of these women university presidents during adulthood. In each of the previous chapters, I have written about a wide range of developmental dimensions. For example, Chapter Three includes information about the women's personalities, schooling, activities, leadership positions and experiences, employment, influential people, significant events and opportunities, and perceptions of the future. Now, this is the first of five chapters focusing on the adult years of these women's lives. Each chapter spans the full adulthood of these women, from their first professional jobs to their current positions. However, each chapter focuses on one major category of leadership development. This chapter discusses the women's career paths and barriers. Chapter Six offers details about influential individuals. Chapter Seven focuses on a variety of development activities, Chapter Eight on work-life issues, and Chapter Nine on overall leadership motivations, styles, and philosophies. This format provides a way to continue identifying emerging themes by analyzing specific categories of the interview data.

During the past few decades, research and dialogue around the topic of academic careers has increased. Of course the topic of career planning and development is important in all kinds of settings and organizations; however, interest in academic career issues is definitely a large and growing sector (Baruch & Hall, 2004a). Within the academic arena, interest and concern now focus increasingly on the academic careers of top leaders, especially presidents. However, research that looks at more than descriptive data is sparse. Although there is some research regarding the actual career paths of university presidents, very little is related to women leaders in academia. The number of women serving as presidents of research and comprehensive institutions remains low; hence, potential participants are few. The good news is that the number of women in leadership continues to rise as significant advances are being made to increase women's participation (at all levels) in higher educational administration (Glazer-Raymo, 1999). Encouragingly, women are preparing, obtaining, and maintaining successfully high-level postsecondary positions of influence, including that of university president.

As for the interview data, each of the university presidents provided a list and details about her career positions, both during the interview and in the form of a vita. I asked them a number of questions regarding how each position helped them develop leadership skills and competencies. I also inquired about any barriers or obstacles they faced throughout their professional career, particularly related to obtaining and securing new positions and promotions. The rest of the chapter describes their responses.

Career Paths

It was particularly amazing to discover the many career paths these women took to ultimately reach the position of university president or chancellor. It's interesting to note that each woman took a different pathway, and none of the women had a specific career development plan that focused on becoming a president throughout the majority of their careers (see Appendix C).

Even with all of the different career paths, there are similarities among some of the presidents in various respects. For example, four started out as K–12 teachers, and four began their professional careers in various positions within higher education. Therefore, eight of the ten presidents began their professional work careers in education (K–12, postsecondary). Although education was one of few acceptable fields for women of that generation, these women clearly had a passion and love for it. Many were drawn to these majors because they wanted to help others. As the last chapter discussed, half of the presidents as young adults chose education majors as undergraduates, and six obtained educational doctorate degrees. They were interested in teaching and learning as a profession. In fact, nine of the ten presidents taught in the college classroom as professors or instructors at one time in their careers before becoming administrators. This academic teaching and research played a significant role in the development of knowledge and skills important to their leadership.

A number of the presidents who progressed along an academic path obtained major grants for research laboratories and experimental research. They spoke of developing many competencies throughout these years related to budgeting, planning, strategy, and managing people (for example, hiring, firing, motivating, and conflict resolution).

Six presidents had academic career paths whereas four followed nonacademic routes. I discovered that only one president followed the *official* traditional male career path (faculty member, chair, dean, academic vice president or provost, and president). Two had chair experience (one department chair, one associate chair). One was an academic dean of a core school; two others were deans of graduate studies and continuing education. Three obtained dean experience through being an associate dean of an academic school or of continuing education. Three of the presidents became assistants or special assistants to the presidents along their journeys. They described these positions as very valuable to their growth and development. Six were, at one time, full-time assistant professors, whereas five continued directly to associate professor status. Although six presidents were full professors, only four of the original six rose through the professor ranks. Two others were awarded the status without going through the ranks of assistant and associate professor.

Other women went through nontraditional career paths related to finance and budgets, community and government relations, noneducational appointments, boards of regents, or commission positions. Each of these positions and experiences somehow provided them opportunities to develop the leadership skills and competencies needed for academic administration.

The presidents came to their current posts from various positions: five were provosts, vice presidents, or vice chancellors of academic affairs; two were vice chancellors or vice presidents of administration and finance, one was a vice president of university relations, one was in a leadership position in a government agency, and one was a president at another institution. The data regarding the positions they held before their current position were similar to data published in 2005 in the *Chronicle of Higher Education* ("What presidents think," 2005) showing that 47 percent of women presidents were previously provosts or chief academic officers. The same source reported that only 55 percent of the presidents sampled had vice president or vice chancellor posts immediately before becoming presidents at their current institutions. Eight of the ten presidents in my study held these positions before obtaining a presidential appointment. The samples are also comparable with regard to educational backgrounds and tenured faculty appointments. The backgrounds of my sample also compared well to another research team's sample of women chief academic officers (Walton & McDade, 2001). In sum, most of the presidents had backgrounds that included teaching, scholarship, curriculum development and evaluation, budgeting, political skills, and the business of higher education. All had positions that helped them learn to work well with all types of people, develop the ability to solve problems, and expand their capacity to provide leadership.

The educational backgrounds and career paths of the ten women university presidents reveal a history of desire and drive for continuous learning and development. Arthur, Claman, and DeFillippi (1995) presented an Intelligent Career idea (academic model) that was based on three dimensions: knowing why, knowing how, and knowing whom (Baruch & Hall, 2004b). The data collected with these women university presidents seem to support these dimensions. The first dimension is *knowing why*. Leading effectively in higher education requires a certain urge to explore, be scientific, and use cognitive and innovative competencies. This is demonstrated by my participants not only in their history of advanced degrees but also their interest, openness, and drive to take on new responsibilities, positions, and opportunities in a variety of areas. They enjoyed challenges and change primarily because of the opportunities these provided for ongoing personal and professional development, as well as the chance to make a difference for the institutions, organizations, or individuals they worked for and served. Their desire to *know why* also relates to their motivation, need for service, idealism, and sense of duty.

The second dimension is *knowing how*. In academe certain competencies are essential for success. According to the Intelligent Career framework, these involve cerebral abilities, emotional intelligence, resilience, and the ability to bounce back. It is clear that these presidents had a deep yearning for *knowing how*. They saw the need for changes and improvements and thought deeply about how to create solutions to the issues at hand. They asked questions, observed, and reflected on how effective individuals were able to have the influence they did. They had the desire to strengthen their skills and found satisfaction when competencies were developed.

The final dimension is *knowing whom*. Studies (Baruch & Hall, 2004b) often associate career success in academics with the right connections and networks. For example, in higher education, finding the right mentor seems to be particularly important. The university presidents developed the unique ability to network and connect (often for life) with influential individuals throughout their educational experiences and professional positions, including mentors, coaches, peers, supervisors, and even subordinates. Although all the presidents do not emerge from traditional academic backgrounds, the search for answers and meaning within these three dimensions provides a helpful framework for understanding the leadership development of women university presidents, with a particular focus on career paths and educational backgrounds.

Formal Versus Informal Career Paths

The topic of career paths (formal versus informal or linear versus nonlinear) has been an ongoing theme of discussion for some time. Literature (Clark, Caffarella, & Ingram, 1999; Walton & McDade, 2001; White, 2003) on this subject reports that, in some industries (including education), women typically have had linear career paths as they rose through the ranks to become leaders. It is important to note, however, that many of the women in previous samples were single (Clark et al., 1999). Yet numerous studies report women leaders having informal and emerging career paths (Aldoory, 1998; Cheng, 1988; Hartman, 1999; Hill & Ragland, 1995; Vinnicombe & Singh, 2003; Waring, 2003). Some of the women in these studies claimed that they took on responsibility but did not aspire to official leadership positions. In fact, one researcher termed them "reluctant leaders." The women in a study (Waring, 2003) of female African American college administrators were either *drafted* by others who identified their leadership potential or were interested in improving the educational opportunities for the students and felt they could make a difference. My sample of women presidents supports the latter position of nonlinear or indirect paths.

When asked whether or not they had a structured career path, all presidents (most, with a smile) answered with a resounding *no*. Therefore, none of the ten presidents had an official career path targeted at becoming a university president. One claimed:

> I thought I was going to be a teacher forever, but I did think I might be a department chair. By the time I was 40, however, I was wondering what I was going to do with the rest of my life. I didn't plan to go into administration. It just happened.

Most stated that they began thinking about becoming presidents when they were vice presidents. One stated, "I never thought that I could possibly be a university president." Another explained:

> I didn't think about becoming a president until after I became a provost. I didn't think about becoming a provost until I was far enough in a deanship and worked closely with the provost. Eventually I thought, "I could do that!"

A third commented:

> Before I became a dean I watched them and thought to myself, "I could do that better than they could." I did the same for all my positions after that.

Still another said:

> I didn't think about a presidency until the president
> I worked for as a vice president told me I could be a
> president. I still didn't believe it until people from the
> community called me, and people at the university en-
> couraged me to do so. I was surprised.

In fact, only one woman thought about becoming a president before
her provost position, saying:

> When I was assistant to the president I became an ACE
> fellow. That is when I decided I wanted to become a
> president. Then I made a plan for next steps and followed
> it.

A number of presidents spoke about their promotions in higher
education. One president mentioned, "The best positions I have
had, I've actually not sought out." Another woman explained:

> I believe what my father taught me. He always said that
> the way to get your next best job is to do as well as you
> can in the one you're currently in.

A third claimed that one of her early mentors said, "If you do the job
you're doing well enough, the next one will find you." She followed
up by saying that she believes that philosophy is true, up to a point.
Three stated in various parts of the interviews that they seemed to
"fall into" new and more challenging positions. When speaking of
her ambitions to become a president, one woman stated:

> I never thought I would end up at the level I did. It was
> never part of my mindset. I did not plan to apply. So
> many people encouraged me to apply, and I couldn't say
> no to these people whom I respected so much.

While discussing their lack of formal career paths, some of the
presidents mentioned the influential individuals around them who

gave them ideas or encouragement to take advantage of opportunities, including new positions, new responsibilities within current
positions, and new institutions. The women were clearly influenced
by those around them who planted small encouraging ideas in their
minds. In most situations, these women did not have one specific
mentor, but they listened to many different voices. One president
explained, "I based my career decisions on other trusted individuals'
ideas." Many of these presidents said that it was primarily men (not
women) who wanted and encouraged them to obtain promotions.
Chapter Six includes more detail about the impact of influential
individuals.

A major finding of my research on this topic is the value of informal or nonlinear career paths for women. This finding supports
those of other researchers (Aldoory, 1998; Cheng, 1988; Hartman,
1999; Hill & Ragland, 1995; Vinnicombe & Singh, 2003; Waring,
2003) in that successful women leaders (unlike many men leaders)
did not intentionally look for leadership positions. Instead they
emerged by working hard, performing to the best of their abilities,
responding to encouragement by others to apply for new positions,
and accepting offers of increased responsibilities and promotions.
None of the presidents expressed regret that they took this indirect
path. None said they wish they had done substantially different
things. All said that each position they filled provided them with
the opportunity to learn important knowledge and develop essential competencies that have been imperative for success in their
current posts. Yet every woman took a different path. This research
supports the notion that various career paths can lead to top leadership positions in academe. When the presidents spoke about their
previous leadership positions, they reminisced about what each had
taught them and how it was helpful in their current presidencies.
Although there is a set of common issues, activities, and competencies that had to be learned for adequate presidential performance,
the presidents demonstrated that these can be learned from a variety of positions and experiences, including membership or leadership on committees, work on research projects and grants, and

opportunities in which they could exert informal influence (Chrisler, Herr, & Murstein, 1998; Twale & Shannon, 1996).

Barriers

I asked the presidents two questions with regard to gender issues they may have encountered: (1) Did you face gender barriers in rising to your current position? (2) Do you think your career would have been different in some way if you had been a man? It is important to remember that these are the women who have broken through the proverbial glass ceiling. As one president articulated:

> When a woman is in a position like being the president of a university, it implies that she *has* broken through the barrier.

Yet their answers were interesting. All participants noted that there may have been issues but none of the presidents seemed to dwell on them. All of the presidents admitted that gender issues still exist. One president explained:

> We are judged differently than men. We have to prove ourselves in a different way. I do think gender does matter.

However, these women did not believe that gender was a major problem or issue for them in obtaining new jobs and promotions. One woman stated:

> I have encountered lots of bumps in the road. They may look different, but I don't think there were more bumps than there would have been with a male. I might have looked at them differently, but I think I have been very, very blessed.

A second explained:

> I don't think it has been more difficult to be a woman.
> I've spent a lot of time being the first woman in the
> job I've gotten. I was the first woman graduate dean. I
> was the first woman administrator in the district. I was
> the first woman provost. I don't think things would have
> been easier or my career path would have been enhanced
> or better if I would have been a man. I like the path I
> have had.

Interestingly, many of the presidents pointed out that gender
was not the only barrier that exists. Everything is not always about
gender. Although they admitted that gender was and is a real issue
from time to time, a number of the presidents were quick to mention
the other career barriers that should be considered. One woman
noted:

> I've worked for wonderful men. Yet, the female "thing"
> is there sometimes. Sometimes you get strange com-
> ments. I must say, however, that gender is not the only
> career issue. It seems that being a male is a problem
> in some environments, being gay is a problem in some
> environments, and being disabled is a problem in some
> environments. My strategy has been to just try to ignore
> what I can and then confront what is not appropriate to
> ignore.

Another president made the following comment:

> I'd been at that institution for a long time. The biggest
> divide was not gender. It was that one day I was a faculty
> member and then the next day I was an administrator. I
> had changed over in the middle of the year, so I still had
> my faculty office because I was still teaching a course.

> I went back to my faculty office, and one of my friends (who I'd known for years) said, "What are you doing here?" That was a lesson.

The third woman not only mentioned a few other barriers but also discussed her philosophy on the importance of finding a good institutional match when looking for a leadership position:

> I've certainly been on many searches where I knew it wasn't going to be a good match. It may have been my gender, background, past institutions, or because of this or that. Who the hell knows? I didn't go to those places because I had the sense not to go and they had the sense not to ask me. However, some institutions were ready (in more or less degrees) to change. That is where I belonged.

A few of the presidents shared some entertaining stories about situations in which specific men had said or done something that demonstrated their incorrect assumptions, lack of awareness, or "downright stupidity" about gender issues. One president explained that these comments sometimes came from men who had been in strong positions for some time and on occasion didn't even know when they were discounting women. Another president chuckled as she told this story:

> I was strong, and I was necessary to people. I had problems with salary and that worked itself through eventually when I was in powerful positions and could deal with it. That doesn't mean that I didn't run into a jerk now and then. Like the Madison Avenue guy who came in and sat in my office one morning. It said "Chancellor" over the door when he entered, and it said "Chancellor" on the desk. I sat there with him and his assistant. We exchanged every pleasantry I could think of. Finally I said,

"I guess I don't know why you are here." He replied,
"I thought I was going to meet with the Chancellor."
I stood up and said, "You did. Thank you for coming."
That was the end of that. I have run into those kinds of
jerks every once in a while, but nothing serious most of
the time.

Another president also smiled as she recalled a situation she had
just experienced a few days prior to our interview:

I don't think things would have been a lot different if I
had been a man, but I do think it would have been easier
in some ways. I don't think I would have done better.
I don't think I've had real obstacles but, like it or not,
it's still there. Let me give you a real example. Sunday
night I was at the airport to get on a plane, and we had
something happen to our airplane. We all got off and
started talking to each other. We, as passengers, hadn't
talked before but this kind of brought us all together.
I was talking to a couple who said they had attended
the university's graduation because their daughter had
just graduated. I said, "Wasn't it a wonderful day and a
wonderful graduation!" They said, "Oh were you there?"
Of course there were 50,000 people there, and I was on
the jumbo tron. I said, "I was there." He said, "Were
you guiding the students?" That was his question. I said,
"No." He said, "What were you doing?" I said, "I was with
the platform party." He said, "Oh, what did you do?" I
said, "I graduated your daughter." He looked at me and
said, "OH!" That's the kind of response women still get.
It is so characteristic, the assumptions still remain that
you are there because you are in a staff position. Here I'd
been in front of so many people, and he hadn't pulled it
together.

Although all presidents didn't believe they were impacted negatively long-term from gender-related barriers, a few told stories of particularly difficult situations. One explained:

> I felt discriminated in a state that prides itself on having all of the ethnic mixes. There was clear discrimination with some of the things I experienced there. It was clear that I needed to remove myself from that environment.

A number of presidents mentioned how important it was not to get offended by statements or situations that might show the insensitivity and unawareness of others. One woman stated:

> I applied for a few different positions where I knew deep down that they really needed to hire a woman for one reason or another. Although some women get terribly offended at that, I had decided a long time ago that conversation was okay with me. Being a woman may have opened a few doors for me in getting initial interviews, but I always knew people would see my experience and competence and hire me for what I could offer to the institution.

Another hardworking, focused, and task-oriented president shared the following story. She became part of the "old boys" club and fit right in with the men:

> I was always an "old boy." My career began in a field where I had a lot of males around. I was comfortable. I was always one of the boys growing up. They saw me as a colleague, not as a woman. As for sexual harassment, I remember telling a colleague that I never felt like people were sexually harassing or flirting with me. He said, "I have been flirting with you for years." I guess it just went over my head. I didn't ever think about it.

Finally, a third president spoke of the type of subtle discrimination that exists particularly at the presidential level. This quotation also includes an interesting and somewhat humorous insight about who can succeed at "disarming" these kinds of men:

> Much of it was not blatant at the presidential level. It was terribly blatant at the lower levels. At the presidential level men had good manners. They were polished and had other ways. However, discrimination was there in some forms. Some of us were somehow able to disarm them (although we didn't realize we were doing it until we looked around and realized we were all short). Somebody should run that hypothesis sometime.

The literature (Appelbaum, Audet, & Miller, 2003; Cubillo & Brown, 2003; Thompson & Marley, 1999) speaks of the fact that women are sometimes their own barriers to leadership positions because of personal and professional insecurities and perceptions. Researchers (Appelbaum et al., 2003; Cubillo & Brown, 2003; Dickerson & Taylor, 2000; Marongiu & Ekehammar, 1999; Thompson & Marley, 1999) argue that some serious internal barriers for women with leadership potential are attitude; fear of failure; lack of confidence in one's skills, abilities, and risk-taking; and a self-concept that is linked to internalized traditional female stereotypes. In fact, in *Academic Medicine* (1996) researchers reported that "women tend to be more modest than men about their achievements and less apt to see themselves as qualified for top positions even when their credentials are equivalent or superior" (p. 805). One president spoke about gender being an issue sometimes for her and others:

> I believe I was in the women's stereotype of what I could do in my earlier years (twenties and thirties). I had a stereotypical female career, so it was a comfortable place for me to be. After a particular move into administration, I quickly became part of the "good old boy network" so gender became less of an issue. However, when I applied for the [chancellor or president] position there were a lot

of issues raised around whether a woman could do that job, whether I was strong enough. There was a quote in the paper by one of the regents who thought I was strong enough. He said I was like Margaret Thatcher. I wondered sometimes if I had the strength or whether I could handle it. You have to make tough decisions and you end up having people not happy. You make enemies of people no matter what you do. It is so political, and you need to be okay with that. I worried about whether I could handle not always being able to help people solve all the problems, not always reaching compromises, or having members of the board not support me. I think that was my Achilles heel.

A number of presidents mentioned that they had a lack of confidence initially in believing they had the skills to become presidents. Although these women were achievement-oriented, as previously mentioned, some believe in the stereotypical view of women's leadership limitations. However, because of the influence and encouragement of people around them, they did move their careers forward.

Final Thoughts

Understanding the experiences and perceptions of these women provides insight into the types of activities, influences, and experiences that are beneficial for women to develop the needed knowledge, skills, and competencies required for effective leadership. As mentioned previously, this will assist (1) individual women of all ages interested in personal and career development, and (2) educators, administrators, and consultants who will be designing future leadership development interventions (training, development, individual preparation, mentoring, career management, self-directed learning).

The career paths of the ten women university presidents reveal a history of desire and drive for continuous learning and development. It is clear from their backgrounds and descriptions that they wanted to know why, know how, and know whom (Baruch & Hall, 2004b). This is demonstrated by their advanced degrees (master's and doctoral) and their interest, openness, and drive to take on new responsibilities, positions, and opportunities in a variety of areas. They enjoyed challenges and change primarily because of the opportunities these provided for ongoing personal and professional development and for the chance to make a difference for the institutions, organizations, or individuals for whom they worked and served. They had a desire to serve and a sense of duty. The presidents saw the need for changes and improvements and thought deeply about how to create solutions to issues at hand. In doing this, they asked questions, observed, and reflected on how effective individuals were able to have the influence they did. They had the desire to strengthen their skills and found satisfaction when competencies (e.g., cerebral abilities, emotional intelligence, and resilience) were developed or strengthened. It was clear that these women also developed the unique ability to network and connect (often for life) with influential individuals throughout their educational experiences and professional positions, including mentors, coaches, peers, supervisors, and even subordinates.

The presidents have a passion for learning and growth. And with this passion has come a desire and ability to learn from nearly everything (formal and informal positions, responsibilities, experiences, mistakes, observations, successes, feedback from others, and even motherhood). Some researchers argue that women should decide early and plan more direct career paths toward their intended leadership goals. However, it is clear that these women became the leaders they are today because of each and every career opportunity. Each president leads differently because of the insights she gained from past lived experiences. All of the presidents found institutions that benefit from the breadth and depth that each of them attained from their lifelong collage of learning. The richness of their current perspectives and insights can be attributed to the powerfulness of the variety of career and service choices and opportunities. Their desire to perform to the best of their abilities in each position or assignment, without the constant questioning of how each task and title would help them attain a higher position, has a quality of selflessness that seems to benefit those who truly desire to make a difference for their students, and in their institutions, communities, and beyond. It is the journey that brings lifelong richness and contentment to any life.

Takeaways

1. Women academic leaders do not always intentionally look for leadership positions, but instead work hard and perform to the best of their abilities in their current posts. They are often offered added responsibilities and new positions and are also encouraged by others to apply for and accept new opportunities.

2. There are many career paths that can be traveled to ultimately obtain positions of leadership in higher education.

3. Leadership skills and competencies can be learned during adulthood from a variety of positions and experiences, both academic and nonacademic.

4. None of the presidents expressed regret that they took an indirect or informal career path.

5. Being a teacher and educator can provide helpful developmental opportunities to learn leadership.

6. Nonacademic career paths can also provide beneficial experiences and opportunities for women to develop leadership competencies needed for top positions in academic institutions.

7. Women in higher education who have potential for leadership positions tend to have strong desires and needs to *know why*, *know how*, and *know whom*.

6

Influential Individuals

In organizations, real power and energy is generated through relationships. The patterns of relationships and the capacities to form them are more important than tasks, functions, roles, and positions.

Margaret Wheatley

Individuals with ability, desire, drive, and opportunity are those who become successful leaders. People often don't know they have *ability* unless they are told and encouraged by others. People often don't display *desire* unless others help them see the options. People often don't focus their *drive* unless they learn from following someone else. And people don't always have *opportunities* unless they are provided them by others. As Margaret Wheatley said, "real power and energy is generated through relationships." I would add that true leadership is all about relationships based on trust.

The ten university presidents spoke in detail about the many people who influenced their development of leadership knowledge and abilities during their professional years. They used a variety of words, often interchangeably, to refer to different people's influential roles: *mentor, role model, coach, advisor, sponsor, encourager, counselor,* and *supporter*. D'Abate, Eddy, and Tannenbaum

(2003) used the term "developmental interactions" as involving "interactions between two or more people with the goal of personal or professional development" (p. 360). Table 6.1 lists roles that are most applicable to this research either mentioned by the presidents or found in the article just mentioned. In my study, the women seemed to be influenced as much by people in these roles (such as advisors, coaches, and counselors) (see Table 6.1) as they were by individuals in particular formal positions (such as deans, provosts, presidents). As other researchers (see Wells, 1998) have noted, women who become leaders report learning leadership from other people.

Based in part on the work of others (Kram, 1988; McCauley & Young, 1993), D'Abate et al. (2003) also outlined five characteristics that can be used when considering why particular individuals were so influential to these women university presidents. First, they found that the positive influence can result, in part, because of the situation or preparedness of the individuals being influenced (that is, age, knowledge level, or career experience). Hence, part of the reason for the influence may have been that the presidents were prepared, open, confident, driven, and aware. Second, the influence can develop, in part, because of the characteristics of the interactions (that is, duration, regularity, mode, or relationship span). The presidents may have been in situations that provided optimal opportunities to interact and be influenced by others. Third, positive influence from others can be enhanced by systems, structures, and settings (for example, hierarchical direction, reporting relationships, or organizational location of participants). The presidents interacted with particularly influential individuals often because of proximity and organizational positions and roles. Fourth, the purpose of an interaction between someone potentially influencing and someone being influenced also determines its potential effectiveness. For example, the goals, time frames (short-term versus long-term), or personalities and

Table 6.1. Possible Roles of Influential Individuals

Role	Definition
Advisor	One who gives advice, counsel, and/or provides information
Coach or peer coach	An experienced individual (typically in a higher position but can also be a peer in the case of peer coach) who instructs, tutors, or trains another
Counselor	A person who gives advice or counsel
Developer	One who develops another through training, motivating, encouraging, coaching, and/or counseling
Encourager	One who encourages, provides help, or inspires with courage, spirit, or hope (Merriam-Webster Online Dictionary, 2006)
Executive coach	(1) An individual who consults managers and senior leaders; (2) one who uses one-on-one interventions with senior managers for the "purpose of improving or enhancing management skills" (Orenstein, 2002, p. 356)

Mentor
  Distance mentoring
  Group mentoring
  Peer mentoring
  Structured mentoring
  Unstructured
    mentoring
	(1) One who "occupies a powerful position at a higher level than that of the protégé, offering guidance and support, paving a path for the protégé, guiding in the development of career goals, and acting in an almost parental role (Scanlon, 1997, p. 42); (2) a trusted guide or counselor; (3) an individual in a position of formal or informal influence who advises, counsels, encourages, teaches, and coaches another

Table 6.1. (*Continued*)

Role	Definition
Role model	An individual whose behavior in a particular role is imitated by others
Sponsor	(1) A person in a leadership role who can "literally pull a person up through the ranks of their organization on the strength of their own power and influence" (Mattis, 2001, p. 12); someone who assumes responsibility for another individual
Supporter	One who supports
Tutor	An individual who instructs and guides another individual

receptiveness of the ones being influenced all have an impact on the opportunity and effectiveness of a developmental relationship. In the presidents' cases, their own goals for development, the timing with regard to learning specific concepts or tasks, and the potential beneficiaries (for example, themselves, organizations, mentor, and department) all influenced the environment that cultivated effective interactions. Finally, these researchers claim that interactions are also influenced by the degree of structure (formality, choice to participate, matching process, preparation and support, evaluation, or the circumstances of the termination). Interestingly, these ten women university presidents flourished primarily through informal relationships with individuals who were naturally connected to them through situations, positions, or opportunities. However, as is discussed in the next chapter, there are a few examples of presidents participating in leadership training in which they were formally paired with specific individuals for the purpose of developing leadership skills.

Consideration of the five characteristics just mentioned is help-ful as information regarding the individuals who influenced the university presidents during their professional years unfolds in this chapter. Clearly, the presidents learned from a variety of develop-mental interactions. As discussed in earlier chapters, the presidents were receptive toward learning from many individuals, circum-stances, and opportunities. The presidents continued to strengthen this skill during their professional years. Chapter Eight (Other Life Roles) discusses the influential individuals outside the workplace (family, spouse, community members, non-workplace friends and contacts). This chapter focuses on influential individuals specif-ically in their own work environments. The chapter begins by discussing general influences and issues, followed by sections on faculty colleagues, peers, superiors, and others.

General Influences and Issues

During their professional careers most of the presidents said they had several individuals who were important to their leadership de-velopment. As one stated, "Certain people helped me formulate my leadership style." Another mentioned that these influential people were "yet more mile markers on this journey of mine." Encourage-ment from others was a powerful force in preparing and motivating these women to continue their development through new opportu-nities and experiences. In fact, all presidents said they took on new responsibilities and positions because of the encouragement they re-ceived from others. For example, one president explained, "People at all levels along the way—leaders, faculty members, friends, and community members—encouraged me to apply for new positions along my career path." Another said, "Many people encouraged me to apply for positions along the way, and this gave me confidence." She continued, "I didn't think I could be successful in certain positions until I saw the confidence others had in me." This encouragement also came in the form of reinforcement. One president commented:

> I got lots of reinforcement in my first major administrative position. Various people (leaders, peers, and subordinates) said things like, "You're doing well," "We like the way you do that," or "You're good at solving problems." The things I did were praised. This reinforcement was a powerful form of encouragement for me.

That being said, it is particularly important to mention one crucial point. Although most presidents gave credit to others for at least part of their development, they were influenced because of who they were. They had self-respect, and because of that they could *hear* what others were saying to them. It was because of their already developed skills of observation and reflection that they could *hear* the positive feedback that was given to them and could accept it. I would argue that many women are given acknowledgment, recognition, and encouragement, but only a small fraction of them *hear* and believe what they are told. Many women have the habit of dismissing comments as not accurate or significant. The presidents in this study had the self-respect and confidence to listen and believe. People can make profound differences to emerging leaders, but only if the leaders let them. In fact, because of these women's high skills in the areas of observation and reflection, many influential individuals probably never knew they had made such a deep impact on these women. People reminded them of their own strengths and competence and sometimes pointed them to opportunities. The presidents were then left to take hold of new options and to apply the new information to their own experiences and lives.

Some of the women believed that, as one president put it, "few achieve anything without mentors and role models," whereas others did not mention individual mentors in their career development. These women learned and developed through observing, asking questions, getting advice, and receiving coaching from time to time. Although this chapter will primarily discuss the positive side of mentoring, it is important to note that two presidents did bring up some negative consequences. One spoke of a concern—that of the mentor not being able to let go:

> The transition from being your student to being your peer is very hard. My mentor couldn't take that step. I found out he was telling people who were trying to recruit me to leave me alone. He had built a fence around me and wouldn't let other universities see my work.

Of course during this period there were more male mentors than female mentors, particularly in higher leadership or administrative positions. Even in higher education today the number of high-level female mentors continues to lag. A few women also mentioned another concern. They found there were women along the way who provided little or no support for other women. In fact, one president explained that sometimes women are their own worst enemies. She said, "As a woman I didn't feel a real support system from other women. Women were still pretty wary of each other." Regarding mentors, writers (Egan & Rosser, 2004; Noe, Greenberger, & Wang, 2002) continue to argue that although cross-gender mentoring relationships have been found to be effective, women who are mentored by women obtain unique benefits. Noe et al. (2002) said, "Based on available research, female mentors may be best suited to prepare their female protégés for the unique source of stress that women face in the workplace, such as discrimination, social isolation, and coping with work-family conflict" (p. 164). Gupton and Slick (1996) contend, "There is a scarcity of supportive sponsors and mentors among women in educational administration as well as executive positions across all professionals . . . Women have traditionally not benefited from having sponsors and mentors to encourage and support their career advancement" (p. 67). It is also important to mention that an official mentor or role model was not always the answer to quality leadership development for these ten university presidents. These women took advantages of other types of assistance and relationships such as advisors, coaches, and encouragers.

Colleagues and Peers

For the presidents who were on the academic career path, faculty colleagues were particularly influential during their assistant and associate professor years. In fact, one previous study (DeNitto, Aguilar, Franklin, & Jordan, 1995) of female faculty members found that women rated fellow colleagues as the *most* helpful factor in their academic environment. Some of the presidents in my study provided examples of faculty members who encouraged them to apply for department chair, associate dean, or dean positions. As one president reflected, "Encouragement to apply for administrative positions from faculty I respected gave me the confidence to move forward along this path." One spoke about the number of faculty who approached her about running for faculty union president. "They knew that I could make a difference for the faculty on our campus and told me they wanted me to run." Another president stated, "The recognition I received from highly respected members of the faculty was very important during those early years." A number of presidents spoke of faculty members more as role models, not necessarily mentors. For example, one president explained:

> After I had been an assistant professor for a year or so, one very influential, highly respected, senior family member—sort of the statesman of the group—took me aside and said, "I'm going to give you some advice, and I want you to listen to it and then do with it whatever you will." He said, "I feel compelled to tell you that you have an uncanny ability to see right straight through

to the core of a problem. You hold back and listen and observe, and at a moment when people are struggling you have this ability to move in and say, 'Aren't we really talking about this. Isn't some of what we have been discussing a bit peripheral to what we are really trying to resolve.'" He told me this was unusual. This was the first time someone in my professional workplace had said something like this to me. It reminded me of my high school English teacher who wrote, "No lesser lights for you" in my senior yearbook. It worked on my mind almost unconsciously. I suppose I was then on a different kind of internal alert about being willing to get involved in university-wide activities. Then, when I would be asked to represent the department on a faculty senate committee, I had a sense of confidence about being able to do it, even though there were very few women.

Once again the presidents continued to hone their observation and reflection skills in new settings. They were developing flexible and adaptable leadership styles as they watched, listened, and made appropriate changes in their behavior. They had role models they could watch and learn from about building collaborative relationships from within and without. One president spoke of watching a particular female faculty member involved in a change project:

She was a faculty member and persuaded the president to put a commission of women together. I watched how she worked with the president's wife to get her involved so that we could work with him through her. This faculty member guided the commission through some pretty tricky politics. The institution took on big women's issues at that time. She did it in a way that would not put the institution in a spot. She gave the president notice so that he had time to fix things, if needed. She was absolutely amazing.

One president spoke of two female colleagues who served as peer role models or mentors. This president learned a great deal from watching them go through some difficult times.

> One woman at my institution was a very strong influence in my life—more of a role model—in those early years. I remember that she was denied tenure, subsequently, and it was a real travesty. I saw gender issues at play during those years. Another female faculty member (a mentor) and I did research together. She was wonderful all the way through. We had different styles, and we had fun tearing things apart. Others didn't understand. She taught me a lot about scholarship that was at a much deeper and sophisticated level than any of the courses and things I'd seen. She was such an extraordinary scholar. She was also denied tenure at the same institution, and she left. I began to understand at some level the deep injustice that can exist within cultures of higher educational institutions.

Another president also spoke of a more senior colleague who provided her with many opportunities.

> I had one mentor who made an enormous difference in my life. Because of his status he opened up many more doors for me than I could have done on my own. As a young assistant professor he got me invited to some of the top meetings as a presenter. Because of him I think I saved all kinds of steps just by meeting the right people at the right time. I think that's what mentors can do. Now that's my job, to save steps for other people. I think it makes a huge difference. It is still who you know!

Past research (King & Bauer, 1988) has reported that peers who are willing to commit themselves to giving support to others are an invaluable source of friendship. This was certainly the case with these women presidents. In fact, peers (academic and nonacademic) were incredibly important during the professional years of all of the presidents. One said, "I think colleagues and peers have been the most meaningful for me." Because the presidents had learned from their childhood to be fairly responsive to feedback, most of the presidents listened and learned. Many noted that the developmental benefits came from watching and observing peers, as well as having them give specific feedback. For example, one president explained:

> When I was a dean, the other deans—peer colleagues— were especially important and helpful in my development and growth. They had so many great ideas and gave me important feedback. I was interacting with people who were confident and who knew what they were doing.

One stated, "It was the colleagues who cared for me that said 'Stop, think, take a breath, be smart, and do your best.'" Peers were so important to these presidents, particularly because of encouraging feedback they provided. A few presidents mentioned experiences in which peers gave them difficult feedback. As they learned to do earlier in their lives, these women recognized what needed to be improved and did not get discouraged. One detail that the presidents didn't expand on was the reciprocal relationship they must have had with these influential people. I'm not certain if they were blind toward or just modest regarding the benefit they were to the people who influenced them. Most did admit, however, that they were often already prepared for the new experiences provided to them from many of these individuals. They just needed the encouragement and opportunities.

One president spoke of the respect she had for a man who was actually a competitor in the running for a dean position. Immediately upon being offered the deanship she persuaded him to be the associate dean. She exclaimed, "That was the smartest thing I ever did." She said he was wonderful, and their diverse backgrounds enriched the leadership of that school. This action demonstrates that she was secure with herself. She was not afraid to assert herself, which stems not only from her childhood experiences with valuing learning and growth but also from the self-assurance that comes with time and experience. One woman spoke of working in a nonacademic environment.

> I worked with a group of employees who had very different backgrounds, socioeconomic classes, and races. I learned a lot about different kinds of people and how to interact with them and also appreciate them.

Another president spoke of the important connections she made with people all over campus—administrators, faculty, and staff. Many became her allies. These friendships and networks made it possible for them to "make good things happen across campus." During their early professional years, these women already understood the importance of stakeholders. This is an example of, as Drucker (1988) wrote, understanding "who depends on me" and "on whom do I depend?" (p. 49).

Peer mentoring or coaching was a powerful source of development for all of the presidents during their professional years; many noted that it remains an important source of continued development to this day. Kochan (2002) described three primary dimensions that must be present for mentoring endeavors (and I would add peer mentoring) to be successful: relational, reflective, and reciprocal. For these presidents, helpful peer mentoring or coaching was based on an effective relationship, the ability to reflect on learning opportunities and experiences, and the reciprocal benefits of the interactions for both parties. For example, one president spoke about her experiences as a dean. She said that her male dean colleagues were very competent leaders. Through watching them, asking them questions, and interacting with them, she learned a great deal. She believed that the other deans and the institution benefited from her continued development. Although they were not official mentors, the deans knew that the strength of each member of the group resulted in a more competent and effective leadership team. Interestingly, it was her dean colleagues who encouraged her to apply for a provost position years later.

One president spoke at length of the profound influence a college peer had on her later life—a type of social support. After college she continued to stay in contact with this individual and watched him from afar as he progressed in his career. He was an exceptional achiever and competitor, yet he had to overcome some very difficult times and did so with strength and courage. He met his goals and objectives. He was an example of strength and endurance to her. Even after his death, she remembers his example as she faces her own challenges and opportunities. She was inspired by his accomplishments and personal ethic. She also learned by watching him push the envelope, stretch his imagination, and take risks. She learned that remaining comfortable provides few opportunities for growth.

A number of women spoke of people in peer positions (faculty, department chairs, associate deans, deans, and vice presidents) on their own as well as other campuses. They believed that others who were in similar positions were particularly suited to give pertinent advice and insight into some of their own dilemmas. The women would ask questions and then receive advice—hence, these individuals served more as temporary advisors for particular issues. The relationships appeared to be reciprocal. The presidents were mindful of choices to establish relationships with others. It was actually people in peer positions who provided encouragement for these presidents to apply for different positions. As one president noted, "Connections and competence are still two of the most important elements of developing leadership." It seems that these women had lots of people who, when needed, coached or advised them on particular issues, matters, or decisions. These individuals facilitated situations in which the women could have powerful learning moments throughout their professional careers. Peer relationships based on trust were essential for the leadership development of these presidents. As Pence (1995) stated, "Traits of trust, mutual respect, commitment, communication, and friendship are the most critical relational factors" (p. 135) in developmental relationships. Mutual acceptance between peers was vital for accurate and honest feedback to be given and received.

Superiors

The presidents shared stories and examples of influential superiors throughout their professional years. During the beginning and even mid-career points, these university presidents were strongly influenced by mid-level managers, directors, or chairs within and without the higher educational arena. These were individuals who, as Astin and Leland (1991) also found, gave the women permission to aspire, to act, and to be themselves. These people gave the presidents permission to "transcend prescribed gender roles" (Astin & Leland, 1991, p. 47), and they also inspired them to try to realize their greatest potential. Although only a few spoke of formal mentors, others used additional words (see Table 6.1) to describe their relationships with influential people.

Although half of the presidents did not mention any strong and competent female mentors or role models, the other half did speak of some during their early professional years. For example, one president stated, "I was positively influenced by my supervisor who was a very strong woman. She pushed me to be more aggressive and outgoing." Another president had a program director who was an important role model.

> She was an incredible teacher and administrator. She didn't have an authoritative style, yet she got so much done. She had built great networks with folks all over. She had been able to accomplish a lot and was very

bright. I observed and learned lots of hard lessons there that I have never forgotten. I remember seeing her grab a notebook and go into lectures and just start talking. I thought that I would be able to do that too. It was bad. It didn't work for me. Maybe that comes with twenty or thirty years of experience. She taught me about the importance of learning for my job and my life.

Another explained:

I worked with two strong women who were expert educators. Seeing really strong women at that time in my career influenced me profoundly. I learned a lot from them, and it was very important for me. They helped me and mentored me. They provided lots of opportunities for me to develop my skills. They stepped back and gave me freedom to be involved in important projects. They were confident in me and my abilities.

One president shared stories about a very positive influence in her first professional job after obtaining her undergraduate degree. She reminisced:

I went to work for a hospital and was the first person hired in this particular position. I had a wonderful supervisor who was a very strong woman. She influenced me greatly. She pushed me to be more aggressive and outgoing. Although I had been the president of many clubs in the past, I was really still timid in many ways. She pushed me, and it was a wonderful experience. As a twenty-two-year-old I learned to speak authoritatively and not be intimidated by others with more experience and more education. This was an important skill to learn at such a young age.

Another president spoke of a wonderful woman who taught her skills that she continues to use in her current position:

> I worked with an incredible woman who taught me some very important lessons about administration. The first one was so simple, but so important. There are two sides to every story. She hammered that lesson home with me. She would not ever make a judgment until she had talked to all of the parties involved. She had a quiet style about her that really inspired me. She was so strong, yet she never raised her voice. She was controlled but very wise and gentle. She was an incredible role model. She and I stepped up and were involved in a very contro-versial project. At that time I had courage, because she had courage. This empowered me to have courage at difficult times later on my own. During those years I began having the feeling that I was a person meant to stand up for causes, do the right things, and make a difference.

She concluded that these and other mentors taught her "how to work within the environment politics and how to be savvy." These women seemed to thrive particularly in an environment where they were given lots of autonomy, responsibility, and opportuni-ties. They were excited when others would let them grow in many different ways. It is important to note that, regarding mentoring relationships, researchers have reported that benefits can include career mobility, career satisfaction, career commitment, career ad-vancement, promotions, higher compensation, and higher reten-tion (Chao, Walz, & Gardner, 1992; Egan & Rosser, 2004; Noe et al., 2002).

When the presidents moved into midcareer positions they be-gan interacting with deans and other administrators at a new level. One woman stated, "I worked for a dean who gave me lots of freedom and opportunities to grow in the job." Most of the individuals in these positions were men, unlike many of those already discussed during the women's early professional years. This is partly because of the generation of women in this study. One president explained:

> In my early professional years I had some women who became my role models. However, as I moved into leadership roles all of my mentors or role models became men. They were all very good. I learned the kinds of things I needed to learn.

For some, male mentors "really opened up paths for jobs along the way." Some of the women felt that their male mentors had a great deal of respect for the strength and skills of competent women. Some universities were encouraging the faculty and administration to be open to women in leadership positions at that time. I asked one woman if her mentor was particularly encouraging specifically because she was a woman. She noted, "It was frosting on the cake for him that I was a woman, but I don't think it was the cake." Another learned from other types of diversity. She said:

> Because I had seen strong women earlier in my career, I never had any doubt that a woman could be competent. As I began moving into leadership roles, I worked with men who did things differently from each other. For example, one was really pretty bottom line, another understood networking in the university and community, and a third was a scientist and driven by data. Although gathering data was not my style (I had more of a big picture style), I learned to do research, pull together numbers, and justify why we should do what I was recommending. I still remember the day that the

data-driven individual finally said, "Enough data, I've got it!" I loved it. These individuals taught me to adapt and adjust when working with various individuals and efforts. I enjoyed learning from everyone.

Again this woman was observant and flexible, when needed. She recognized when she needed to adjust to others' needs. One president described her experience as she decided to take opportunities provided for her because of previous relationships with these individuals:

> Two individuals I had worked with as a graduate student were now in powerful positions within the university. They were my mentors and were so supportive. I realized that these men had widespread respect across campus. They were so eager for me to come to work with them. I knew that they saw potential in me, and they gave me absolutely marvelous opportunities, which I took full advantage of. These early opportunities showed my competence to others.

Academic presidents, provosts, and vice presidents were particularly influential for the women as they progressed into upper administrative positions where they could interact with leaders within their own institutions. One woman gave this example:

> I received wonderful mentoring from a new president and provost. They delegated very well, and I knew I had their confidence. I had an enormous sense of being in charge of important areas of the institution. They continued to hand me huge areas of responsibility, which helped my confidence even more. These two men were just extraordinary leaders. In fact, they were unbelievable supporters of mine as references for my current presidential position.

Another president learned a great deal from a fellow vice chancellor, whom she described, because of his experience, as more of a mentor.

> I had the most amazing partnership I ever could have imagined with another vice chancellor. We were peers, but I learned a lot. He was really a mentor. He would say to others about me, "She runs this place." We had a common vision. He is one of the most brilliant people I know. Working with him was an absolutely wonderful learning experience.

The presidents of the institutions where these women worked asked them (particularly those on an academic career path) to be involved in some important tasks and to lead specific committees. One of the women had a situation in which her president requested that she move from the position of faculty member to that of assistant to the president. Having the support of these leaders was particularly meaningful to the presidents when they were in subordinate positions, especially when these leaders had appointed them to various positions. Most of the women mentioned that the support of a then-current president was particularly important to them and their progress, even before they were vice presidents or provosts. One president concluded:

> My primary supporters and encouragers have been men. I could give you a list of five or six who, to this day, still support me in formal conversations. When I became chancellor I also had informal supporters that I would talk to from each of the different campuses. These are people who I also respected and supported. These individuals knew I could succeed in top leadership positions. When times get tough, these are the ones who still say, "You can do this. You're the right person for this job. Don't waver." This has been important to me through

the years. I sometimes still have a few of those southern female doubts that creep in: "Who am I to think I can do this?" Women feel that way more than men. Sometimes we have one view of ourselves, and I suspect other people have a very different view. I wouldn't have applied for chancellor if people hadn't come to me and asked me to apply.

Although the women had confidence, some still did not let themselves believe they were competent enough to obtain presidential positions.

Fels (2004) reported that, even when discrimination is not a factor, women have "much more difficulty than men developing relationships with people who have the power to advance their work" (p. 58). She continued by saying that "actively pursuing advantageous connections runs counter to the classic ideal of femininity" (p. 58). It did not appear that the presidents in this study had difficulty—particularly as they began advancing in their careers—developing relationships with key stakeholders. In fact, many found it very natural to do so. As explained in previous chapters, they were accomplishment-oriented and very driven. They wanted to make a difference and chose the appropriate paths to do so, most of which included developing relationships with stakeholders.

Interactions with good leaders were particularly beneficial for all of the presidents. One president explained, "Meeting with the provost helped me with my political astuteness, networking, and especially how to get along with people." For one woman, just observing the president and provost during the planning process was helpful in preparing for when she was responsible for it herself. Another had a similar experience.

The provost was very good at his job. I learned the kinds of things I needed to learn from watching him and interacting with him. I learned to work with people who did things a little differently. I learned from all of them about things like networking, politics, the bottom line, community, and data. Learning from the people around me has been one of the secrets of my leadership development.

In their developmental interactions with top administrators, the women continued to use their observation and self-reflective skills to improve themselves. They also reflected on others' actions—a systems perspective—and how those behaviors affected the institution as a whole. Again, the women gave credit to others for assisting them in their learning, but it was clear that they took responsibility for their own development. The women were not carried through advancements by any mentors or leaders. They worked hard and earned advancements because they were high performers.

For many of these women, as vice presidents, being mentored or coached by a competent, effective president was integral. One woman said that she had never thought of being a university president until her president said, "You could be a president." Another spoke of some mentoring characteristics:

> The president gave me—a vice president—so many new opportunities. He was a mentor and a sponsor. He listened to folks, and he always shared the credit. He involved us (the vice presidents) in overall university issues, so I had lots of experiences before I became president.

Another stated:

> The president told me that he could get a new vice president in one of two ways. He could go out and hire somebody who already had the expertise but didn't know the university and the community, or he could hire somebody who knew the university and community and could develop the expertise. He told me that he chose to do the

latter and hire me. So I started out on another learning adventure. He gave me new opportunities, and I learned so much from him. I don't think I would be in this position now if he hadn't been supportive of me. Because of his leadership style I was able to be involved with decision making beyond my own area. I was able to analyze many situations to figure out what worked well and what did not. I didn't want to make the same mistakes again. It just was incredibly helpful to have that kind of base of experiences that I could draw on. From the president I learned how to go through the decision-making process on very difficult issues. I had already been part of discussions. I had been part of the dialogue.

The women were smart enough and certain enough to take advantage of the opportunities given to them. And in many cases, they created their own opportunities through seeing institutional needs and being high performers. As Louis Pasteur said, "Chance favors only the prepared mind" (Scanlon, 1997, p. 55). Again, the presidents did not always discuss the reciprocity of these relationships. However, these presidents did benefit the individuals who influenced them. One woman acknowledged this reciprocity:

The president became my mentor. He was a very experienced president. If we were going into a meeting, he would take the time to talk through who would be there, what they would say, why they would say it, what would happen, what he would do, and what would happen as a result. Then it would happen just like he would say. Although I think he was probably talking over the situation so he could think through it himself, he also did it to prepare me. It was fabulous teaching. He was a very experienced administrator, and I was not. He really helped. He saw potential in me and supported me in many ways.

Interestingly, once these women became vice presidents or provosts, their own presidents would sometimes become "great and wonderful friends and advisors."

A number of women also mentioned examples of leaders who were influential to their leadership development because of their negative examples. One explained:

> I learned by watching very poor leaders make mistakes.
> I learned by watching leaders who didn't have courage
> and strength to do what was important and right.

One spoke of a woman leader who was vicious. She watched this woman lose the respect of the campus community because of her poor behavior. Many presidents gave examples of great learning experiences from watching the unethical behavior of leaders for whom they worked. They also noted a few examples of superiors who seemed to be threatened by their success, "although it made them look great." They saw how others viewed this behavior as childish and inappropriate. One president told a story of a K–12 school administrator who discouraged her from seeking a Ph.D. when she was employed as a teacher. He could not look ahead and see a vision of how people could develop and emerge into more competent and skilled individuals. "He could only see here and now." Because of negative examples, these women have been particularly careful not to fall into these leadership traps themselves. According to one president, "Not being able to respect superiors made a substantial impact on my development—for good and bad." The *examples* of others were often more powerful than their *words*.

Others

The presidents also described some individuals outside their immediate institutions who said or did things that made some kind of developmental difference. For example, one president told of the work she did on a particular multicampus task force. Someone from that task force on another campus called and told her that he had watched her work on the task force and was inquiring to see whether she would consider a new job opportunity. Another president explained that people on and off campus must have known of her leadership ability because they appointed her to chair committees and offered her positions. She noted, "The ultimate statement about a person's belief in another's leadership ability is to offer them leadership positions and opportunities." Three presidents spoke of the importance of networking with colleagues at other institutions. One colleague suggested that one of the women in this study consider heading up an important statewide commission. It was this suggestion that lead to a "change in plans and the opportunity to embrace new experiences." Some of these colleagues became "wonderful friends and advisors" to these future presidents. In a few situations, it was actually colleagues at other campuses who nominated the women in this study for leadership positions at these other institutions. Networking contacts appeared to be important sources of advice and encouragement for the women. One president spoke of the importance of staying in touch with colleagues throughout the years. She stated, "I stay connected with many people and, even after moving on, some nominated me for positions. I have stayed friends with people for years and years."

Some of the women mentioned being influenced by people they heard speak at conferences or in leadership training courses (see Chapter Seven for more details) who had "overcome odds." Listening to others who had children issues, gone through a divorce, and dealt with the death of a spouse, and were now successful faculty members or administrators, was a very important form of encouragement and motivation. One president explained, "I was impressed at how one speaker got so many things done. I decided if she could do it, then maybe I could do it too." Another woman was profoundly influenced by some of her struggling students who couldn't read well. She said, "I was really very inspired by my students when teaching philosophy at a public college." By listening to many women speak, they would "take pieces of people who influenced" them to improve themselves. The presidents were also influenced by people who worked for them. One president noted:

> I was influenced by the difficult circumstances some of the people who worked for me had to endure. I learned from them as I observed them and had to deal with them at work. Working with people in difficult circumstances during this time in my life helped me strengthen my interpersonal and management skills.

A few presidents, who had substantial years in careers outside higher education, were particularly influenced by leaders in the government and community. Many of these were role models more than mentors or coaches. For example, one president relayed the following about a particular role model:

> In high school I had an AP English teacher who was a real role model during those years. She was brilliant. I heard of her years later because she had become a principal at a major high school and was, at that time, the only woman in secondary administration in the entire state. I had been interested in secondary school administration, and when I heard she was an administrator I decided that I could go into administration as well. She was definitely a role model during my years working in K–12.

One president said that various contacts who knew her capabilities and talents asked her to take new positions. When she moved into those new positions, others around her assumed she was only hired because of gender and race. She was not offended by that assumption because some were being hired for those reasons. She stated:

> These individuals were pleasantly surprised when I opened my mouth and spoke. They figured out very quickly that I was qualified for the positions and really knew my stuff.

The women gained a lot from observing others in various positions—possibly more often than when they had official mentors or role models—and were influenced by observing people who showed strength and determination when going through struggles and challenges.

Final Thoughts

This research supports the categories and characteristics of D'Abate et al. (2003) to describe reasons for successful developmental interactions. The qualities and preparedness of the individual being influenced was a powerful indicator of success. In addition, the interaction situation, the positions and proximity of the influential individuals, the purpose for the interactions, and the degree of structure all played an important role in the opportunities in which these presidents developed leadership.

As past researchers have also found (see Wells, 1998), the women university presidents in this study learned through relationships and connections with others. In fact, influential individuals were vital in assisting these women to continue to obtain a deeper understanding of their own capabilities, talents, strengths, and weaknesses. Others assisted them in exploring their own sense of identity, strengthening their own self-awareness, developing their own voice as a leader, and finding authority of self, as Caffarella and Barnett (1997) similarly noted in their research. My findings show that they did this somewhat differently from that reported in past research. Corporate leadership studies (Hennig & Jardim, 1977; Kelly & Marin, 1998; Morrison, White, & Van Velsor, 1994) decades ago claimed that all women leaders reached the highest levels of their occupations through mentoring support. Other researchers (Dunlap & Schmuck, 1995; Kelly & Marin, 1998; Moore & Amey, 1988; Pankake, Schroth, & Funk, 2000b) also praise the effectiveness and necessity of official mentors. Although some of the presidents in my study had mentors, over half of the women did not. They built and developed their own relationships and were often more profoundly influenced by unofficial mentors such as coaches, counselors, advisors, supporters, tutors, confronters, and developers. As many (Cullen & Luna, 1993; Growe & Montgomery, 1999; Wesson, 1998) have argued, to obtain leadership positions in the twenty-first century, women need to have means of support to obtain advice, encouragement, moral support, informational contacts, ideas and methods for constructive ways of dealing with frustration, and forums for open and honest discussion and feedback. I found this to be the case in my research as well; however, it is important to remember that each individual woman develops differently. Leadership development is an individual process. Hence, providing women opportunities for self-reflection and self-exploration is imperative. Helping women understand themselves through a wide range of opportunities can provide the most important developmental experiences they can have.

Takeaways

1. Although mentoring is a powerful career development tool for women, it is only one of many potentially effective methods to develop leadership knowledge and skills.

2. Women with self-respect can accurately hear and accept compliments, and they are not afraid to believe and act.

3. Developmental interactions are most powerful when women are prepared, observant, and reflective.

4. The most effective developmental interactions occur between people who trust each other.

5. Trusted professional colleagues and peers can provide a valuable source of feedback, encouragement, and support.

6. Providing women opportunities for self-reflection and self-exploration can greatly enhance their development.

7

Developmental Activities

The only real training for leadership is leadership.

Anthony Jay

Leadership is much more an art, a belief, a condition of the heart, than a set of things to do. The visible signs of artful leadership are expressed, ultimately, in its practice.

Max DePree

Researchers (e.g., Galambos & Hughes, 2000; Weick, 1983) have believed for some time that "all human beings possess an inherent push for growth" and that this force serves as a "catalyst for developmental change" (Galambos & Hughes, 2000, p. 22). This desire for growth is stimulated by "innate curiosity, a need for stimulation, and a desire for fulfillment" (p. 18). The presidents in this study clearly had all of these. Cooke (2004) articulated this desire well when she said:

> A life fully lived must be one of constant discovery, openness and acceptance to deviations from the chosen path, and a thirsting curiosity to uncover and participate fully in what Parker Palmer (1998, p. 183) defines as our one great thing. This expedition is a wonderful quest to uncover what is important and what will make a person

whole, happy, true to self, and productive to society. Hopefully along this path one also discovers maturity as an individual and eventually the greater goal of true wisdom. (p. 2)

For these presidents, a life fully lived included the development of strong leadership skills and competencies so that they could satisfy both their internal drive for accomplishment and their desire to make a difference. Yet recognizing and understanding leadership development in all its dimensions and complexity is a challenge for researchers and practitioners alike.

This chapter discusses a number of developmental activities (experiences, situations, and opportunities) that the presidents believed were particularly beneficial for them. Chapter Five has already outlined the women's basic career paths, Chapter Six discussed the individuals who influenced them during their professional years, and Chapter Eight will present information about the effects of nonwork issues (motherhood, marriage, extended family, nonpaid community work, and so forth) on the leadership development of the presidents. Hence, this chapter will focus on the specific development they received from work-related professional positions and assignments, leadership training programs, professional organization involvement, and work-related challenges.

The presidents spoke of how much they learned from watching and observing people (as discussed in Chapter Six) and situations. They watched human systems without necessarily being intrusive. They often made decisions about what they wanted to do with their careers based on these observations. Some presidents found it fascinating to observe bad examples and learned what worked and what did not. As already mentioned, the presidents reflected on their observations. This continues to be a strong theme throughout the chapters encompassing adulthood. With observation and reflective skills, these women went through a "discovery process of finding and recognizing" (Micas, 1991, p. 21) the voice that now guides their vision of leadership. As Ahn, Adamson, and

Dornbusch (2004) noted, "to be effective in leading others, leaders must start from a position of authentic self-knowledge" (p. 123). This chapter continues the discussion of how these women learned to understand themselves.

Positions and Assignments

Although there were many influential individuals and experiences along the career paths of these women leaders, it is clear that the most effective means of developing leadership skills and competencies was experience itself. McCall, Lombardo, and Morrison (1988) reported that the most potent leadership development forces do not necessarily occur in a formal classroom setting but instead occur in the context of ongoing work. Development is not a "matter of mere experience; rather, it depends on how the experience is organized and interpreted" (Day & O'Connor, 2003, p. 15). Experience can be an effective means for promoting development, provided that it causes individuals to think in different and more complex ways. As Anthony Jay said, "The only real training for leadership is leadership" (WorldofQuotes.com, 2007). For example, the presidents became politically astute through their past experiences with politics. They learned to manage conflict by dealing with conflict in a variety of settings. They became expert strategists by creating and implementing strategy in positions along the way. Opportunities to learn from actually "doing" provided these women with the skills to become top leaders.

Learning from experience takes time, as one president stated:

> I always just believed that if I worked hard at something that I could do it. People gave me opportunities. Sometimes I took them, and I wasn't always patient. It takes time to build experience. It takes time and even though you can accomplish and do a lot, it takes seasoning, and it takes experience. That is something that I didn't understand early. At some point in time I thought competence was just it, that if you were just really

competent and you really worked hard then you could make things happen. Now I understand. Early on I didn't know that I needed to learn more about relationship building, working with others, and bringing them along with you. This was a very important lesson for me.

Another woman reiterated saying, "Learning how to lead takes time. It just takes time to build experience." A third commented, "Time and seasoning has taught me invaluable lessons, and even now my leadership skills continue to be refined and strengthened." Competence is enhanced by work experience. Emerging leaders need time and experience to practice leading. As Lyman (1995) said, "the most trustworthy knowledge comes from personal experience" (pp. 206–207).

New Positions and Assignments

Throughout their careers the women presidents thrived on new opportunities, either by taking new positions or by accepting new assignments within current jobs. They intentionally looked for opportunities to learn what they didn't know rather than looking for ways to show what they could do. One president stated, "New positions really helped my confidence, which in turn facilitated my development even more." They loved "challenge and complexity" and wanted to "make a difference" and have "some kind of impact." It seems the presidents entered into leadership positions not to impose their will on others but to learn. They took pleasure in learning and found excitement in "figuring out how to incorporate new ideas, concepts, and skills" to improve themselves. For example, one president stated:

When I needed to be involved in fundraising, I went out and tried to soak up everything from everyone related to how to raise money, including what I should do and what kinds of things I should put in place.

They had the ability to retain data in their minds until better or more complete information emerged. In most cases they seemed to enjoy learning new things by building on what they had already learned. As one president explained:

> This new position required an amazing blend of all the analytical, budgeting, instructional researching, strate-gic planning, and political skills I had learned and devel-oped in the past. It was invigorating to be able to learn by building on to the knowledge and skill foundation I had already begun to develop.

For many of the presidents, their academic disciplines provided the foundation for this learning. The women brought with them knowledge and skills from their own disciplines to solve prob-lems and make decisions. Although some of them did not come from academic disciplines in which they studied human behavior, they learned about human systems along the way through various positions.

A number of presidents spoke of learning epiphanies they experienced in certain assignments. For example, one president recalled:

> A huge awakening for me was when I figured out where the intersection of policy and politics was. I suddenly realized that analytical stuff and policy analysis wasn't going to mean much unless we figured out how to make it a part of the organizational capacity. After this realiza-tion I was then able to learn how to get policy adopted in highly political environments—not just by the people on Capitol Hill—but little people.

Others noted that new positions that gave them opportunities to work with the legislature and finances were "very interesting and helpful." One president took a year sabbatical and worked on a statewide educational commission. She explained:

> Opportunities to meet with the governor, members of the board of regents, and legislative leaders were very helpful. While working with a commission I could see agendas, levels of interests, and watched the friction between the board of regents and the speaker of the house. I got a bird's eye view of what this dynamic looks like. It was not frustrating at all. I was thinking, Why is he doing that? What is going on there that is not on the table? I think I added "chess playing" skills during this time. It isn't just the next move, but it is figuring out the next three moves after that. I was watching all of that complexity and dynamics with a room full of 800-pound gorillas. It was *fun!*

The presidents took great pleasure in watching themselves learn and develop. In many situations, like the one just described, the presidents became participant-observers. They not only watched others and situations, but they also observed themselves interact and react in these settings. Then they reflected on their experiences. This notion of the link between leadership development and being a participant-observer is quite powerful.

"Fun" was a word mentioned by most presidents throughout the interviews. Although they sometimes mentioned "fun" in the context of working with certain individuals, they used the word more often to describe intellectual fun in acquiring new abilities, solving problems, and meeting and conquering challenges. As Fels (2004) noted, "doing a thing well can be a reward in and of itself. The delight provided by the skill repays the effort of learning it" (p. 53). This reward and delight was often termed "fun" by the presidents.

Now, just because they thrived on new opportunities and challenges did not mean they did not get nervous and fearful at times. But even with uneasiness they often enjoyed new challenges. A number of presidents spoke of the first times they began working with both the legislature and the press. One president recalled:

> At first I was scared to death. I hated the idea that I might not have immediate answers. I was very uncomfortable. However, I got better with experience. The confidence came, the steadiness came, and the nervousness and fear subsided.

In working with these groups, the presidents used words such as *courage*, *toughness*, and *strength* to describe what they had learned from related experiences. One attribute that was consistent across the ten presidents was that these women were persistent in the face of skill deficiencies. In the interviews, they often admitted their weak areas, and then spoke of how they strengthened them. Lacking skills can be intimating for many individuals. Yet these women were not intimidated by the lack of skills and abilities, and they had confidence that they could learn if they were open and persistent. They understood that they could "prove their worth by performing and delivering" (Olsson, 2002, p. 246).

Special Assignments

Astin and Leland (1991) found that future leaders who participate in purposeful assignments can "test their competencies, take risks, manifest values, and simultaneously receive support, counsel, and validation from more experienced leaders" (p. 69). The presidents shared examples of special assignments they were given when they were faculty members or early administrators that gave them these experiences. One said, "Opportunities to work on task forces and committees was very helpful for my development." Another woman spoke of her experience in leading a particular task force:

> Because of past smaller opportunities, when I was asked to lead a high-level task force I already had the confidence I could do it well. I met with the president and

provost regularly. I met with colleagues and administrators across campus. I had unbelievable experiences in terms of opening up my mind to all the other types of work that goes on in the university. It was amazing. I could see beyond the academics. I could see strategy, and I could see how the people at the top interacted with each other and the board of trustees. It was exhilarating. I learned about admissions, financial aid, and capital planning. I was able to see how the various disciplines interacted. I learned that people in humanities go about their work differently than people in physics. They had different ways of attacking problems and had different cultures. This experience was mind-expanding and energizing.

Again, the presidents were able to put themselves in a participant-observer role to learn the most they could in these experiences. Another president spoke of being put in charge of creating a strategic plan for the campus. She pulled together a committee of deans, faculty members, trustees, and students, and she learned a great deal from the committee members and the process. Most researchers (Collins et al., 1998) agree that women can gain valuable experience by "participating in a wide variety of campus committees" (p. 201), since these can teach them about administration, policies, budgets, processes, negotiation, reports, and stakeholders. Researchers note that women often do more service than men but do not often have opportunities to chair prominent or strategic committees that will provide them the best training. Twale and Shannon (1996) blame some of this on women themselves by saying that "women remain less savvy about networking that would aid their nomination or appointment to key governance posts on prestigious campus committees" (p. 11). These researchers and others (Burke & Collins, 2001; Collins et al., 1998; Sagaria, 1988; Twale & Shannon, 1996) believe women can develop leadership by volunteering and accepting strategic and highly visible assignments in areas where they do or do not yet have experience, as well as being open to filling challenging positions where they can gain a sense of their own personal capacity and competence. The presidents in my study were successful in doing just that. In fact, they often created their own developmental experiences from the opportunities before them, although others facing the same situation may not have received any developmental value. Development is in fact enhanced by the characteristics of the learner.

One president, as a faculty member, became the faculty union president and learned "valuable leadership skills." She said, "I learned so much about negotiation from staying up all night trying to negotiate contracts." She felt that "good things happen from relationships outside of normal faculty work." Another president became the director of field experience at an educational institution. This position gave her valuable experience in balancing a variety of constituencies (university, students, parents of the children, school districts, and school unions). She said, "I had some really great learning experiences. When I became chancellor I knew every mayor and superintendent in the whole area because of my previous responsibilities." In very different ways, the presidents learned the language, concerns, and interests of stakeholders. They learned to listen and understand the various constituencies in the higher educational environment and beyond.

Faculty Duties and Assignments

Half of the presidents spoke of the valuable leadership development that came from regular faculty duties and assignments. As one president noted, "Having been a faculty member is very helpful in my current position. It is beneficial to know how faculty members think and how the faculty is organized." Teaching responsibilities taught the presidents time management, organization, confidence, presentations skills, and people skills. Regarding academic service, another stated:

> As a faculty member I think my committee work and service have been extremely helpful in my development. Any time you are put in a position to plan, organize, or lead, it really stretches you. It also calls upon you to draw on your resources and delegate. It teaches you a lot of things.

Scholarship-related activities (research, publishing, grants) also provided opportunities for growth and development. One president believed that research and publishing prepared her for a graduate dean post. Three presidents spoke of research-related conferences and travel being very beneficial for the development of leadership. One explained:

> I traveled internationally and learned to get along with individuals in the high society (i.e., snobs). I got to see a different way to organize an educational system.

Others said that international experiences taught them diversity, new perspectives, multitasking, dealing with the unknown, and other life lessons.

Receiving grants helped build the presidents' confidence, and managing grants helped teach them leadership, hiring, budgeting, administration skills, and multitasking. One president stated:

> My research and lab skill work have been helpful in developing my leadership abilities. I love to start new things. I like to make things happen. When I have new ideas, I always write things down coherently as far as I can get. Then I research what has been done before and figure out some good ideas. Next I talk about it with other people. It is fun. I love to do research, learn new things, and get my hands in deeply.

Another president spoke of her work in directing a lab. She worked with prominent people from all over the world who came to work in the lab. She had a lot of responsibility and practiced motivating employees, getting things done, managing conflict, dealing with difficult situations, understanding behavior, hiring and firing employees, encouraging people to move on if they had better opportunities, and working with people who had personal problems (e.g., alcoholism, depression). She said that she "learned from all of it." One last president said the following in reference to research:

> If one does research, one understands how to deal with complex problems. One learns to take a complex situation and think about what key questions to ask or what key themes there may be that run through it. They learn to figure out how to shape them into theories or questions. Even if you can't solve them you can still make a lot of progress. Doing research uniquely informs management and leadership.

Nonacademic Positions

Although some of the presidents did not begin their careers in higher education, opportunities in their workplace helped shape their values and influence their career choices, as they did for the women in the study by Astin and Leland (1991). The presidents in my study found other leadership experiences to be very important developmental opportunities. For example, one was a high school principal and learned many transferable skills such as motivating others, managing conflict, understanding stakeholders, listening to different perspectives before making judgments, organizing and facilitating meetings, and managing employees. Another, who was a high-level leader in a noneducational public environment, explained:

> I learned leadership skills from other positions along the way. I learned about budgets, speaking, time management, negotiations, sizing up complex problems,

international travel, and dealing with high level individuals. These positions did a lot to prepare me for this
presidency. My experience with this organization was
probably one of the most transformative events in my
life.

One president who worked outside higher education was actually able to serve on educational boards that gave her an awareness
of related issues and constituencies. She felt that "having the blend
was helpful" because she could "understand issues of concerns to
students, faculty, and administrators." Another president had substantial management experience in a health-related field. In this
position she coordinated and managed employees, administration,
a police force, as well as other departments. She said:

I had experience that helped me learn to handle crime,
deal with death, solve problems creatively, make a difference, negotiate strategically, persuade stakeholders, create and work with teams, network wisely and effectively,
and continue to develop financial skills and astuteness.
I had so many learning experiences during these years
that helped me become the leader I am today.

Another president was a hospital social worker, which was difficult
work. She learned to speak authoritatively and was not intimidated,
even by doctors. She said, "I learned a lot. I learned to care deeply
and had to make hard decisions that influenced people's lives."
She noted that she now has to do the same as a president, so
she appreciated the learning experience when she was a young
professional. She explained:

In this early position I learned how to work in teams, get
along with different disciplines, make tough decisions,
accept that there would always be enemies, deal with
political issues, handle not always being able to solve

problems or reach compromises, have members of the board not support me, and work with aggressive clients who hated me. I continued to strengthen my abilities to do all of these things in other positions. They are all important skills when one becomes a president or chancellor.

Work experiences outside higher education were clearly beneficial for the development of leadership for many of these women.

New Institutions

Some of the presidents spoke of "opportunities to do new things and continually develop" by accepting "new assignments in new institutions." One president recalled:

Going to different institutions helped me enhance my general leadership skills, meet new people, network, advance my interpersonal skills, and more. I think the different environment gave me different exposure. That variety helped me develop a much more comprehensive vision of how to manage, which I believed has helped me a great deal.

Another explained that it was a beneficial learning experience to take on "similar responsibilities in new settings" as well as learning from the "addition of new responsibilities." She simply stated, "I learned a lot on the job." One president spoke of taking new positions with a board of regents in a state across the country from where she had been employed. She said:

My learning curve went straight up, and I loved it! It was a very different kind of environment and it was just a marvelous, growth experience for me. It gave me the appreciation of the additional complexities and inefficiencies of public higher education in contrast to private higher education.

Another president had previously attended and worked at private institutions until she accepted her first position at a public institution with many immigrant students. She spoke of what she learned from finally being exposed to what public higher education is all about, including its philosophy and what it does.

Overall, throughout adulthood the presidents continued to seek learning in everything they did through observing, listening, reflecting, remembering, practicing, enjoying, and experiencing. The pleasure they found in growth and development continued to drive their desire to learn leadership skills and prepare themselves to contribute within the larger society.

Leadership Training Programs

The presidents spoke about the formal training and development programs (courses, seminars, workshops, lectures, and sessions) they attended. They mentioned the following:

- American Council on Education Fellowship
- American Council on Education National Identification Project for Women (ACENIP)
- American Council on Education Network
- American Council on Education seminars and workshops
- Association of State Colleges and Universities
- Bryn Mawr Women in Leadership Institute (linked to the HERS program; see below)
- Delta Kappa Gamma Fellow
- Doctoral Course in Educational Administration and Leadership

- European Higher Educational Roundtables

- Harvard Institute for Education Management

- Higher Education Resource Services (HERS)

- Other leadership seminars and workshops (information-based and skill-based)

- Professional organizations and memberships

- Related research and publishing (as a faculty member)

- Position-specific (for example, provost, dean) conferences, meetings, and groups

- Women-only training and groups

Nine of the ten women presidents specifically mentioned the American Council on Education (ACE) programs as being influential in their leadership training and preparation. In talking about these programs, the presidents summed up several of the advantages of participation, including increased confidence, new positions of authority, personal and professional growth and development, and broadened contextual understanding of management in higher education.

Three presidents participated in the ACE Fellowship program and spoke highly and fondly of their related experiences, growth, and personal and professional development. One president explained:

> They put me with thirty to forty really smart people from higher education and brought in great people to teach us. We went everywhere—to national meetings and various campuses. They got us pumped up and ready to be presidents.

Another discussed a very real, immediate benefit of her participation in the ACE program:

> I went to all of the ACE events and had access to everything that was happening at that level. When I came back to my own campus, the chancellor immediately asked me to be his assistant.

One president summarized her experience: "ACE is the best and broadest of anything you could do. Everyone there has something to teach and learn."

Four presidents mentioned the ACE/NIP or ACE Network, which was established in the late 1970s to identify women in higher education and help prepare them for promotions. They explained that it was a valuable forum for women to get together and "find their voices." From these experiences women "gain confidence that they can do it, and they learn they are smart, competent, and can move into new positions." According to another president, these workshops "helped validate their own points of view and also helped them hear and understand that there are other points of view that might be equally valuable and helpful." Women participants "come to really value the group as a way to help them learn and grow. Their understanding and confidence grows. They open up and share well, and it is fun!"

The presidents spoke of a number of other formal training and development experiences. Many women mentioned ACE seminars and workshops (in general) as helpful. One president said that she found ACE-specific training beneficial because she acquired new ideas and had old solid ideas reinforced. The presidents explained that the opportunities for building and extending networks at these types of events were very effective and important. One said, "All of these have been helpful and contributed to my leadership development in different ways. In each one you create a new network you can use to find out and learn what you don't already know."

Three of the women presidents mentioned being accepted to the Harvard Institute for Management Education program, but due to other constraints only one attended. The president who did participate described the program benefits, saying that the week-long seminar was

> targeted at some of the issues that a president would face like time management, fund raising, dealing with multiple constituencies, and such. It was helpful. It gave me things to think about and to learn more about. I learned where I needed more information. I created a network of other presidents which was helpful. In fact, I remain in touch with some of them to this day.

Three of the women mentioned attending HERS as presenters or attendees. They spoke highly of its positive influence on future women leaders in postsecondary education. One participant spoke of European higher educational roundtables. She stated that presidents meet and discuss the "leadership of higher educational institutions and those issues that impact universities." She found these very enlightening and beneficial. She explained:

> It's important to draw from those who are in similar situations and also understand the differences as well. There are common things all institutions deal with in higher education and it is helpful to listen, discuss, learn, and reflect.

Another stated that "AASCU [American Association of State Colleges and Universities] does a great job in developing presidential leadership," while another declared that she liked the Delta Kappa Gamma Fellowship classes on "transforming operational leaders to policy leaders." Finally, many of the presidents spoke generically of other information-based and skill-based leadership seminars and workshops. In fact, many still attend because they are presenting. One mentioned:

> I have been at a multitude of training and seminar sessions. I have learned from every single one of them. I always learn from what other people think, even if only to reinforce the kinds of things I have been thinking. What I find repeatedly is that there isn't any magic to postsecondary leadership. It's just a whole lot of common sense. Ultimately, all of us pretty much come to the same conclusions. I hear the same stories over and over.

One president said that she primarily attended training or meetings that were informative versus skill-building. She wanted to

> be with other leaders, to get together with peers and have the opportunity to be around them sharing stories, listening to see what works and what doesn't work. Sometimes I think, "Wow, that person is really effective," and then I watch them to see what they are doing.

Another president said she prefers skill-based training versus information-based training. Training on facilitation was most helpful for her. She stated, "I learned different ways to make decisions and to design group processes. I immediately used these new skills at my university and saw immediate results."

Most of the presidents spoke of the positive influence that comes from meeting with other individuals with analogous job positions (provost, dean) and the same types of responsibilities. Whether they gathered in training sessions, as groups, or at conferences, the presidents agreed that meeting with individuals from other campuses, states, or countries was very useful. One participant stated, "Some of the best learning opportunities are going to sessions with people in your same position from different universities. I love hearing ideas, innovations, and what other people are doing." Another said, "Conferences or meetings with people doing your same job are critical." A third explained:

> Getting together with people who do your same job at other campuses is helpful. I've done that for a long time. We stay in touch informally through e-mail and events. We give and take advice freely. It is a powerful leadership development tool.

Eight of the ten presidents discussed their perceptions of women-only training sessions and groups. All felt that these experiences can be positive and insightful opportunities. However, no president believed that all training and development programs should be women-only, but that occasional women-only sessions were refreshing, informative, motivational, and enriching. According to one president:

> Women are very candid about themselves. Men are much more guarded. I was on the president's panel at an ACE network regional meeting, and we all talked about our own experiences, and we discovered that they were so similar. Everyone was candid about what they didn't do well and about where they made mistakes. I don't think you could get a group of male presidents to ever talk like that. I don't think you could talk like that in a mixed group either. I wouldn't.

Another stated, "Women's groups can be very candid and collegial, and there really is a kind of sisterhood. It doesn't matter where you are from; women from all backgrounds, races, classes, and ages really connect well." It is important to note that these experiences were not particularly highlighted with regard to official leadership training and development opportunities. Often they spoke of women-only groups within professional organizations, academic conferences, and community groups, to name a few. Two presidents made it clear they don't like to attend or belong to women's groups that focus on women as victims in the "glass half-empty" mentality. However, these women enjoyed discussing challenges and opportunities in an open and positive environment.

Women-only training has been discussed somewhat in the literature by a number of writers (De la Rey & Suffla, 2003; Jurgens & Dodd, 2003; Koonce, 2004; Lewis & Fagenson, 1995; Vinnicombe & Singh, 2003; Watson, 1988). Most of the authors speak about the benefits of this type of training for the women involved, addressing many of the issues the ten presidents spoke about. Some writers describe women-only leadership training as "crucial," whereas others stated it was "helpful and beneficial" and that it could provide a unique networking opportunity (Koonce, 2004). As the presidents also addressed, Koonce (2004) found that leadership training programs can be very beneficial to rising women leaders because they "provide a confidential environment in which women can candidly discuss both personal concerns and organizational challenges in ways they wouldn't feel comfortable doing in a mixed-gender program" (p. 82). For these programs to be effective, researchers believe that they should be designed to help women find their voices (Lyman, 1995; Micas, 1991), learn more about themselves (Cooke, 2004; Lyman, 1995), claim the value of one's self and knowledge, and then speak and act in new ways (Lyman, 1995). Training should provide women opportunities to interact with and talk to leaders about leadership challenges and opportunities (Dickerson & Taylor, 2000). As Kaminski (2003) outlined in her stages of development, leadership development should include opportunities for women to develop basic skills, figure out politics, and mobilize others. Further, Boatwright and Egidio's (2003) findings suggest that successful leadership development should include "experiences that validate women's relational identities, increase women's awareness of how their relational strengths may enhance their leadership effectiveness, and enhance women's psychological resistance against negative leadership evaluation" (pp. 666, 668).

One research team (Ebbers, Gallisath, Rockel, & Coyan, 2000) proclaimed that without leadership training in general, "a major source of potential future leaders would be lost" (p. 376). Research does confirm that there is a link between leadership training and development and enhanced advancement opportunities (McDonald & Hite, 1999).

In sum, the university presidents found a variety of leadership training and development programs, seminars, workshops, and experiences helpful in their learning and growth. Same-gender training was helpful for most, but none claimed to believe that all training for females should be women-only. They felt that same-gender training is helpful as one of many types of training programs. In fact, these women took advantage of a variety of training opportunities, including same-gender, mixed gender, international, domestic, same role or position, mixed role or position, and so forth. A wide range of training opportunities provided well-rounded developmental experiences for these women.

Professional Organizations

Most of the women also spoke of the value of belonging to and staying involved with professional organizations. One stated, "Belonging to professional organizations was and is helpful and important." Some presidents spoke about their continued involvement in their discipline-related professional organizations. One stated, "The colleagues I made as a scholar from professional organizations were very important even though I had moved into administration. I wrote for years with colleagues from other institutions." Others spoke of the higher educational academies and organizations (for instance, student affairs, academic affairs, accreditations, and position-specific groups), as well as general education associations like AAHE and ACE. One explained that she brings back (even now as a president) "what others are doing and how other people are thinking, whether it conflicts with or adds to what we are considering and doing." Two talked about the leadership experience they gained from actively leading such a group. They felt that networking had been very helpful throughout the years. One president said that professional organizations were "very important in terms of my development, not only seeing the dynamics but watching the process and staying connected (past, present, future) to the bigger picture within the industry." Another believed that involvement in international conferences added depth and insight in her work:

> My professional organizations are important for continued development. I travel abroad to go to major international conferences. It has always been important for me to strengthen and broaden my global understanding and experience. It has helped me have a multicultural and multinational perspective that is very valuable in my current leadership position.

Professional organizations have provided important networking opportunities for these presidents. It provided them with practice in looking for systems and connections. Women sometimes struggle with developing strong networks. Murphy and Riggio (2003) stated that a major problem for women in educational administration is the obvious lack of positive role models, adequate networks, and support systems. Many women believe that enhanced support systems would be helpful (Gupton & Slick, 1996; Murphy & Riggio, 2003). According to De la Rey and Suffla (2003), effective networking can help women obtain and be successful in advanced leadership positions. In fact, Pini, Brown, and Ryan (2004) reported that "women have a higher level of reliance on outside networks for developmental functions than men" (p. 287). In academic environments, professional organizations can broaden networks, as they did for the women in my study. These women developed the capability to continually develop and expand helpful networks that have served them well throughout the years. Their networks were based on learning and support. They continued to connect with individuals who could, in some way, help them learn and develop, and they associated with those who could provide support and encouragement in their goals. This is not to say that these women did not network to provide support and assistance to others. They were highly focused throughout their careers on the development of others (see Chapter Nine for details).

Difficulties

Difficulties and struggles continued to provide developmental opportunities for the university presidents. Van Velsor and Hughes (1990) reported that women obtain most of their learning and development from three areas: assignments (43 percent), other people (28 percent), and hardships (22 percent). Twenty-two percent is a lot of learning obtained through this medium. As Jack Mezirow (cited in Van Velsor & Hughes, 1990, p. 37) once said:

> What we perceive and fail to perceive, and what we think and fail to think are powerfully influenced by habits of expectation that constitute our frame of reference, that is, a set of assumptions that structure the way we interpret our experiences.

The presidents seemed to learn from pain and struggle through self-examination and reflection. As one set of authors stated, "Reflective self-assessment is a natural and healthy reaction to challenge" (Van Velsor & Hughes, 1990, p. 28). Bennis and Goldsmith (2003) believe that self-reflection (on both successes and failures) is a critical step in becoming a leader. Most of the presidents have gone through some very difficult situations that gave them the chance, as one president noted, to "test how sturdy my constitution was, and to understand how resourceful I could be." She explained, "These moments in my life, whether it was a failure or a near disaster, have been among the most important growth experiences that I have had." These women intentionally tested and pushed their boundaries by accepting challenges and stretching themselves. Yet many of the difficulties they encountered unintentionally tested and pushed them as well. Again, many women learned more from the difficulties than from their successes. Chapter Five already discussed some career and gender challenges. Three presidents spoke of painful experiences in dealing with negative press. One explained:

> It was a very new experience; it was one that led to a lot of deep reflection. I had to ask myself what I had learned, and what I could have done differently. The pain from something that difficult and painful never goes away totally. Yet I think that was good. It is very hard when you are in a position that is so visible and powerful to avoid those experiences.

The presidents were very resilient, and were able to recover relatively quickly from difficulties. This is not to say that the effects may not have lingered. However, these women did not and would not let struggles and challenges discourage them enough to stop performing. They had the ability to pick themselves up and recover relatively quickly when many others may have quit. Cubillo and Brown (2003) found in their study of educational leaders that women leaders display qualities of remarkable resilience, courage, and self-reliance that come from dealing with difficulties. Their motivation for resilience came from their driving needs for both self-actualization and altruism. Similar to findings of one research study (Olsson & Pringle, 2004), the ten university presidents' focus was not on barriers but on openings and opportunities.

Half of the presidents shared stories of working with unethical leaders or in situations in which unethical activities were being tolerated. One president spoke of some difficult circumstances with a previous institution. She stayed long enough to protect the institution and took a beating in the press. She said:

> I learned a lot from this. I learned that there are some realities you cannot change. I think up until that point I thought I could change the world. I learned that I couldn't change some individuals' value systems that are different from my own or the academy. I learned that sometimes you just need to get out of a situation.

Some of the presidents felt that working with difficult or unethical leaders was one of the most stressful things they had to endure. In fact, several attribute stress-related medical conditions to some of these situations. One president even felt that her belief in the "redeeming qualities of all mankind" and her determination that "if only I had tried harder this could have worked out" had caused her some grief and gotten her in trouble here and there throughout the years. She had to come to terms with understanding that things were not always under her control, and that she could no longer trust everyone.

One president spoke of starting out with thin skin in difficult circumstances and then learning to toughen up. She said, "I learned that I could step on toes and survive. My skin got thickened appropriately, which was necessary." Others learned from union strikes, hurtful rumors, and failure. As one president explained:

> I think reflection helped me be more successful. It kept me engaged and involved at the university. As an assistant professor without tenure I learned that if you are not failing, then you are not learning. I didn't realize how important that was until I started to fail once in a while. Reflection has been an absolute lifesaver.

The presidents hated making mistakes or failing, but the ability to learn from these was a very powerful gift. Leadership experts

(Bennis, 1989; Lombardo & Eichinger, 2000; Pankake et al., 2000a) have agreed. Looking at failure as an opportunity to learn and grow rather than denying mistakes or blaming others is a quality that makes an exceptional leader. As already mentioned, learning from failures, mistakes, and difficulties was one of the most significant forms of learning for the presidents. As Cooke (2004) so profoundly stated, "From these times of chaos and uncertainty, individuals become more than just the outside facade, but grow to know and recognize their inner selves as well as the outer reflection in the mirror" (p. 2).

Final Thoughts

All emerging leaders need a wide range of developmental experiences and opportunities. As Sullivan (2003) explained:

> Even natural leaders, however, need education. For the veterans, perhaps it is reflection. For those with quick minds but few years, it is experience. But it cannot be done in isolation because an education in leadership is not so much about learning how you learn, but understanding how others learn. Being a leader is about understanding how individuals work differently from one another, and how they can all work together with the most efficiency. At its highest point, leadership is understanding how you can teach another to see the same. (p. 51)

These women were able to understand the technical and human skills and systems necessary to comprehend higher education in general. They were also able to find their own voices and to understand themselves. They displayed remarkable resilience, courage, self-reliance, work ethic, and observation and reflective abilities. As Gupton and Del Rosario (1997) outlined in their research, the women in this study also understood the importance of appropriate education, meaningful experiences, ongoing networking, strategic career development, and having a record of improving and updating their professional qualifications. They continued to develop basic skills, figure out politics, and mobilize others (Kaminski, 2003). And finally, they found learning in almost every experience.

Takeaways

1. The best developmental experience for learning leadership is practice.

2. Developing the ability to learn effectively is essential in leadership. Women should not be intimidated in the face of skill deficiencies. Having the confidence in one's own abilities to learn and develop throughout one's life is imperative.

3. Increasing observation and reflection skills throughout one's life will bring continuous and lifelong growth.

4. Effective leaders are those who thrive on challenges, take pleasure in complexity, and enjoy solving problems.

5. Learning to become participant-observers can be a powerful tool in understanding one's own behavior in relation to other individuals and situations.

6. Effective networking is foundational for successful long-term leadership. Networks are important means for further development, opportunities, collaborations, creativity, assistance, and support.

7. Women-only leadership programs can be an effective and helpful way to develop academic leadership knowledge and competencies.

8. Any academic discipline can be helpful in many dimensions of the development of leadership.

9. Future leaders should find pleasure in their own development as well as that of others.

8

Other Life Roles

A good leader inspires others with confidence in him; a great leader inspires them with confidence in themselves.

Leaders are like eagles. They don't flock, you find them one at a time.

Professional employment and experiences are not the only things that provide women with opportunities for leadership development and growth. All aspects of women's lives must be explored to understand how they have prepared themselves to become effective high-profile leaders. Leadership skills can be developed throughout an individual's life in a variety of arenas (Galambos & Hughes, 2000). Personal roles such as those of spouse, daughter, friend, parent, sister, and volunteer provide opportunities to learn skills, values, and abilities that are useful at work. In fact, researchers (Ruderman, Ohlott, Panzer, & King, 2002) report that multiple roles are related to enhanced leadership skills. Although studies continue to report that women who choose to work outside the home experience more role conflict and possibly stress (Carlson, Kacmar, & Williams, 2000), the positive impacts of multiple roles on women are also being explored (Greenhaus & Powell, 2006).

Research findings (Ruderman et al., 2002) have provided at least partial support that women leaders committed to multiple roles seem to be very satisfied with their lives, have a strong sense of self-worth, and accept and acknowledge multiple aspects of self— meaning they have some understanding of themselves and their own complexity. These women believe they can be successful, contribute, and add value to the world in every venue they choose.

Interest in the interplay between different life roles has grown substantially in recent years. Although some employers continue to look at the multidimensional aspects of women's lives particularly in their early professional years as a disadvantage for today's workplace (for example, in higher education as faculty members and early administrators), it is clear that this is not always the case. In fact, the phenomenon of women's multifaceted lives is now viewed as advantageous both for leaders and organizations (Astin & Leland, 1991). Ruderman and colleagues (2002) confirmed my earlier findings (see Chapters Three and Four) that women learned leadership through personal experience, including participation in community, religious, and volunteer organizations. Taylor and Conradie (1997) wrote that "Women's *life* experiences were used as a springboard for development education and women's empowerment. The approach which underpins development education is that people are in a process of lifelong learning" (p. 53). As one participant in their research study said, "We have been taught by life itself" (Taylor & Conradie, 1997, p. 47). And, as Fels (2004) so eloquently stated, "Life must be a creation of sorts and also an assertion of values, priorities, and identity" (p. 53).

Caffarella and Barnett (1997) corroborate my earlier findings that it is critical for rising women leaders to explore the concept of identity, discover the importance of self-awareness, find the authority of self, and develop their own voice. These characteristics allow women to not only perform effectively but also to be heard as distinct from other leaders. This chapter provides insight into how ten women university presidents were able to strengthen these and other characteristics from the non-employment-related-aspects of their lives. These include their experiences and insights related to marriage, family, friends, motherhood, personal difficulties, and community involvement.

Committed Relationships, Family, and Friends

Seven of the presidents were married between nineteen and twenty-two years of age, two after twenty-five, and one has a long-term partner. Five women have remained in their first marriages throughout the years; four others are in committed relationships, with two having been married twice and one four times. Three of the four divorcees said that separations were related to their career choices and advancement ambitions. Currently, eight say they are in happy, committed relationships.

Most of the presidents spoke in detail about their marriages, relationships, and lives in general. The five who have remained in their first marriages seem to be, to this day, wonderful friends and companions with their husbands. Many women noted that it takes a very special man to be married to a woman with such ambition and drive for accomplishment and success. One president who has remained married to her first husband described her situation:

> My husband was so supportive. We talked about the twenty year plan. The first twenty years I followed him, and the second twenty years he followed me. He was always very supportive of my desires, ambitions, and needs, and he has been throughout our married life. He was great with the kids. He coached baseball and supported them in all of their activities. He was very, very encouraging to me. He enjoyed my accomplishments, and he felt satisfaction and joy at my successes. He has truly been my friend.

One president noted that her first and only husband is "tolerant and supportive." She spoke of his great capacity for listening to her throughout the years. She said:

> He knew that I needed to do certain things, and he supported me as much as he could. When I struggled, he just listened and waited, and eventually I would work through issues and make the decisions I needed to so that I could move forward.

Another said she has a husband who lets her talk incessantly at nights. A few presidents, who were once professors, married men who were also academics. In one case, the president and her husband were in the same field and worked together for many years. She explained:

> My husband was very supportive. When our first child was born, we complemented each other in terms of the skills that we brought to our family and our various projects at work. It was a good working relationship and was extremely collaborative. He supported me in my goals, and I supported him in his. Life was very complex and challenging with young children, but it was wonderful. I was a wife, mother, and professor; my husband understood who I was.

One president, married to the same man for over forty years, spoke of dating someone else before her marriage and what she figured out about herself.

> My high school boyfriend and I had wisely gone to different colleges on purpose, but he came back into my life at the end of my senior year. I realized that he still wanted to go back to our hometown when he finished medical school. He thought that we'd live in a house on

> a hill and have a station wagon full of kids. By the end
> of my undergraduate degree, I figured out that I didn't
> want to do that, because I didn't think that was going
> to be enough for me. So, I spent most of my senior year
> making sure I didn't get married, and I didn't.

By this time in her life she had learned more about herself and knew that, in addition to raising children, she would need to have flexibility in her life to pursue her desires and ambitions. Although it wasn't the norm at that time, she understood that she needed more.

Other researchers (Astin & Leland, 1991; Pankake et al., 2000a) who study women leaders confirmed that support, guidance, and encouragement from spouse or partner also helped immensely in their development. Spouses were described as helping the women do whatever was necessary to help them succeed. These men listened, brainstormed when asked, and took over the full family responsibilities when the women traveled or were particularly busy at work (Astin & Leland, 1991). The spouses were typically strong and confident individuals who had the unique attributes needed to be successful in these relationships. Researchers (Goldwasser, 1988, cited in Wells, 1998) report that husbands also helped wives increase their feelings of competency. Woo (1985) stated that a large majority of the women in her study said that "their husbands' support had been a crucial factor in their careers" (p. 287). Others (Clark et al., 1999) reported that the women leaders who are most successful in balancing professional and personal lives usually had supportive spouses.

Several reasons for divorces were similar among the five presidents, yet others were unique. Women who were married to men who either had insecurities or were unwilling to support a highly ambitious woman divorced in at least three of their first marriages and three later marriages. All of the women who divorced said they learned a great deal about themselves through these experiences. Three presidents spoke of early divorces (before children) because of lack of support or the recognition of the wide gap in life goals and desires. One president explained:

> It was clear after a few years that my husband wanted a different life than I did. He wanted me to quit work and join groups and clubs in the community. I wasn't crazy about how he saw the rest of our lives. I packed the car and left. I knew I wanted an advanced degree and had been accepted to a program I knew I would love. I didn't intend it to be a divorce, but it was. Maybe subconsciously I knew this because I did pack and ship out my china!

Two presidents spoke of husbands not being supportive of their continued desires for advanced education, and two also mentioned first husbands not being supportive of successes. One stated, "I didn't realize it would be such a big deal to him that I could be more successful than him." One divorced president spoke of what she and her husband figured out about themselves:

> My second husband and I were great friends. After our divorce we remained friends, so we talked occasionally and had very civil kinds of interaction. One day he said, "I thought I could be married to the president of the United States if it was a woman, but I've learned I can't do that." I think marriage is hard for all of us. It is challenging wanting to balance and have both a career and family. I wasn't successful at doing that, and I have now realized that is part of the price I have paid for my success.

Another president spoke of being married to a wonderful, kind man who, unfortunately, was very closed and nontalkative. They had a formal, comfortable relationship, but it was more of a business relationship than a marriage. She said, "We were in the business of raising children." They divorced after the kids were older, and she spoke of the joy and peace she now has with a man who is truly her friend. "He is just great. I was in administration when we married, and he has always been absolutely supportive and has done anything he could to help me succeed."

Friendship and support were the foundational elements of good marriages for these women. The presidents said that they have learned a substantial amount from committed relationships in general, good and bad. These relationships provided many opportunities for them to practice skills such as compromise, negotiation, support, encouragement, development of others, interpersonal communication, and so forth.

Personal friends and extended family were also very important support systems for these women. They continued to be influenced and taught by parents, in-laws, grandparents, siblings, friends, church members, neighbors, and colleagues from community work. One said, "Family members encouraged me to apply for an associate dean position even though I didn't think I was ready. My sibling said, 'If not now, when?' She followed his advice. Some of their childhood, adolescent, and college friends (men and women) continued to be good influences for development later in life. One spoke of a group of girlfriends from high school and college, as she said, "My girlfriends were kind of my role models. They have all been very successful, and I've been able to watch and learn." Another stated, "I have stayed in touch with good friends for years. They still provide me with support and encouragement."

The ten presidents had people in their lives who would ground them and provide candid, open, trustworthy feedback. As Wells (1998) also found in her research with women entrepreneurs, the presidents in my study felt that "images of themselves were formed as they were rewarded and reinforced by those closest to them in their lives" (p. 123). Support from family was listed in one study as particularly vital to the women's leadership development (Pankake et al., 2000a). Cubillo and Brown (2003) confirmed my earlier writings (see Chapters Two, Three, and Four) that family support was an important, positive influence for women in their pursuit of education and career progression. Other researchers (Goldwasser, 1988; Hartman, 1999) also verify my earlier findings that support from families and friends enhances women's ability to function more effectively as leaders, and that female competency in general is strengthened through supportive relationships with parents and spouses.

Motherhood

Nine of the ten presidents have children. One president has four children, one has three, four presidents have two children each, two have one child, and one has a stepchild. Most of these presidents reminisced throughout the interviews about their families and children. Many are currently proud grandmothers and love that role. Their children were, and continue to be, central in their lives, even with the presidents' busy and pressing schedules. The women's families have brought much joy to their lives throughout the years.

The women learned a great deal from the experiences and responsibilities that came with parenthood. Five of the eight women chose to work part-time while they were bearing and raising young children. All had opportunities to be involved in part-time professional employment during these years, which was somewhat unusual for that period. This was important because they were able to continue their careers while focusing significant time and energy on raising children. These women worked part-time until their children were in school full-time. One woman hadn't considered even working part-time until certain things came together in her life.

> It seems like I've always lived along the fault line of social change. When my first child was a year old I was asked to teach college part-time. I told them, "Women with

children just don't teach!" Later that week my next door neighbor had come over for coffee, and we talked about the offer. She said, "Oh, couldn't I just take care of him? You could go two mornings a week, and I'll come over and watch him." She wanted a huge family and only had one child. Our son ended up having a surrogate mother. It was a good situation for both her and me.

Another president had a mother who lived close and helped while she worked part-time and then later full-time. She said, "My mother clearly helped make it possible for me to imagine a professional life without compromising my commitment to my family." A different woman started teaching part-time after her third child was born and then full-time after all of her kids were in school. One mother of three stopped working full-time after her first child was born and then worked two days a week while the children were small. She simply said, "I liked working. This was a way I could be a mother and work, both of which I loved." These women enjoyed being with their kids at home during those years, although it was not without its own set of challenges.

Many of the women had pregnancies and children during their schooling. Two had pregnancies during their undergraduate degrees, and a total of seven women had children before completing their doctorate work. Particularly during their advanced degrees, some presidents found that faculty and colleagues temporarily wondered about their ability to juggle both children and school. One president stated, "I think my Ph.D. advisor wondered if his investment was down the drain when he saw that I was pregnant again." This situation made her even more determined to do well. One president was a teacher's assistant while in her Ph.D. program. She said, "I finished my finals and went into labor with my second child with bluebooks under my arm for the test I was supposed to be grading." These were tough women! A number of presidents spoke about the challenge of finishing advanced schooling with the dynamics present in having children at home. One of the major issues was the presidents' desire to do things very well. They hated to do less than excellent work in every way. One explained:

> I had to take some classes for my doctorate degree after my children had been born. I remember my husband saying, "I'll give you 100 dollars for every B you make." I told him I didn't know how to get Bs, and he said, "I know, that's why I'm trying to bribe you!" I had to work very hard for As sometimes, but I didn't know how to *not* do all that I could do. I wasn't comfortable with less.

Three presidents chose to continue working full-time with young children during those years. One president described her situation as follows:

> When my first child was born, we had just received a very large research grant. I had always been productive, so I thought it would be easy to keep working on the grant. Because my time was paid for on the grant, I had no teaching responsibilities. However, my new daughter did not cooperate, and it was challenging to get the work done. She never slept! I was trying to be home with her full-time as well as work, and after three long months I knew it wasn't going to work. I hired a wonderful caregiver. Probably half of our disposable income went to her. We wanted a stable situation with little turnover, so we paid well. She was wonderful. I don't think I struggled with that decision. I struggled more with the fact that I couldn't get my work done. I had two more children in the next three to four years and had the same caregiver. I also earned tenure during these years.

A second woman spoke of the wonderful assistance her mother provided, which made it possible for her to continue her career full-time. She said:

> Our child was born about one year after we were married. My parents had moved out to be with us. My father died, and my mother chose to stay close to us. My mother really needed our son, so she and he became as close as they could be. This gave me freedom that I would not have had without my mother, so I continued to work full-time. I worked the day he was born and went back a week later (I know that was bad!). My mother wanted nothing more than to take care of my son. We bought her a house a block from ours, and they became best friends. He would live at her home some days of the week. They loved it, and I didn't feel guilty because he was with her. Without a doubt, my son was truly the most important thing I've done in my life.

A third president said that she was at peace with her decision to work full-time, and she tried to involve her children in her work whenever possible. All three of these presidents mentioned that a good caregiver was the key to feeling peace. One said that she actually had a caregiver until all her children went to college. When speaking of working part-time or full-time while their children were young, the first topic the presidents spoke about was their child care. Having peace regarding the care of their children was the first priority. Without that confidence, many of the women would have chosen not to work. This is also the case for many women in the workplace today. Those who have support to help them with child care (families, spouses, money, and so forth) are often those who take advantage of employment opportunities, whereas other very talented women may not have that choice.

The presidents spoke of challenging family experiences that taught them a lot. One women and her husband took their very young children to Europe on sabbatical for a year. Although it was challenging, they loved it. It was complex but a wonderful learning experience. Two presidents took new positions later in their careers and had to start their new jobs without their families. It was very difficult for them to be without their spouses and children, but they reflected on how much they learned about themselves (strength, endurance, competence, for instance) during those times. Three of the women spoke in detail about feeling judged by neighbors, church members, or extended family members for making the choices they did about school and work. The women struggled with these issues for many years. Two spoke of serious difficulties with rebellious children; difficult teenagers provided heartbreaking experiences for some mothers. One of these women spoke of finding calmness in the midst of judgments and concern regarding a child. She said:

> I learned to be okay with a lot of things in my life that I thought I never would have been okay with. I've had to come to grips with a lot of issues and find peace that I am doing the best I can even though I have felt terribly judged.

The presidents also spoke of work-family conflict that often existed throughout the years. One said, "When I began in leadership in higher education I felt an intense conflict between my family, traditions, and work. It wasn't a comfortable fit for many years." One president had a daughter who had a serious disability, which altered some of her career plans. She explained:

> This is really why I stayed in a university setting. It gave me much more flexibility than any other kind of role or occupation. I chose not to do anything full-time until after both kids were in school and could read. This was important to me.

Several presidents spoke of dealing with guilt. They often felt guilt when they had to miss a child's game or event because of an important meeting. Conversely, they also felt guilt when they missed a work meeting to attend a child's game or event. There was guilt either way! One said, "Learning to deal with guilt is help-ful now as I can't do everything as a president. I have to pick and choose, and sometimes I feel a little guilty for not being at certain events because I must be at others." Even with the ongoing guilt, some women felt they needed the complexity and challenge in-herent in juggling their various roles and responsibilities. For these women it seemed to provide them with positive development and growth. Some researchers (Hammond & Fong, 1988) have found that women who occupy multiple roles have the highest level of physical well-being and lower levels of depression. Crosby (1991) argued that "women who combine significant life roles are better off emotionally than are women with fewer roles" (p. 15). In fact, there appears to be some evidence that juggling actually enhances physical as well as psychological health (Hill & Ragland, 1995).

I asked the presidents about their work-life strategies, particu-larly when they had children living at home. Interestingly, only a few described an integrative approach between their work and family lives; most spoke of using the compartmentalization work-life strategy. Other studies (Caffarella, 1992; Clark et al., 1999; Enkelis, Olsen, Lewenstein, & Applegate, 1995; Shakeshaft, 1989) have made different conclusions, as they reported "women most often do not separate the private or personal aspects of their lives from their professional work" (Clark et al., 1999, p. 67). But it is clear that the participants in this study were able to leave their work at work, and when they came home they were able to focus entirely on the family. One said, "I'm good at compartmentalizing, but sometimes the stacks of compartments get pretty high." This compartmentalization was very important, particularly for some of the presidents. One recalled:

> I really think this was always very important when I had children at home. I really kept those worlds separate in that sense. My children came first, and the college knew

that. I did everything I could to be at everything the kids
did. They needed me to do that because, although their
father loved them, he just wasn't available much.

The compartmentalizing presidents said that it was important for
them to be able to walk in the front door and leave all of their
work responsibilities behind. They wanted to be mom and wife
when they were at home. It is possible that compartmentalization
may have been a tactic for some women to have a more integrated, satisfying balance between their professional and personal
lives. The bottom line is that these women had support that allowed them to focus on things that they enjoyed. Clearly this
is not always the case for women who have emerging leadership
potential.

The presidents also spoke of the enjoyable things they did with
their children, partners, siblings, and extended families—even now.
They spoke of family trips, sports, four-wheeling, hiking, backpack-
ing, camping, games, garage sales, skiing, and other types of family
activities. These women love being mothers. One president stated,
"I can't say that I loved everything about being a parent, but certainly I can say that there were amazing things at every stage. I
enjoyed my children and would never trade being a mother for
anything in this world."

I asked each woman to describe what leadership competencies
motherhood has helped her learn and develop. The nine presidents
who have children or stepchildren, all felt strongly that motherhood
is a powerful preparatory role for the development of presidential
leadership skills and abilities. Table 8.1 outlines the fifty-two competencies the women mentioned. Notice that every one of these
is included in the leadership literature as critical competencies for
leaders.

The development of the abilities to both multitask and prioritize
was the most often cited competency attributed to motherhood by
the presidents. Every woman with children said that motherhood

Table 8.1. Competencies Developed Through Motherhood

Motherhood helped me learn to . . .

Accept that everything can't be perfect	Handle judgments
Accept what I can do	Learn communication skills
Accept what people can do	Learn conflict management skills
Appreciate different learning styles	Learn from difficulties
Appreciate unique personalities	Learn patience
Be self-disciplined	Learn to think during chaos
Build and function in teams	Manage others' poor behavior
Compartmentalize work and family	Manage stress
Comprehend human and organizational systems	Manage time
Cope with everything	Multitask
Cope with others' inaccurate perceptions	Negotiate
Deal with bad attitudes	Organize complex events
Deal with guilt	Organize life
Deal with harshness and meanness	Outlast persistent people
Deepen relationships in difficult times	Outlast stubborn individuals
Empathize with parents	Pay attention to how I affect situations
Endure through difficulties	Pay attention to how others affect situations
Facilitate meaningful conversations	Pick up the pieces and start over
Figure out I can't always take myself seriously	Reach the best match given the circumstances
Figure out one has little control over life	Recognize that things can't always be aligned
Get people to open up and share concerns	Reconcile conflict
Get up when I fall down	See the good during difficult times
Handle conflict and teach others the same	Set priorities and goals

The following entries appear in the right column only:

- Accept that everything can't be perfect → Handle judgments
- Learn communication skills
- Learn conflict management skills
- Learn from difficulties
- Learn patience
- Learn to think during chaos
- Manage others' poor behavior
- Manage stress
- Manage time
- Multitask
- Negotiate
- Organize complex events
- Organize life
- Outlast persistent people
- Outlast stubborn individuals
- Pay attention to how I affect situations
- Pay attention to how others affect situations
- Pick up the pieces and start over
- Reach the best match given the circumstances
- Recognize that things can't always be aligned
- Reconcile conflict
- See the good during difficult times
- Set priorities and goals
- Support others in their interests
- Take time to breathe and relax
- Teach people to understand others
- Understand others' perspectives
- Understand parental concerns
- Understand youth and college students

naturally and inherently taught them these abilities. One president explained:

> Motherhood taught me that I could not be linear and do one thing at a time. It became very comfortable to get multiple things accomplished often in a nonsequenced way. When I was confronted with that in the workplace, it was just business as usual. I see women with children having far less trouble with that than others. I think women are far less linear thinkers because they've never had the luxury of being able to think through one issue at a time. There are always split screens that have to be dealt with, and my ability to do this well came first from motherhood.

Another president stated:

> I had to learn multitasking very early, and motherhood helped me do that. I can be talking to someone and also thinking about the next chore over here. I can do something while talking to somebody else about making sure something else is being done. Sometimes people find that a little unnerving. It is just that I know what you are going to say, and I am past that already.

A third president described her experiences as follows:

> I was a single mother and had to travel a long distance for work and daycare. I had to figure out each day how to get everything done. Between groceries, cooking, cleaning, driving, working, daycare, children's sports, and other activities and responsibilities, I learned to multitask effectively. I must say that the complexity of a university presidency is almost (not quite) as complex as raising my teenagers and handling divorce.

A fourth woman spoke about doing her doctorate work with multiple children at home. She didn't have the luxury of hiring help, so she just learned to do many things at the same time and deal with noise and chaos. She had to learn these skills so that she could continue her educational goals. Past research (Collins & Killough, 1992) also reports that because women must balance work and family demands, they develop skills to be able to handle competing tasks, deal effectively with interruptions, and be accessible while making efficient use of their time.

Most of the presidents also mentioned that motherhood helped them learn to deal with conflict more effectively. One president explained:

> Reconciling conflict is a very important part of being an effective leader, whether it is conflict in schedules that you have to align or whether it is a conflict on issues or differences of viewpoints. Two obstreperous young boys who didn't always have the patience with others helped me to learn about dealing with conflict. My boys taught me that it was okay to have a difference of opinion, but that you need to convey that in a way that was both loving and respectful.

Another spoke of learning to resolve conflict more effectively through the necessity of needing to teach the skills to her children.

> As a parent I had to work with young children as well as teenagers to help them overcome their rivalries with one another. I had to talk to them about how to discipline themselves in many ways. These conversations always provided an opportunity for me to think about my own actions in this area.

The presidents also spoke about learning organizational and time management skills from motherhood. One woman said that she learned coping, self-discipline, planning, and organizational skills through being a mother, but she had to give up a lot of sleep so she would have time to do it all. Three presidents talked about perfecting organizational skills through planning long family vacations and camping trips with their spouses and multiple children.

Most women mentioned the word "patience" when speaking of things they learned from being a mother. As one explained, "I learned a lot more patience. I learned that I couldn't lose my temper." She said that her sons' feelings would be hurt when she lost her temper, and then she would feel bad. When this happened she would remember that she shouldn't treat others this way because it would upset them in the same way. Other women also said that they learned to be careful about what they said because their kids would sometimes be negatively affected by harsh and blunt words. A president shared this experience:

> Never assume that you are the only one who has had a bad day. I think that is one thing that I have learned from my kids. Sometimes I would come home and get a little cross with my son never realizing that he may have had a bad day too. He would let me know. Now every time I have a bad day I remember this. I really hurt his feelings badly once, and that memory stays with me.

Although patience was mentioned by nearly all of the presidents, a few smiled and said they didn't know how much they had actually learned and changed. For example, one president bluntly stated:

> I would like to say I learned patience, but I don't think I developed it. I honestly don't. I would go back and do it differently if I could. I wasn't patient then, and I'm not patient now. I guess I didn't learn anything on that score.

One president described her experience with a teenage stepchild. She spoke of the years of patience and tolerance it took to get to the place they are today, communicating civilly. She spoke of the years it takes to develop trust with certain individuals in blended families and workplaces alike. This president actually felt that the leadership skills she had already obtained by that point in her life were very useful in this situation.

> Thank God I had some leadership skills and interpersonal skills before we started this relationship. I practiced a whole lot of skills with this teenager. It wasn't as much about conflict management, as it was about communication and attitude. It took me several years of deliberate communication strategy to get to where we are. Her behavior was totally foreign to me, so I learned from that.

The presidents also mentioned a number of other competencies they learned. One spoke specifically of systems. She learned to pay attention to how her children were affecting others, which caused her to reflect more on how her actions affected her children, spouse, and colleagues at work. Several presidents spoke of learning to be okay with less than perfection. One said, "I figured out that I couldn't align every part of my life and that I needed to make the best decisions given the circumstances." A few spoke of how much they learned from the persistence and stubbornness of their kids. One president said:

> My children were terribly persistent and stubborn, and I learned that I could outlast them from the first temper tantrum to the last teenage emergency. No matter how persistent they were, no matter how hard they pushed back, I learned I could just plain outlast them. They sometimes said, "I hate you," and I would say "That is all well and good, but I'm still here and I love you." This is what we need to do in life. When things don't go well, we need to pick up the pieces and move on.

Another president also spoke of moving forward during difficulties and how she taught that to her children. She said:

> We stumbled over a few stones in the road together as a family and just rewrote our own style. When we fell down, we just got back up and brushed ourselves off. In fact, through the years we completely restructured how we interacted as a family. This has enriched and deepened my leadership ability.

When raising children, mothers learned to blend toughness, patience, compassion, negotiation, and the ability to cultivate flexibility with support. Helgesen (1995) added that managing households, raising children, and juggling careers give women a capacity for prioritization in a leadership role that others do not possess. All of these traits helped them become excellent situational leaders, which is particularly useful in today's workplaces. However, it is important for me to acknowledge that women without children also become competent leaders. Motherhood is clearly one of many ways (as my research has evidenced) for females to learn leadership competencies. In fact, anytime a woman is in a committed relationship to another individual (spouse, partner, child, sibling, parent, or friend), they can learn and develop a host of skills useful for successful leadership in various settings.

Caffarella and Olson's (1993) work substantiates my research; they explained that a "woman's web of relationships (e.g., primary family, husband/children, and friends) is central to her identity formulation" (p. 134). They found that for most women, having a career was a secondary concern and that they needed to integrate components of care and relatedness into all of the components of their lives. They believe that, although it was important for women to become their own separate individuals as part of formulating their own identity, for development to actually occur it was very important for them to maintain a sense of connectedness and affiliation with others, particularly their immediate families.

Women's development of "self" involved "integrating a capacity to respond to the needs of others with an ability to meet one's needs" (Caffarella & Olsen, 1993, p. 134). The women in my study believed that their relationships were central in the formation of their own identities and that their "self" included a portion of all the roles they occupied. These women had skills in understanding themselves, but the complexity inherent in giving birth and raising children helped them search deeper to understand themselves in these new roles.

Personal Struggles

Personal health issues seemed to teach these presidents a substantial amount about themselves and life in general. As one president noted, "Having a serious illness was a reflective time for me." Another, who had "burned the candle at both ends and became very ill," said:

> I was diagnosed with ulcerative colitis and was out of commission for a couple of months. It was a wake-up call for me. I have had some terribly difficult moments in my life that have been among the most important growth experiences that I have had. I had to continue to test the sturdiness of my constitution and figure out how resourceful I could be.

A third spoke of getting very ill at the same time that her kids had the chicken pox and her family was having some other difficulties. "Everything went wrong that could go wrong." The doctors could not determine what was amiss. They just attributed it to stress and gave her tranquilizers. She was having trouble functioning at a basic level, let alone accomplishing anything else. She actually had a roaring kidney infection and ended up in the hospital. She had to call her mother to help, which she hadn't even done when she had her babies. She learned that there were times that she needed help from others. She also learned that she needed to be assertive when she knew things were not right. A few presidents spoke of trying to do too much, for a time. One said, "I had to sort of pour myself into bed many times as it was approaching midnight. I had to do some serious reflection about how long I could do that and how it was affecting us."

In a few cases, the women had to commute or move to different cities or states before their families. One described her experience with a temporary position in another city. She lived in an apartment for much of the week and then traveled home on the weekend. She said, "I learned how to adapt and take care of myself. I really hadn't lived on my own before like this."

Several women spoke about the lessons they learned from difficult marriages. They learned that things don't always work out as planned, no matter how much work and effort is put into the situation. As one woman stated, "My self-confidence as a woman was low because of the marital situation." Another explained, "I thought I would get married and stay married the rest of my life. I thought I could resolve issues with anyone. I found that there are some things that just can't be fixed." She learned that there are times that an individual just needs to make a decision and then move on. Another woman said that certain situations can "take everything out of an individual." She said:

> I learned that you have to concentrate on what you can do, not on what you can't. A valuable lesson as a chancellor alas. I learned that you should concentrate on helping people to the extent that you can, and then you just need to go home and sleep. Losing sleep at night because of things you can't control doesn't help anyone!

Traumatic events continued to give them opportunities for reflection and growth as well as a time to make choices on what was most important. A few described "life changing nights." The deaths of siblings and parents were particularly painful and reflective times. Pankake and colleagues (2000a) found in their research with women superintendents that the loss of loved ones was one of three major categories related to turning points in their lives.

Even during adulthood, the presidents had deep connections with their parents. Although none professed to have perfect parents, the depth of respect and commitment the presidents had for their parents was admirable. Two quit work for a time to care for a parent. A number of the women had parents live close to or with them during times of illness. They felt a close connection and responsibility for their parents as they aged. On a positive note, even while healthy, parents stayed very involved in their daughters' lives in various ways. The parents of four presidents were caregivers, at least for a time, for their grandchildren. The presidents spoke fondly of particular parents who provided selfless service, support, and encouragement. This support was central in helping some of these women deal with personal issues and struggles.

Some experts (e.g., Sullivan, 2003) believe that leadership is a learned capacity. Because women's lives are often nonlinear, contextual, and interwoven with personal concerns (Cheng, 1988), these experiences play a particularly powerful role in "shaping core values that motivate people to act" (Astin & Leland, 1991, p. 66). In fact, the most impressive individuals in the world have typically gone through difficulties, challenges, and trials. Experts (e.g., Bennis, 1989; Pankake et al., 2000a) confirm my previously stated findings that learning from difficulties and challenges is a sign of a good leader. In fact, we have found that successful leaders learn more lessons from personal experiences (in general) than do moderately successful or unsuccessful leaders. Successful leaders also seem to have a more optimistic view of dealing with their hardships. These ten presidents learned as youth to discover insights from their difficulties. They have continued to use this skill throughout their lives. They currently believe that developing the ability to discover insights through hardships is important to more effective and efficient growth and development.

Community Involvement

The presidents have all been involved in various community service positions and activities at least occasionally throughout their careers. When asked about specific involvement, the presidents listed the following:

- Brownies and Girl Scouts leader

- Chamber of Commerce member or leader

- Children's educational program director

- Church activity coordinator or teacher

- Civic organization member or leader

- Community group member or leader

- Community partnership coordinator

- Corporate board member

- County school board association chair or member

- Economic council member

- Professional nonprofit organization member

- School board member

- School district search committee chair

- School classroom volunteer

- United Way, chairman of the board

Although they didn't provide specific names of all organizations and service assignments, most presidents did give their perspective of the value of such involvement and work. One president explained:

> My voluntary work was very important for my development, as every experience is helpful. I had never had a supervisory role, so leadership in these organizations was important for me. I learned to organize and motivate people in a different way. As you know, it is quite different to do these things with a volunteer organization.

Another president made a similar statement:

> When you lead a community board it is different than working in higher education. The members are not going to do something just because you say they should. You have to figure out how to get them on board and supportive. My community involvement has been incredibly important in my development.

Another president spoke about the value of obtaining a different perspective from community involvement experiences:

> I think community activities are very helpful for one's development. When I'm involved in external activities, I get a very different sense of how people think outside of academia. Like it or not, we are very different. We are academics, and that's a mind-set I know very well. Yet that's not the way the rest of the world thinks. It has been important for me to get out into the community and interact with these other leaders and see the passion they have for advancing the society as a whole. I have learned a lot from them about my own community. It reminds me that it's about people.

The most important concept that one president learned from serving on a school board pertained to politics. She said, "It gave me an abiding respect, which I think has served me well over the years." The presidents used the following words to describe the types of competencies that community involvement has helped them develop:

- Community insights and perspectives

- Community systems

- Coordination

- Empathy

- Facilitation skills

- Legislative experience

- Listening

- Management skills

- Motivating others

- Networking

- Organization

- Political skills

- Stakeholder insights

- Taking responsibility

- Teaching

- Teamwork

Other developmental insights came in different ways. One woman was heavily involved in a professional nonprofit organization and began working with the board of regents and legislature (unpaid) when she was teaching part-time and raising children. Another provided insight regarding the reasons she chose to become heavily involved in community work during part of her career. She said:

> I became United Way chairman of the board when I didn't have challenges at work. I learned a lot of things, made a lot of connections, and did things that added richness to my life. It was very fulfilling. Community leadership helped because I was in an unfulfilling organizational setting during that time and knew I wasn't going to advance any more. By working with individuals who had very different backgrounds than mine, not just persons of color but people who were in different industries and of various ages, I learned to appreciate what each brought to the process and then how to build consensus with such different perspectives. I chaired all the planning and allocation and loved it. It was a challenge.

Finally, a president summed up the feelings of a number of the presidents:

> Once I found places that I could get involved, make things happen, and make a difference, I got really connected and engaged in the community. I learned all kinds of things from these experiences that I use daily in my current position.

Community involvement gave the presidents opportunities for social interactions and practical management and leadership experience. One research team (Ayman, Adams, Fisher, & Hartman, 2003) explained that leadership development must include chances for social interactions. Others (Galambos & Hughes, 2000; Rayburn et al., 2001; Ruderman et al., 2002) have found that community settings provide opportunities for growth and refinement in skills that can transfer directly to paid workplace environments. Community involvement provided some of these women the chance to gain experience with leadership, learn how to achieve goals through others, become skillful at developing and implementing organizational systems, and develop comfort in authority roles (Ruderman et al., 2002). The women in the research study of Shaw-Hardy (1998) said that volunteer work was in fact a primary key to obtaining and succeeding in later paid occupations.

Final Thoughts

Spouses, partners, families, friends, motherhood, personal difficulties, and community involvement were all important components of successful leadership development in the ten women university presidents' lives. The support, encouragement, and experience these women obtained were helpful to each president in her personal developmental journey toward successful leadership. These experiences provided the assistance needed for the presidents to claim their own values and develop an authentic voice (Lyman, 1995). They helped these women learn to live more effectively with ambiguity, share control, and to listen, guide, and follow others (Dunlap & Schmuck, 1995). According to Caffarella and Barnett (1997), "a woman's development is characterized by multiple role patterns, role discontinuities, and a need to maintain a sense of self" (p. 4). Throughout a woman's life, the mingling of the importance of relationships with the need for self and identity is a critical issue. As women change their roles, move from job to job, and juggle many life roles, issues of identity are continually changed. With the skills the university presidents had developed during childhood, adolescence, and early adulthood, they were able to continue discovering and understanding who they were (Caffarella & Barnett, 1997), and they ultimately developed the skills to become who they wanted to become.

Takeaways

1. The complexity of committed relationships provides opportunities and experiences for learning leadership. These leaders learned through managing difficult relationships, and, after all, being a leader is all about relationships.

2. It takes a unique and unusually supportive partner to be married to a woman with ambition and drive for leadership at the top administrative levels.

3. Women leaders have learned to do what they had to do to become what they have become.

4. The support of others is a critical factor in influencing whether a mother can pursue leadership ambitions.

5. Women can learn leadership from nearly every element and experience related to motherhood if they are reflective.

6. Successful leaders develop the ability to learn from their mistakes, failures, and difficulties. They have the strength to be persistent through these experiences and continue to decide what matters, what they want to learn, and what changes they would incorporate into their future behaviors.

7. Working women who are mothers (and maybe those in other interpersonal roles) sometimes have to get used to living with some guilt.

8. Community involvement can provide powerful opportunities for women to develop and strengthen competencies needed for successful leadership in higher education and other settings.

Part III

Leadership

9

Leadership Motivation, Styles, and Philosophies

Leadership is not magnetic personality—that can just as well be a glib tongue. It is not "making friends and influencing people"—that is flattery. Leadership is lifting a person's vision to higher sights, the raising of a person's performance to a higher standard, the building of a personality beyond its normal limitations.

Peter F. Drucker

Leadership motivation, style, and philosophy are sometimes viewed as generic and vague terms. Much of the extensive work in this area before 1990 was summarized in the seminal *Bass & Stogdill's Handbook of Leadership: Theory, Research, and Managerial Applications* (Bass, 1990), and now there are a multitude of books published on this topic. In addition, thousands of academic, scholarly, and practitioner-oriented articles have appeared in publications throughout the past three or four decades, and the number continues to rise each year. As most academicians and practitioners will attest, there are a variety of differences between higher educational and corporate environments and perspectives. Although much is published based on corporate leadership, current publications share little about the leadership motivations, styles, and philosophies of actual university presidents, particularly women. In fact, scholarly research on this specific topic for women in higher education has not yet been published—until now.

Motivation for Leadership

I have always been interested in why people make certain choices in their lives. The choice to lead, even during childhood and youth (directly or from behind the scenes), is of particular interest to me. I asked the women university presidents various times throughout the interviews why they accepted or sought out informal and formal leadership roles. I analyzed each woman's responses to discover the themes and then compared the multiple responses among all ten participants. The top nine motivations for leading became quite clear:

1. *To accomplish and achieve.* All ten presidents had strong accomplishment and achievement needs even during childhood and youth. One woman said, "I love to start new things. I like to make things happen." Another said, "I have felt driven to accomplish a lot throughout my life." A third president explained:

> I had strong accomplishment needs as a youth and now throughout my life. I have constantly felt the need to do my best, learn all that I can learn, and achieve all that I can achieve.

2. *To make a difference, contribution, or impact.* Their desire to do things that mattered was also easily recognizable when analyzing the data. One president stated, "I wanted to make a difference." Another said:

> I felt like I was making a contribution, making a difference, making some impact, and that was very important to me.

A third explained:

> I have always wanted desperately to make a difference.
> I believe we're put on this earth for some reason, and I
> believe that very strongly. We must not squander that.
> There are so many people who can't speak for them-
> selves, and they must have a voice. When we can be
> that voice then our lives are really worth living.

3. *To be involved in meaningful and important work.* These women
accepted or often sought out opportunities to be involved in things
they believed were meaningful. In the previous quotation, under
motivation #2, which is related to this one, the president who made
the comment believed that being a "voice for others" is meaningful
work for her. While rising through the ranks, other women spoke
of the drive they felt to be involved in strategic areas in the school,
college, and university. They seemed to be systems thinkers. They
enjoyed the "big picture," the "breadth," and participating in the
"integration" of all of the pieces into a large, effective "system."
One president explained:

> Although I loved the job I was in and did well at it,
> I often found myself looking and analyzing how things
> could be changed and improved at various levels on
> campus.

4. *To have challenges and complexity.* The women in this study
actually smiled when they spoke of how much they enjoyed a good
challenge, whether it was a new project, new responsibility or position, or even a different complex situation or dilemma. The presidents made statements such as:

> I love the challenge and complexity of leadership, espe-
> cially in higher education.

> I thrive on challenge. I thrive on doing different things all of the time. I like variety. I like trying to work through and find solutions to things . . . figuring out your way through issues. I like to help make things happen.

5. *To have fun and enjoyment.* All of the women spoke of the enjoyment they found in leadership positions, and half of them actually used the word "fun" when speaking of why they became leaders. In fact, they used these words when speaking of many of the terms in this list of the nine top motivations for leading, for example, challenges, complexity, making a difference, accomplishing tasks, developing, and enabling others. One president explained:

> I liked having a work family. I had a secretary and coworkers in the president's office. I had the president, who was a great mentor. They cared if I showed up. We really worked together. It was really different from being a faculty member, which you do by yourself (which by the way is stupid, and we shouldn't do it that way). I had fun, and I made change.

6. *To do work that I knew I could do.* Because these presidents had developed the confidence that they could do things successfully, they yearned for opportunities to do this. They knew they were good at tasks and projects and had the ability to make things happen. One explained, "I was good at it, people listened, and changes happened." They knew they could do the job of president well.

7. *To enable others to develop and succeed.* All of the presidents spoke of the satisfaction they felt when they were able to provide opportunities or assist others in some way to succeed. They spoke of the enjoyment they felt when they watched someone they had helped move into a new position and take new opportunities. One said, "I learned that I really do like making things happen for people. I like helping others be successful." One explained that this

satisfaction and ability to get satisfaction from others' success is a sign she uses now in determining whether a faculty member is "made" for administration:

> A litmus test I use is to determine whether a faculty member can move from being a faculty member, where all of the satisfactions are individual (activities, publications, presentations, office, and such), to being a dean where the satisfaction comes from enabling all those things to happen for others. It is never satisfying to some people. It gets even bigger at the next level. Although when you are president you get credit for a lot of things, you have to be very quick to say, "WE". Presidents can get into trouble believing they did things all by themselves.

8. *To have power and influence.* Eight of the presidents discussed the word *power* and eight admitted that they enjoyed the power that positions of influence embodied. They used the word *power* in the same sentence with many of the other items on this motivation list. For example, "I like the power to make things happen for others"; "I believe that power can be useful in serving others and moving efforts along that can truly make a difference." They liked the ability they had to influence, make changes, and serve others. Another argued:

> I like power, and you have to be comfortable liking power. Many women leaders are not. I think power, if used well, can really advance you and your organization. I think I enjoyed it but I also wanted to do good by others. I felt leadership allowed me to do that.

9. *To serve.* When asked why they became leaders, a few of the presidents just said, "To serve." They had strong desires to serve the public (or mankind, as some of them termed it). They explained

that it was an "honor to serve" in their various capacities. Two presidents spoke of believing that the "good Lord" has a purpose for all of us, and that "we are all meant to accomplish certain things with our lives." One stated, "I was raised to help others."

Leadership Styles

In order to understand the presidents' leadership styles, I asked them two questions. (1) If I were to ask your university administrators and staff to describe your leadership style, what would they say? (2) What is your personal leadership style? Table 9.1 summarizes these findings.

The results show that these women's styles fit into a number of models of leadership style. First, they demonstrated an emergent style of leadership that is "more collectivist in nature, assuming a 'relational context' in which leaders share power, information, and decision-making with other group members" (Nidiffer, 2001, p. 108). These types of leaders are participatory, flexible, ethical, authentic, connective, and team-oriented. They have developed and apply skills such as empowerment, communication, collaboration, and healing. Regardless of their official position, individuals who are perceived by others as influential are often known as emergent leaders. These emergent leaders often become assigned leaders (Collins, Chrisler, & Quina, 1998).

Second, the presidents also demonstrated an androgynous style of leadership. Androgyny leadership theory appears to have characteristics similar to the emergent leadership theory. It predicts that the most effective leader will be highly instrumental (a stereotypical male quality) and expressive (a stereotypical female quality) (Korabik, 1990). Individuals with this style typically have greater flexibility and a broader repertoire of behaviors than individuals who use only skills and techniques traditionally aligned with a particular gender (feminine or masculine). Hence, women and men who use androgyny as a style have access to "both traditionally

Table 9.1. Leadership Styles

She is . . .	She . . .
A consensus-builder	Communicates well
A risk-taker	Delegates
A strong communicator	Develops others
An analyzer	Does not micromanage
Appropriate	Engages others
Business-minded	Gives credit to others for successes
Committed	Has a deep understanding of the issues
Confident	Has a strong personality
Collaborative	Has detailed knowledge
Cooperative	Has high standards
Decisive	Has strength
Demanding of self	Hires the best people
Demanding of others	Involves others in decision making
Focused	Listens well
Inclusive	Uses loose leadership
Engaging	Uses soft leadership
Ethical	
Facilitative	
Fair	
Honest	
Nice	
Not afraid	
Open to criticism	
Open to learning from mistakes	
Perceptive	
People-oriented	
Plain spoken	
Productive	
Results-focused	
Supportive	
Team-oriented	
Service-oriented	
Visionary	

feminine qualities and also masculine task-oriented ones" (Korabik, 1990, p. 288). In fact, Park (1997) stated that an "androgynous leadership style can be the most appropriate for achieving high performance in many organizations" (p. 166). Park outlined three premises for androgynous leaders: (1) they will have a wider range of possible reactions for any situation; (2) they will have the "capacity to assess a situation and to determine the most appropriate response" (p. 168); and (3) they will have "greater success in their encounters with the world than other leaders" (p. 168). Of course, this would depend on the subordinates' willingness to accept a leader who combines the qualities of the traditionally task-oriented and relations-oriented gender divisions.

The findings that emerged from my data support the androgyny theory of leadership, as other researchers have also noted in their results (for example, Korabik, 1990; Leonard, 1981; Waring, 2003). Others have reported that successful women leaders in male-dominated settings (and leadership in higher education remains male-dominated) tend to use a combination of female and male leadership traits. One president provided a good example of this type of leadership in a description about her own leadership style:

> I have a deep understanding of the issues; I can engage an individual in any position and come away knowing whether he or she is trying to do the right things or if they are not. They would say that I have a fine detailed knowledge and that it can be a little "off putting" at times, but it's typically coupled with this soft style, lots of delegation, and communication. I do more of this at 30,000 feet rather than at ground zero, but I can go to ground zero whenever I need to.

The descriptions in Table 9.1 show this combination of task-oriented and relationship-oriented attributes.

Third, both androgyny and emergent leadership theories speak of flexibility and adaptability, in the sense of being able to change leadership style based on different situations. This is highly emphasized in situational leadership theory. Leadership is "a network of relationships, a polyvalent phenomenon that can only be defined in the context of the leader's relationship with his specific constituency" (Ahn et al., 2004, p. 123). A variety of studies (Farkas & Wetlaufer, 1996; Ahn et al., 2004) found that this situational responsiveness to context is a key to successful leadership. Researchers have argued that adapting to specific strategic situations is more effective than employing a single leadership approach. According to Ahn et al. (2004) "it was their responsiveness to company culture and their ability to refine and adapt it to new strategic needs that was one of the critical elements of their success" (p. 114).

The presidents believed that situational leadership is not only helpful but also necessary in higher educational administration today. With the various stakeholder contingencies, the variety of governance bodies or structures (legislature, students, faculty, local government, governance boards, and state educational administration), and the current challenges in higher education, a president must be able to use a variety of leadership techniques or styles dependent upon the need and appropriateness of the context. In fact, one president diplomatically told me that asking her about her "leadership style" was a stupid question. She explained:

> If you have a specific leadership style then you're in big trouble! It has got to grow out of the needs of the times. If the house is on fire, you'd better be very directive. If you are going to revise the promotion and tenure guidelines, you had better be very participatory. If you have a style and somebody can say, "You're always going to do this," you're going to be a disaster because you don't have enough sense to read the situation and know what's required.

Another president admitted that early in her career she preferred one main leadership style. However, through various challenges and experiences she learned to modify her style

> ...based on the folks that I am working with, what their needs are, and what it takes in a particular given situation.

Finally, one woman stated:

> I believe finding commonalities is much more important than a particular leadership style, especially at a time when globalization is creating all kinds of authentic kinds of interdependencies.

Overall, these findings support other research (Collins et al., 1998; Nidiffer, 2001; Park, 1997) (albeit centered on different contexts) that spoke of effective styles of high-level leaders as being androgynous, emergent, and situational. It also supports the literature (Aldoory, 1998; Dunlap & Schmuck, 1995; Haring-Hidore, Freeman, Phelps, Spann, & Wooten, 1990; Matz, 2002) that focuses on successful women's styles and preferences as being consensus-oriented, committed, positive, empowering, participatory, collaborative, interactive, and so forth.

Leadership Philosophy

To look deeper into these presidents' ideas of leadership, I asked them to respond to questions about their own leadership philosophies. An analysis of their responses resulted in the generation of six primary themes: (1) hiring the right people and firing the wrong, (2) power and empowerment, (3) ethics, honesty, and openness, (4) developing and supporting others, (5) collaboration and teamwork, and (6) creating a vision.

Hiring the Right People and Firing the Wrong

All ten presidents explained (some briefly, some at length) that hiring the right people was central to successful leadership in higher education. When asked about their leadership philosophies, over half of the participants mentioned that getting the "right people on the bus" (two even referred to Jim Collins' book *Good to Great*) was foundational in higher educational strategies, improvements, changes, and overall leadership efforts. One president stated:

> There is no question in my mind that the most impor-
> tant thing you need to do when you get to a position of
> leadership is to be hardnosed about hiring really good
> people. You can't be soft hearted and hire someone be-
> cause they are a nice person. You have to hire very
> competent people to surround yourself with very bright
> individuals who will speak their minds to you and peo-
> ple you can truly respect. You must respect the people
> who work for you. Everyday you need to think, "Boy, I'm
> lucky that these wonderful people are working for me."
> That's what I tried to do in every situation.

Another president explained:

> I believe that it is important to hire good people to work
> for me and know when people need to leave.

Interestingly, the issue of hiring and firing is not directly addressed in much of the postsecondary literature on effective leadership. The current focus is on the development of managers and
leaders (McCaffery, 2004). Outside of the educational arena, hiring the right people and firing the wrong people are topics of more
open discussion and debate (Collins et al., 1998). Unfortunately,
higher education often focuses on how and when to move ineffective people to positions that will not have such devastating,

negative consequences on the institution. However, over half of the women in this study openly shared examples of firing people for a number of reasons, including ethical improprieties, lack of "fit" with new strategies or focus, incompetence, lack of ability to motivate others, and inability to move efforts toward bottom-line results. Considering the high response of comments about this topic in my study, it is evident that more needs to be written on the courage to fire in higher education.

Power and Empowerment

All ten presidents shared their philosophies of empowering others. After ensuring that the best people were working for them, the presidents believed that giving these individuals the power to do their jobs and make their own decisions was a strategy that proved to be effective for them throughout their administrative careers. One president explained:

> It is important to understand that the more you share power the more you have. It is wonderful when others make you look good!

A second explained that she did not enjoy micromanaging others in executive leadership positions.

> We have a provost who is much more of a traditional academic than I am. I think faculty wonder how we worked together. The fact is that we work together extremely well because I am not in the middle of his business all the time, yet he knows that he has to deliver.

Another president claimed:

> It is essential in higher education that you share your leadership. I think the more you give power away, the more power you actually have. To me empowering

others is probably the most important thing you can do. However, you must expect less than perfection when you do this. So many of us think we can do it better ourselves, and maybe that is true. But, at least in some areas, you have to accept less than perfect if you want to engage people who will stay with you.

To illustrate her point, one president said that she didn't do anything around her campus. She stated:

> The real work on this campus is done all around me. I don't teach the classes, I don't mow the grass, I don't clean the toilets, I don't serve the food, and I don't do the counseling. Other people do it, and they have to want to do it. I have found it works best to have people working on projects they want to work on. So, what I do is I encourage them and empower them. Sometimes I choose among the things they want to do and decide which I think will help the campus move forward in the long run. If someone comes to me with a great idea, I say, 'That's a good idea. Go do it'!

This notion of empowerment and sharing power for effective educational leadership is supported widely in the literature (Astin & Leland, 1991; Fennell, 2005; Haring-Hidore et al., 1990; Matz, 2002).

Eight of the ten presidents also mentioned the term *power* in this context. Most admitted that even if a president believes in empowerment, she still needs to be comfortable with power. In fact one president purported that one must actually like and enjoy power at some level to be effective in high-level leadership positions, especially as women. Interestingly, these women used the word *power* when referring primarily to influence and accountability. They also used the word when speaking of decision-making responsibilities. For example, one president stated:

> I also believe that if the buck stops with me, I'm going to make the final decision. I have to be very comfortable with that decision. I make sure people understand that well.

Ethics, Honesty, and Openness

In all of the interviews, the presidents discussed their commitment to ethics and honesty in their personal and professional lives. One woman proclaimed that presidents should be "models of integrity." A second president stated:

> It is so important to tell the truth. This is actually more than being ethical. Someone can be ethical and not be particularly good at telling the truth. Sometimes it's not easy to always tell the truth.

A third explained that her philosophy of leadership includes a "commitment to fair and scrupulously honest interactions on every level." A fourth remarked:

> My staff would say I am ethical and honest. I really pride myself on being honest. I don't lie. I just simply tell the truth. I'm honest in a way that is nice when sometimes I probably need to be honest in a way that is tough or harder on people.

A fifth president spoke about ethics, honesty, and integrity being part of a personal "core" that can be developed through hard work. She explained:

> I think that leadership cuts so totally to the core of an individual's character and personality. We should try to

identify one's character and who they really are instead of their leadership style or philosophy. I think a lot of candidates in colleges get in trouble with bad matches because the candidate goes in and tries to be who they think the university wants, and universities let them get away with that. My best advice to a candidate is to go in and be as much as "who you are" as you possibly can. After this interview today I would hope when you leave you will know who I am in a way that you wouldn't if I just answered some well-defined questions in a very detailed and deliberate manner. These kinds of questions and responses will not tell you who I am or what my character is all about. Universities hire leaders for the crises. In a crisis we all go immediately into that core of who we are and what our values are. We can't help it. It is just a human thing that happens. In a crisis you've got to be sure a leader has enough substance in his or her core. If the core is weak, you are not going to have a leader. If that core is not one that is whole and can move with very deliberate actions, you're going to be in trouble.

When I confronted some unethical situations at one institution, somebody said, "Why did you stand up? Didn't you know it would get you in trouble?" I said, "It never occurred to me not to stand up. I didn't think about options. It was a crisis, and I went immediately to my core." My core knew there were things that were wrong. There were things that had to be done, and as a president you're the one who has to do them. The core kicks in when it's tough. When an individual doesn't have a core filled with ethics and character then the institution is in trouble. You have to develop that core if you want people to have confidence in you. You need to know who you are before you can be authentic.

The topics of ethics and honesty in leadership are mentioned in some of the postsecondary literature, but actual in-depth scholarly research and writing in this area is sparse. Interestingly, because of recent scandals in corporate America, articles and books on ethical leadership in business are becoming commonplace. Many of the women in this study shared stories about being in situations that required an ethical stand (some at the expense of their past positions). They spoke of working with individuals who were clearly unethical and the choices they had to make because of that. So why is it that we sometimes protect unethical leaders in higher education? And why is it that we are just beginning to speak and write more openly about these issues? This is something that needs to be considered.

With regard to openness, five of the ten presidents prided themselves on their willingness to be candid and plainspoken. They explained that this is important for them in developing and maintaining trust and respect from those on their campuses, and in their communities, legislatures, and other stakeholder constituencies. Although they found it difficult at times, these presidents also spoke about a willingness to hear criticism and to act on it when and where appropriate. Eight of the ten spoke specifically about acknowledging and understanding their mistakes and failures but seeking diligently to learn from them to become more effective in their positions and relationships. A majority of the presidents also spoke of the importance of being open as a means of self-growth and development.

Developing and Supporting Others

Another strong theme that emerged from interviews with the university presidents is their leadership philosophies relating to their interest, motivation, and passion to assist others in personal and professional development. As discussed earlier in this chapter, this was also one of the nine primary motivations for decisions to accept and seek leadership positions. The presidents used a number of terms (*coaching*, *mentoring*, *assisting*, *developing*, *teaching*) to refer to developing others. One president reflected:

> I have mentored a lot of young graduate students who have become very successful. I've picked them out, in a sense, like I was picked out, because they are bright, they are hard working, and they are wonderful people. I love to develop people. I've created opportunities for faculty to have administrative experiences, so they can discover if they enjoy this kind of challenge.

Another president explained:

> I help develop people; the stronger they are the stronger we are. I want the best people that I can find for a position. I don't want to micromanage them, and I want them to take hold of their areas. We talk about the expectations related to what they want to accomplish and monitor whether we are making progress in those areas. If not, we decide what we have to change or discuss other options or opportunities. I have pretty high expectations for folks, and I like to let them find their own best way (as I like to do). In the end we focus on results, and I give them the credit.

One university president discussed some specific types of developmental strategies she utilizes to develop some of her administrators and staff:

> I don't get angry if something goes wrong. Failure is okay. You can never make me yell at you because you did something bad, stupid, or wrong. I just say, "Oh, it didn't work. How come? What can you do better?"

> I have an open door policy. People come to my office, send me e-mail, or call me on the phone. I want them to feel comfortable with me. I believe in developing others. That is the only way to be more successful as a leader.

The presidents also spoke about the importance of supporting others around them. They believed that this support is central to the success of the leadership team and the campus as a whole. A part of showing and displaying support is to respect and believe in colleagues. A few of the presidents mentioned that one way to respect and support their subordinates was to be on time and prepared for meetings. One president talked about being supportive:

> I try to be very supportive of those who report to me and help them. Sometimes I have to ask them to do difficult things. In these cases I ensure I provide them with enough encouragement and support to help them succeed.

Another president said her deans would say that she will ultimately support their final decisions. "They did not believe I would do this at first, and they had to find out for themselves." She explained that they tried her out on a few issues and, according to this president, "Now they believe me."

These findings support prior literature in the postsecondary and business arenas. Women leaders who have emergent and androgynous leadership styles are said to be interested in the development of those who work for them (Bass, 1990; Nidiffer, 2001). Other higher educational and business literature also discussed the desires and concern of women leaders to assist in the development of those around them (Aldoory, 1998; Waring, 2003; Wells, 1998).

Collaboration and Teamwork

Collaboration and teamwork was a central theme that emerged from the presidents' statements about their leadership philosophies.

They used related descriptive words or phrases such as "team-oriented," "building consensus," "respecting people around you," "facilitative leadership," "involving others in decision making," "participatory management," "listening to others," "team of inter-changeable parts," and "partnership between leaders and followers." One president had people say to her "If I was chancellor or president, I could make things happen in a second." However, she has learned that the top leader really can't do anything.

> You can only get teams of people together, very good people together; and they are the ones who will make things happen.

Other sample statements made by some of the presidents on this topic include the following:

> They can tell me when they think I'm wrong. If they want me to be a good leader, they'll tell me. If I'm head-ing over a cliff and my administrative team doesn't say "Watch out," it's their fault, too.

> My team would say that I like a team of interchangeable parts where we all know the whole organization and the baton can be seamlessly passed from one person to another. Someone may have special responsibilities, but we are all trying to create the same organizational capacity behind the vision we have created. We do it in different ways, but I believe in cooperation, delegation, soft leadership, and loose leadership

> I believe that leadership is a partnership between the leader and his or her followers where together you dis-cover the best of all of you. This is how you can move the institution forward to its benefit. Any benefit that accrues to you has got to be a side effect; it can not be the goal. It is not about you. It really is true that if

you want to be the sole source of inspiration, the sole source of good ideas, and the sole source of decisiveness, a university is not the place to be a leader. Everybody is smarter than you are; everybody knows a heck of a lot more about a lot of things than you do. They all have dreams and aspirations that are grounded in expertise, assertiveness, and achievement. The best thing you can do is to catch that wave, ride it, and be part of it. You have been successful if your administrators, faculty, and staff believe you have helped them achieve their goals.

Six of the presidents specifically spoke about the importance of listening to the people around them. One stated:

You have to hear the people, and you can only do that if you are quiet enough to listen to what they are saying.

The presidents explained that they hire the best people so they can make better choices and decisions as a leadership team. Every member of the team makes distinctive contributions and embodies unique skills and perspectives. However, if they are not heard and trusted, there is no reason to hire the best and brightest. These results also support the previously published literature. In fact, much of the current literature discusses how important teamwork and collaboration are to women leaders, both in business and educational settings (Aldoory, 1998; Astin & Leland, 1991; Dunlap & Schmuck, 1995; Fennell, 2005; Haring-Hidore et al., 1990; Matz, 2002; Waring, 2003; Wells, 1998).

Creating a Vision

The sixth and final theme of leadership philosophy that emerged from the presidents' responses was the importance of creating a vision. They believe that presidents must recognize the need to look ahead and think globally. Two of the presidents mentioned

Jim Collins' (2001) book *Good to Great* in terms of creating a vision, building an image, focusing on what the organization does really well, and building on those strengths. One president explained:

> Although we create a vision together, the people want to hear your perspectives. Share with them your vision. I learned that if I didn't speak clearly and forcefully about what I wanted to happen, everybody got nervous, including the regents, my staff, and the presidents. They all wanted to know where I stood on things and where we were supposed to be heading. I learned that you have to be clear. You must provide a pathway for people to follow, and you can't be wishy-washy. It was hard for me because every issue is like that. I'm very clear about some issues yet unclear about others. I see the complexity, and sometimes I'm not always quite sure. I've found that you work your way through the issues, and then take a position. That is what helps the people around you. This surprised me. People liked it when I would be decisive and could lay out where we needed to go. I believe effective leaders need to do this. It is also important to recognize that many others help. They tell me about potential unintended consequences of policy change and political feasibility.

These findings also support past research that found that creating and leading with a vision is necessary and central to effective leadership today (Aldoory, 1998; Wells, 1998).

Final Thoughts

After analyzing the presidents' leadership motivations, styles, and philosophies it is clear that these presidents have always yearned to make a real difference in the lives of students, employees, colleagues, and community members. This conclusion supports the limited existing literature on the desires and motivations of women university leaders, as most women participants in other studies also speak of their desire to truly make a difference for a variety of constituencies (such as Collins et al., 1998; Dunlap & Schmuck, 1995; Nidiffer & Bashaw, 2001). The university presidents in this study seem to thrive on making progress in areas that they and those around them are convinced truly matter. These women strongly believe that it is their task or calling, as well as their ethical and professional responsibility, to leave a place or situation better than they found it. In fact, this desire and commitment has provided a firm foundation for the presidents' personal and professional choices throughout the years.

Takeaways

1. It is important for emerging leaders to seek out (or at least be receptive toward) jobs that provide opportunities to accomplish and achieve, make a difference and contribute, be involved in meaningful and important work, and have challenge and complexity.

2. Competent women leaders-in-training want opportunities to do work that they know they can do, enable others to develop and succeed, have power and influence, serve, and have fun and enjoyment.

3. Women university presidents have emergent, androgynous, and situational leadership styles. They share power, information, and decision making with others and are participatory, flexible, ethical, and connective. They have a wide range of possible reactions for any situations. They adapt their leadership approach to specific strategic situations.

4. Hiring the right people and firing the wrong or ineffective people are important skills in successful leadership.

5. Women leaders enjoy empowering others to do their jobs and make their own decisions. Sharing power, teamwork, and collaboration are important philosophies and values to these women.

6. Ethics, honesty, and openness are highly valued traits and characteristics of women university presidents. They demonstrated direct application of these values during times of difficulty.

7. Effective women leaders find satisfaction in developing, nurturing, and supporting others. They enjoy providing opportunities for others to learn, grow, and develop.

10

Presidential Advice and Perspectives

Each time [a person] stands up for an ideal, or acts to
improve the lot of others, or strikes out against injustice,
he [or she] sends forth a tiny ripple of hope, and crossing
each other from a million different centers of energy and
daring those ripples build a current that can sweep down
the mightiest walls of oppression and resistance.

Robert F. Kennedy

Now I become myself,
It's taken time,
Many years and places;
I have been dissolved and shaken,
Worn other people's faces . . .

May Sarton, "Now I Become Myself"

During these women presidents' remarkable lifetime journeys, they have stood up for ideas, acted to improve the lot of others, struck out against injustice, and sent out ripples of hope. These successful women have learned about leadership throughout every stage of their lives. They have yearned to make a difference, and they have. They have been driven to develop and grow in their knowledge, skills, and abilities, and they did. And throughout their lifetime of experiences they have become themselves—a gift to so many who have had the opportunity to be influenced by them.

At the conclusion of each research interview, I asked the presidents what advice they would give to girls and women about leadership development. I also asked them to share their feelings about the position of a university president or chancellor in higher education. This chapter focuses on these two broad areas: presidential advice and presidential perspectives.

Advice

The presidents said that they have been asked often during their presidencies to give advice on leadership development to girls, young women, and women not only in higher education, but also in government and business settings. After analyzing the advice of each president, I categorized it into seven broad suggestions: (1) prepare early; (2) become proactive in your own career development; (3) be a lifelong learner; (4) develop strength and trust in self; (5) embrace challenges; (6) develop general leadership competencies; and (7) look beyond yourself.

Prepare Early

The presidents were very insistent that leadership development should start as early in life as possible. They suggest involvement during high school and college (or earlier) in a variety of activities, including sports and community, and participation in "critical growth experiences that can become embedded in an individual's skills and habits" as early as possible. One president stated:

> Young women should take any opportunity they have to develop leadership. They should volunteer to do things, to participate in the community in strategic ways. I have enjoyed those kinds of experiences throughout my life. Young women should find ways to stretch themselves during adolescence, college, and their early professional years. Every time a young woman challenges herself, she becomes less intimidated and she can find a place for

herself. She must see herself as a leader early so that she can consciously make decisions that will help her learn and develop competencies throughout her life.

One president shared her belief that women need to prepare themselves educationally with the skills needed to have opportunities. She said, "There are certain union cards you have to have. Once you have these cards then you can enjoy what you are doing and look for opportunities when you are ready for a new challenge." One woman spoke of the importance of learning early to build networks and develop healthy individual relationships with people in all settings. She was quick to say that the development of leadership competencies is not a linear process. These suggestions and other types of preparation can be integrated into a variety of experiences.

Service opportunities such as community involvement and academic service were recommended by many of the presidents. One president said many women have come to her seeking advice throughout the years. She said that they tell her of their desire to be leaders, but then complain that they have had no opportunities to gain applicable leadership experience. She told the following story about one particular young faculty member seeking advice:

> I had a young woman come to me recently and say, "I'm not a leader, and I would like to be one. How did you get to be a leader?" I asked her some questions. "Do you run a lab? Have you written a grant? Do you manage a budget? Do you belong to professional organizations? Do you chair committees?" After each question I paused, and she said "Yes." Then I explained that she needed to use service to her advantage. I told her that all of those things should count as leadership. Leaders don't have to have titles. I advised her (and have advised others as well) to consider all the things they've done where they have had to make decisions and manage. All of these experiences count in your portfolio of experiences.

Various types of service can provide both experience and visibility. Two presidents suggested that women should intentionally seek visibility particularly during their early professional years if they are interested in leadership. One stated:

> It is very important to be visible in a positive way. You need to be recognized as someone that people can work with. You need to be seen as someone who can make things happen. You need to be identified as one who is trustworthy, ethical, and strong.

Being prepared early was mentioned by various presidents as one way to obtain more challenging opportunities. One president spoke of the importance of "seeing yourself as a leader," but warned that this can become "harder the higher up you go. If you haven't done the job before, you may need to grow into it." Another woman gave the following advice:

> You can obtain challenging tasks, assignments, or positions by developing your own unique talents so that you can become the very best that you can be. You must learn to lead by sharing your talents, interests, energy, ideas, and by contributing to the innovations needed in whatever discipline you settle upon. Experience is foundational in doing this.

Become Proactive in Your Own Career Development

The presidents spoke about the importance of "gaining experience, moving through the ranks, and challenging oneself to do and learn different kinds of things throughout one's career." This doesn't specifically mean that careers need to be structured and planned well in advance. In fact, some presidents outright discouraged this. As Chapter Five explained, the presidents did not have formal career plans, but they did have a wealth of unique experiences, positions, and opportunities that provided them the knowledge, skills, and abilities needed to lead. One president explained:

> To develop leadership you need to have had experiences that lead you from one step to another. In my judgment, I would also say that it is not a very good idea to have it all planned out. If you do this then it will make you crazy. You won't enjoy what you are doing at the moment. The most important preparation for whatever comes next is to be the best you can in the job you are currently in and love every minute of it!

Another president reiterated this with the notion that doors are naturally opened when women are high performers in their current jobs. She explained, "I thought each position was the greatest job in the world." She believes that "being focused and committed to what you are currently doing is crucial." A third woman declared, "You must do well in every single task you are given. Everything is important, and you must do your very best in all that you do." In fact, every president made a similar statement advising young women to do the "absolute best job in whatever it is" no matter how important or seemingly insignificant it may appear. As one president noted, "You must lead by seizing opportunities when they present themselves."

The presidents also believe that women should accept positions they are truly interested in. One stated that accepting a position just because it provides a "different" experience is not a good enough excuse. The presidents advised that women should closely consider their interests and passions. As one president said:

> A truly exciting experience is when an opportunity comes along that you find interesting. If you have appropriate experience, then you should do it! However, sometimes you don't think you have the experience,

when in fact you do. As women we tend to devalue our skills. But it's the interest level that is so important! If it sounds like a challenge, and you really think, "Boy this would be fun to do," then you ought to do it. In most cases, you will have the skills that you need. Women have so many skills already. The women I talk to are often women who have raised children and never worked. The skills they gained raising children are powerful. This has all been true of my life. I accepted every job I've ever had because it was really interesting to me. Sometimes I wouldn't have thought of putting myself forward, but people have encouraged me. Ultimately, I think everyone has an obligation to reach beyond themselves to improve society.

The presidents provided some suggestions regarding how to obtain challenging assignments if current assignments do not provide these opportunities. One woman advised:

Look for gaps, things that are not being done. Don't sit back and say, "Why isn't someone doing something about this?" Instead you should say, "How can I help?" Although the focus is on the organization, by looking for gaps and volunteering to find solutions you make a difference and gain experience.

One president spoke of looking down the road at some career goals, and figuring out generally what kinds of skills you'll need to do those future jobs successfully. She explained:

If your current job doesn't require doing those things, ask somebody to give you those responsibilities. Offer to do that work and say, "I don't know anything about the budget of this university. I need experience." Say, "I have no experience working with the legislature, and I want a career in public higher education. Can you help me work with the legislature?" Seize the experiences that you need to have; don't wait for them. You may not need all of the formal steps along the way in various positions, but you do need to make sure you have the opportunity to develop and practice the skills critical to authenticity.

Some of the presidents recommended that emerging leaders need to be very careful about position choices, particularly if they are interested in high-level educational leadership. For example one president advised, "Don't start your career with a community college if you want to be in a research institution, and don't take a job in student affairs if you want to obtain an academic leadership or presidential position down the road." The presidents believe that women should take new and challenging assignments, but that they must be cautious to make sure the experiences will be credible and are related to the leadership goals they may have in mind.

Three presidents said specifically that women need to have an academic background if they are interested in academic leadership. They suggested that women need to consider their career choices early in their lives to determine whether there is a specific route to some choices. One president stated:

> Academics should run universities because the most important decisions are the ones that reaffirm the values and the traditions of the academy. That judgment is not available if you aren't part of it. I would suggest that if you want to be a university president, you should come up through the academic ranks. If you don't have this background, the rest of us have to teach you the other things you don't know. In fact, if you are not an academic often you won't clearly understand what you don't know. You'll just assume you get things when in fact you do not.

A majority of the presidents spoke of the value of being a faculty member for eventual academic leadership. One woman explained:

> My advice to young women interested in academic leadership is that they become faculty members if they can. This is important because faculty is what differentiates this sort of place from any other kind of place. If women don't know what it is like, then they won't get it, and they're just not going to be as effective as they might be otherwise. Even if an individual can teach part-time, that will be helpful. Even if women are not going into high level academic leadership, being a faculty member can still help individuals understand the students, which is important in any type of position within higher education.

The presidents were very clear that rising leaders should take responsibility for their own career development. Some women are given opportunities by mentors and others, whereas other women are not. As one of the previous quotations outlined, women need to look for gaps and assertively suggest projects and solutions. A woman can volunteer to do work that helps her learn specific things she doesn't already know. The bottom line is that each individual must take responsibility for her own career development. If she wants to become a leader, she must consciously look for opportunities and then embrace them.

Become Lifelong Learners

Taking opportunities to continuously develop and learn more about themselves, others, and the world around them was an important component of the presidents' advice for rising women to become lifelong learners. The themes of lifelong learning that emerged from the interviews focus on the following: the search for opportunities; observation, reflection, and assimilation; education; self-knowledge; and competence versus authenticity.

The presidents recommend that women of all ages continually seek and obtain ongoing development and learning. Continuous improvement in knowledge and skills is the only way one can develop effective leadership capabilities. They suggest that women develop the ability to learn from everything around them—opportunities, situations, and other individuals. One president made the following statement:

> You encounter choices and decisions all along the way in everything you do. Most of them are small, and many seemingly unimportant. Yet each requires a special clarity, the ability to see beyond the immediate issue, to contemplate the broader one, to weigh the benefits, to be aware of consequences, and to be informed and knowledgeable. We can all learn from these choices and decisions, and they can help us become strong and inclusive leaders.

Learning from a large number and variety of people has been important to most of the presidents. As one explained:

> I don't just have one or two role models. However, there are so many times that I have learned from just watching. Sometimes it is their speaking or negotiation skills. Often I watch how people interact effectively in meetings, and I implement those behaviors. I remember when I was a very new administrator with no experience in meeting facilitation. I used to watch people run meetings, and I think that helped me a lot. Watching and paying attention to how people do certain things has been a great help to me. I'm certain it can be helpful for all.

One president spoke of President John F. Kennedy's statement "Leadership and learning are indispensable to each other." This president added, "Take this tool on your journey to leadership, and you cannot go wrong." Two presidents spoke of the importance of learning by "doing your homework" on all aspects of your job and higher education in general. Two presidents also added that rising women leaders should be readers. One of them said:

> Read stuff. Most people know their discipline, but they don't know anything about higher education. That was one of the things that happened to me when I was an ACE fellow. I started realizing there was a literature about teaching and about higher education. It was so interesting to me, and I think it is interesting to anyone interested in administration down the road.

Being a lifelong learner leads not only to continuous personal development but also to a more complete and in-depth understanding of oneself. The presidents felt that the most effective and successful leaders are those who (1) can understand themselves, and (2) have the self-monitoring skills that allow them to see themselves accurately in the eyes of those around them. Coming to understand oneself through self-reflection is central to success. As one president noted, "I really think the most important reflection is what goes on inside your head about the kind of person you are, what excites you, what drives you, and what makes you feel good about yourself." This self-knowledge is an empowering element in personal and professional development. Another president said:

> Reflection can be the most enriching experience if you are willing to deeply acknowledge your own frailties and your own limitations, and then let that knowledge empower you when you turn to take the next curve in the road. You see it coming and this time you are prepared and recognize it.

If you truly understand who you are, then your decisions and behaviors will be based upon more accurate information. This can be helpful in putting yourself in situations where you are most likely to be successful. For example, one president stated:

> If I were at a small liberal arts college where I had my arms around details everyday, I would be nuts, and I would be making the people around me crazy. I have to have the complexity inherent in a large institution. I know that about myself, so I wouldn't take a presidency just to take a presidency. It must have the right set of characteristics and challenges. I really think it is important to spend time reflecting on who you are.

The presidents believe that rising leaders must be clear about their own principles of leadership. One president explained:

> I believe what works today is value-driven leadership, which is the sum of competence and authenticity. Competence refers to your experiences, preparation, and accomplishments, while authenticity refers to your character. It is important to know how you see your place in the world while being confident, centered, and committed to your own values. Understand how you choose to work, think, handle disappointment, and connect with people. Understand how you react to fear, anxiety, and frustration. You must have a sense of self. And finally, you need to understand which traits are important to you in this value-driven leadership you are developing in yourself (for example, empathy, sincerity, compassion, humility, ethics, moral standards, veracity, trust, integrity, openness, communication, courage, relationships, diversity commitment, willingness to serve others, learning, intellectual vigor, and/or the ability to focus and motivate).

The presidents advised that emerging women leaders should ask questions and be as informed as possible. Women should look for areas of curiosity and interest, and then study and learn about each of them. They should "allow differing ideas and perspectives to stretch their thinking." They should find opportunities that allow them to use creativity, innovation, and discovery. Finally, they should have positive experiences in ethical and respectful environments that allow for the effective development of leadership.

Develop Strength and Trust in Self

Knowing yourself leads to trusting yourself and your leadership capabilities. This, in turn, leads to increased confidence, both in yourself and those you lead. All of the presidents spoke of how critical it is to be an individual and a leader who trusts herself and has internal and external strength. One president stated, "Successful leaders have a personal and professional strength that gives them backbone and energy to lead." Although the presidents spoke highly of the ability to collaborate and compromise when needed, they said that values are never something to be compromised. One woman stated, "Be sure your values are in sync with your organization, and never compromise them!"

Another study participant spoke of the importance of trusting yourself.

> Trust your own judgment. Hold fast when you think you're right. Don't back down. If you back down when you really believe you're right, then you loose credibility. In fact, the next time you make a firm decision, nobody will believe you. They'll say, "She'll change her mind." I really believe you have to trust yourself. If you find out you're wrong, you can certainly back down and learn from the experience. But if you make a hard decision and you believe you have done the right thing, it's really very important to stay with it.

Other presidents used the phrase, "Listen to your gut." Learning to believe in yourself and your abilities is foundational in developing leadership throughout a lifetime. This internal strength and self-trust should eliminate, or at least decrease, fear. Fear breeds insecurity, which, according to one president, "isn't a good thing when it comes to leading." As another president noted, "To lead one has to be unafraid to make decisions and then act." It is personal strength and confidence that removes fear.

Embrace Challenges

The willingness and ability to embrace challenges has been a strong emerging theme throughout this book. It is no surprise then that it was one of the seven primary streams of advice the women believe is important for emerging leaders to hear. One president said simply, "You must embrace challenges and learn from them." Another stated, "Continually challenge yourself to do different kinds of things." A few women made statements such as, "Don't be afraid to think and dream big." Having the right set of challenges available is particularly motivating to individuals who are driven and ambitious.

Girls and young women can learn early in life that it is acceptable to take certain risks. They need to have experiences in which they demonstrate self-esteem and self-concept by challenging themselves and having many successes and occasional failures. As one president noted, "These experiences increase self-efficacy and the desire to continue accepting and seeking challenges." If this habit is created early in life it can be particularly useful in the ongoing development of emerging leaders. One president explained, "You need to find ways to stretch yourself. Each time you do you become less intimidated and more confident." The presidents suggested that women should not fear putting themselves forward to take on new challenges.

The presidents believe that rising leaders need to clearly understand that stretching and challenging yourself is a lot of work and may result at times in certain unintended consequences. One president explained:

> Young women need to clearly understand that becoming and then being a leader is a lot of hard work. There's a great deal of personal sacrifice that comes with it, including some that affect your family. I think my ambition has actually been a strong contributor to my divorces and other family struggles. However, I have clearly enjoyed what I have done, and I don't have any regrets about it.

If you decide that you want to challenge yourself and assertively develop leadership skills and competencies, one president gave the following advice:

> You have to learn how to not stress out about the little stuff. You need to develop the skills to be able to handle large amounts of data and tasks. You have to learn to be flexible and ride with things. Although I had some preparation and experience, I didn't feel the load and complexity until I actually had a substantial leadership position. It's not just the weight, but it's the amount of stuff. Remember, universities are little cities.

One president gave this summarizing advice:

> If there is any advice I can share it is that, if you are lucky, life is long, and life is good. However, no successful leader escapes this life without having her share of bumps, bruises, and sometimes fractures. It's never pleasant, but if the difference you can make outweighs those bumps, bruises, and fractures—it is worth it. Those people like me who thrive on challenges are driven forward. If you want to make the kind of difference that matters, embrace challenges and start preparing yourself now.

Develop General Leadership Competencies

The ten participants provided a number of recommendations regarding the development of leadership competencies. I have summarized these in the following list:

- Be clear with yourself about the skills needed to be successful in leadership.

- Hire the right people, have confidence in them, and then get out of their way and let them do their jobs. Focus on building a great team.

- Gather around you people from diverse backgrounds, perspectives, experiences, and viewpoints—seek commonalities and new approaches. Let the differences freshen and inform your thinking.

- Involve, engage, enlist, and profit from including others in everything you do.

- Always do your homework so you are prepared.

- Accept that the position of a leader is a position of power. Embrace power. Take it, and then give it away. The more power you give, the more you have. You lose power when you fail to empower others.

- Have a positive attitude. A positive outlook, even on a bad situation that others may have created around you, deters the naysayer from the next level of criticism. Understand the nature of public scrutiny and criticism, and then continue to focus on the positive.

- Be aware of the language you choose when talking about issues, and engage in discussion, exchange, and debate. Language helps set the tone and can be inclusive or exclusive. Language has the capacity to elevate the discussion and bring out the best in others.

- Don't take yourself too seriously.

- Build powerful support systems with family, friends, professional organizations, colleagues, peers, bosses, researchers, and so forth.

- Participate in leadership training and networking opportunities.

- Always be ethical and honest.

- Remember that gender is only one of many issues to consider when there are challenges and issues.

- Build the ability to see beyond the immediate issue so that you can contemplate the broader ones.

- Consider whether you are an organizational or individual contributor. Figure out if you are interested in effectively enabling others. This brings clarity of understanding if you have the capability to lead such a complex organization.

- Articulate a forward-looking, poignant, encompassing vision to set the tone and direction of an organization by developing the courage to aim high while remaining realistic and seeking wise counsel.

- Learn to put yourself into another's shoes and have that kind of empathy. It's hard to serve and lead others without an understanding about what motivates or discourages them.

- Learn to create an appropriate structure to support the vision.

- Have strong change agent skills.

- Understand what it means to leave behind a private life.

- Avoid burnout in a pressured environment by learning and doing new things.

- Insert and find humor in everyday things—including yourself! Remember to make yourself a priority at times so that you can be renewed.

- Move on when you need to move on. Leave a position when the excitement is gone.

Look Beyond Yourself

Leadership is not really about the leader herself. It is about the organization, followers, and those who are being serviced. The presidents believe that leaders who are focused too much on themselves lose sight of the true organizational needs. These individuals fail to recognize the interplay between all of the subsystems within and without the larger organizational system. One piece of advice given over and over by the presidents was that leaders need to "think beyond themselves." Three presidents spoke specifically about the role of a female leader to lift other women. One explained:

> You must lead by example for those who are coming up behind you. You must lead by reaching back and helping others. That is a responsibility you have.

Another stated:

> Always remember that as you climb up the ladder you've got to pull up other women with you. I really believe that it is our responsibility as women leaders to bring others along. There are many amazing women who just need opportunities.

A third spoke of this responsibility for all positions, including that of a faculty member. She explained:

> Even faculty who are strong researchers need to reach beyond themselves and create better places for their students and for their community, whatever that may be. In today's world the pressure is on faculty members of the higher education community to be selfish and to do whatever it takes to take care of themselves. They believe that they have to do that. Yet it's still a world that requires people to give of themselves over and beyond the job. It's still a world that needs individuals to help make things better around them. It is clear that there is a tendency to look after ourselves, but that is a pathway that will not lead to a happy life.

A number of presidents recommended that, although they have encouraged women to take opportunities that give them personal and professional development, a leader-in-training should focus first on the needs of the organization. Leadership development should never be done at the expense of the organization. One president said she always thought to herself, "What do I need to do to support this organization, help this organization, and build programs that support this organization?" She said that keeping the focus continually on what is good for the organization has provided her with plenty of opportunities for personal experience and growth.

The women explained that if presidents are truly looking out for those around them instead of focusing on themselves, they typically do a few specific things. First, they give their best in all that they do, even behind the scenes. Second, they take time for others. Third, they are "honest and ethical—beyond reproach—throughout their lives." This is crucial if the leader cares about the institution and those who are served by it. Fourth, they respect others. One stated, "Always remember the words *respect* and *trust*. It is essential to earn the respect and trust of your immediate colleagues and to return the favor to them." Finally, they serve as leaders with a spirit of sincere care and concern for others. One president explained, "You can build a reservoir of good will that will come back in a time you need it."

Presidency Perspectives

The presidents also shared some interesting perspectives related to the office of a university president and higher education in general. Three presidents spoke of early women presidential pioneers and the lack of mentoring they provided. One explained:

> Women who were about five years ahead of me in major administrative posts were, as a group, unwilling to get involved in supporting other women in leadership development. They were intent upon being very male-like. Women of my generation were much more willing to reach out. We didn't think that it made us look weak to reach out and support other women. On behalf of these first women academic leaders, I'm not sure any of us can ever really understand what they had to go through to break through that glass ceiling during those years. They are all retired now, but they were pretty chilly to the rest of us. There is no excuse for this now. We must support each other.

Another participant in her late sixties provided some very interesting insights on her theory about the reasons some women were able to obtain positions in earlier years. Of course these are only one woman's feelings, but the theory does provide an interesting and humorous perspective.

> I predict that generations from now will never understand what I'm about to say. Those of us along the fault lines do understand. I was the kind of woman that was

not threatened by male leaders. I dressed like their wives dressed and looked like their wives looked. I didn't show up at work without a bra and in sandals. I looked smart and knew what their expectations were for me. A lot of very talented women felt compromised if they didn't flaunt the fads of the day, and they would come in deliberately braless and in pony tails. It was totally inappropriate. In fact, no man could have gotten ahead that way either. It was a bad road that some women went down early on. I never saw dressing and acting professional as a compromise.

Interestingly, I remember having a discussion when I was an ACE Fellow. One woman said, "I hate these clothes." I said, "Actually, I kind of like them. If you hate them, why do you wear them?" Her response was, "If you are going to assassinate Caesar you've got to dress like Caesar's guard." There was a lot of that in the beginning.

I was already part of leadership groups before the men figured out that I was going to lead the group. That was an important survival skill for early women presidents. You'll notice that, with the exception of Hannah Gray who always would have dressed the way a man would have dressed, many of us are short. We were not physically intimidating women. In fact, many of us presidents were gathered at an event one day, and we laughed as we realized that we were in a room full of midgets—we were all short women! We jokingly decided that we got to our positions because we were short enough to walk between the men unnoticed. Because we were not intimidating in that sense, we concluded that maybe we had disarmed them long enough to become known. And after we were known, there was no longer an issue. The men knew what we could do and supported us.

The presidents then spoke briefly of their feelings about the presidential position specifically. One noted, "I have a great deal of respect for the office of the president and the leadership role it embodies." Another president explained:

> I just can't tell you what a privilege and honor it is to serve as president of this university. It is not one that I earned. It is a place that is so important and so valuable, and I just don't want to screw it up. Like the Athenian state, it is our responsibility to make it better and more beautiful by the time we are done.

A president with responsibilities for a state education system shared these insights on how this position can make a difference for the larger society:

> I really believe that a president or chancellor can truly make a difference with regard to important things for others. It is a matter of doing the right things. I have worked really hard to make things better. I think that's what ethical leaders do. When you get into these positions, you have the opportunity to carry out your values and to make a difference at such a large scale, even globally at times. You can spend an awful lot of your time doing other stuff, but you must try to keep your eye on what key issues are important to you, the students, the institutions, and the state. If you do this you can make a difference that will matter to many.

Although the office of a president should be respected, one woman spoke candidly of what makes a large impact on that the office.

> I have a great deal of respect for the office of the president and the leadership role, but in the end all of us are smarter than one of us. It is not about me, and it is not

about the president. It is about us and about building the best team we can. It's about being willing to talk candidly about the problems we have to take on and the challenging changes we have to work into the culture.

Finally, a different president provided some profound insights regarding her position:

I have learned not to confuse the high office I hold with the human frailties that I am. It is easy, when your first name is president, to think you are more than you really are. You have to really be honest with yourself about the office and not the person. You see this in corporations too, where leaders loose sight of that fact. They forget and think that since they are so important that all their ideas must be great and anything they want should happen. So many leaders in business and higher education are full of themselves, and *that* is what their success is. The office is noble, but the individual in the office has human frailties that he or she should never forget! Leaders who are both successful and ethical do not.

Three of the presidents, very close to retirement, spoke of the position being exhausting. One explained, "I couldn't have done this job earlier in my life. I was in my mid-fifties when I took office, and it is all consuming. It takes everything I've got." Another explained:

I am a marathoner (I don't mean literally), and I am a sprinter. But I can't sprint a marathon, and that's what it feels like sometimes. Before 8:00 in the morning I'm on my e-mail dealing with some accreditation problems on one campus, athletic problems on another, an audit issue on a third, and that is all before getting the daily paper. When the morning paper comes I must address all of the issues it brings. Often these issues stack up, and I have to deal with them simultaneously. The mind is willing, but the body numbs. I have wondered how many years I can take of sleep deprivation. This job is all encompassing.

The presidents generally seemed to believe that leadership in higher education has become more complex through the years. One president said:

In the past, leadership has relied on the strength and determination of a single individual. This still holds, but leadership today must also address greater complexities at multiple levels. By that same token, past leadership ultimately was answerable to a relatively small, contained homogeneous community, making ethical leadership easier and clearer. Leadership challenges are no longer single or simple. They intertwine and reach beyond a single community to touch communities across the entire planet.

A number of presidents also agree that higher education should be involved in social change as one of its major purposes. One president stated:

Leaders in higher education can lose sight of this role amid the issues and demands of the moment. It is easy to slip back into a comfort zone, passing on the difficult position, and not rising to the challenge or taking the risk.

Finally, four additional themes that emerged focused on the presidents' beliefs that (1) higher education should be the very essence of change and, therefore, should be a leader in the community; (2) in today's world, education should be responsive and adaptive to the changing environment; (3) faculty, staff, administrators, and students should be prepared and open to change; and (4) higher educational communities should be more concerned with the "common good" versus the "entitlement" perspectives of the past.

Final Thoughts

By the time this book is published, some of these presidents may have retired, changed institutions, or possibly changed occupations; but whatever they go on to do, they will always be leaders. It is in their blood, it is in their hearts, and it is in their souls. They yearn to make a difference. They already have, and they will continue to do so throughout their lives.

Studying the lifetime developmental journeys of these ten women has provided me opportunities to think about my own goals, ambitions, and life. I have learned to self-reflect at a level deeper than I had previously done. This has provided moments of uneasiness, moments of amazement, and moments of peace. I would encourage you to allow this book do the same for you as you reflect back upon its content, insights, and advice.

Developing leaders is a crucial issue in today's higher education, business, and public arenas. We need strong, prepared, and ethical leaders in our homes, schools, businesses, nonprofits, churches, communities, states, nations, and world. Women *can* and *must* make a difference. Let us prepare ourselves to become those leaders and, more important, let's reach out to help prepare the girls and young women who can make a phenomenal impact in years to come.

APPENDIX A

Research Methods

Based on an extensive review of existing writings, I created a detailed list of open-ended probing questions designed to obtain a wide array of information about the presidents' past experiences and perceptions. Two experienced leadership researchers provided feedback on these questions, and adjustments were made accordingly (see Appendix B for the question categories).

After spending months writing proposals for small grants and recruiting funding for travel costs and support, I was able to secure the basic funding by January 2005. I then sent invitational e-mails and letters to twenty-five women university presidents or chancellors across the United States requesting their participation in the study. Twelve presidents agreed and I was able to interview ten of the twelve presidents who could meet with me between March and June 2005. Traveling to the presidents' university offices for a face-to-face interview was imperative in obtaining the type, quantity, and quality of data needed for this research.

Analysis included:

1. *Transcriptions*: resulting in about 600 double-spaced pages.

2. *Preliminary analysis*: resulting in a categorization of all responses within each interview.

3. *Combined categorization*: resulting in a combination of all related responses (comments, perspectives, and stories) from all

ten interviews into separate categorized documents (examples of categories include responses about mothers and fathers, sibling order, childhood personalities, influential individuals during childhood, important childhood events, childhood activities, youth employment, influential school teachers, and so forth).

4. *In-depth analysis:* resulting in the identification of key ideas and phrases about the presidents' experiences related to each category (these were based on a reread of each interview transcription and preliminary analysis).

5. *Theme generation:* resulting in an assembling of the emerging themes based on the interview phrases or statements on each topic and category. The presidents then reviewed the themes and results, section by section, and provided corrections or additional perspective and insight that may not have been captured in the original interviews.

To ensure accuracy, the presidents read and provided feedback for each chapter in this book. With this type of research method, it is very important that the analysis and writings accurately represent the presidents' true perceptions and experiences.

1. **Personal information** (age, ethnicity, vita/résumé, work positions)

2. **Childhood**

a.	Family background:	Parents/guardians, occupations, home environment, siblings, birth order, extended family, hometown, expectations, era
b.	Activities:	Sports, 4-H, art, plays, choir, clubs, church, business ventures, etc.
c.	Influential individuals:	Parents, relatives, neighbors, teachers, church members, coaches, role models, mentors, other
d.	Significant events	
e.	Challenges and opportunities	
f.	Childhood personality	

3. **Youth**

a.	Change:	Family structure or situation, hometown, responsibility, etc.
b.	Activities:	Sports, 4-H, dance, art, plays, choir, clubs, church, etc.

c. Influential individuals:

Parents, relatives, neighbors, teachers, church members, coaches, friends, role models, mentors, peers, boyfriends, authority figures who recognized leadership ability

d. Significant events:

Influence on leadership development, leadership training and development, stories, challenges, opportunities

e. Employment:

Paid and volunteer

f. Leadership positions:

Formal and informal

g. Recognitions:

Awards, titles, other

h. Style and values:

Leadership, personality, self-esteem, strengths, learning preferences, important values, work ethic/experiences

i. Competency development:

Events, individuals, opportunities: networking, leading change, interpersonal skills, viewing barriers/crises as opportunities, learning from mistakes, inspiring others, accepting and learning from feedback/criticism, reflection, problem solving, focus on results, taking a stand, confidence

4. **Young adulthood and college years** (3a–i and the following)

a. Background:

Age, living situation, family influence, social influences, degrees/coursework, career plan

b. Leadership opportunities:

Types, reasons for seeking them, responsibilities, factors that influenced interest in leadership

c. Educational preparation:

Focused on leadership

d. Personal characteristics:

Traits, abilities, skills, self-esteem, self-efficacy

5. Professional positions and experiences

a. Short history:
Official positions, travel, work hours, informal leadership roles and influence, committee/service work (assigned/volunteer), passion, interest, drive

b. Leadership motivation:
Desire to serve, need, self-actualization, desire for achievement or accomplishment

c. Influential individuals:
Mentors, coaches, role models, peers, those who recognized leadership abilities

d. Developmental activities:
Leadership training and development, research/publishing, teaching, job rotation, stories, mistakes, challenges, networking, service (explore links to development of leadership competencies)

e. Support systems:
Policies, colleagues, supervisors, peers, staff, culture, flexibility, and visible work assignments

f. Personal development strategies:
Learning preferences

g. Recognitions:
Awards, titles

h. Competency development:
See list in other sections.

i. Career path:
Formal, informal, details

j. Style and values:
Leadership, personality, self-esteem, strengths, important values and ethics, attitude

k. Self-knowledge:
Self-monitoring, self-directed learner, sense of uniqueness, personal power, need for acknowledgment

l. Career goals, aspirations, motivations
Satisfaction, areas for improvement, final goals, barriers/glass ceiling perceptions, things that may have been different if you were a man

6. Non-work roles

a. Background/ influences:	Marital status, spouse/significant other's role, children (number and ages), parental influences, family support, religion/ spirituality, health, career breaks, personal sacrifices
b. Activities/ involvement:	Community, volunteer, schools, politics, neighborhood
c. KSA developed from nonwork areas:	Motherhood, volunteer work, community involvement, hobbies, social opportunities, networking
d. Work–family strategies:	Compartmentalization, integration, priorities, multiple roles, conflict, challenges, benefits
e. Influential individuals:	Role models, mentors, friends

7. Leadership philosophy

8. Leadership advice

APPENDIX C

Previous Positions Held by the Ten Women Presidents

The following table lists all of the ten women presidents' previous positions, providing both position titles and the number of presidents who served in each position. Review and reflect on this information, as some interesting themes emerge.

Title	No. of Women	Title	No. of Women
Accreditation officer/coordinator	2	Associate dean for academic affairs	1
Adjunct college instructor	3	Associate dean for continuing education	1
Assistant professor	6	Associate director of continuing education	1
Assistant VP for academic affairs	1	Associate in H.E. opportunity	1
Assistant VP for community partnerships	1	Associate professor	5
Assistant VP for finance	1	Associate VP/VC of budget and finance	1
Associate chair	1	Board of regents administrator/ consultant	3
Associate dean, academic school	3		

(Continued)

Title	No. of Women	Title	No. of Women
Budget analyst	1	Full-time instructor	4
Business officer (non-education)	1	Instructional developer	1
		Instructor of special programs	1
Commission on H.E. administration	1	Interim/acting president or chancellor	2
Consultant	2		
COO (educational setting)	1	K–12 classroom teacher	4
		Manager of budget/planning	1
Curriculum development, chair/coordinator	2	Non-educational agency director	1
Dean, academic school	1	Principal	1
Dean, undergraduate programs	1	Professor	6
		Research fellow	2
Dean, graduate school	1	Researcher, lab	2
Department chair	1	Special assistant/ assistant to the president	3
Director of community leadership program	1		
Director of finance	1	Teaching assistant	1
Director of graduate programs	1	Vice provost	1
		VP of community relations	1
Director of institutional research	1	VP of government/ community relations	1
Director of office of field studies	1		
		VP of research	1
Director of outreach	1	VP/VC for administration	2
Director of professional development	1		
		VP/VC for finance	2
Education coordinator	1	VP/VC/provost of academic affairs	5
Faculty union leader	1		
Family counselor	1		

References

Academic Medicine. (1996). Increasing women's leadership in academic medicine. *Academic Medicine, 71*(7), 799–811.

Ahn, M. J., Adamson, J. S. A., & Dornbusch, D. (2004). From leaders to leadership: Managing change. *The Journal of Leadership & Organizational Studies, 10*(4), 112–123.

Aldoory, L. (1998). The language of leadership for female public relations professionals. *Journal of Public Relations Research, 10*(2), 73–101.

Anonymous. (2005). Girls work in teams. Boys take it on themselves. *Management Services, 49*(1), 12–13.

Appelbaum, S. H., Audet, L., & Miller, J. C. (2003). Gender and leadership? Leadership and gender? A journey through the landscape of theories. *Leadership & Organization Development Journal, 24*(1/2), 43–51.

Arthur, M. B., Claman, P. H., & DeFillippi, R. J. (1995). Intelligent enterprise, intelligent careers. *Academy of Management Executive, 9*(4), 7–22.

Astin, H. S., & Leland, C. (1991). *Women of influence, women of vision: Across-generational study of leaders and social change.* San Francisco: Jossey-Bass.

Atwater, L. E., & Yammarino, F. J. (1992). Does self-other agreement on leadership perceptions moderate the validity of leadership and performance predictions? *Personnel Psychology, 45*(1), 141–164.

Ayman, R., Adams, S., Fisher, B., & Hartman, E. (2003). Leadership development in higher education institutions: A present and future perspective. In S. E. Murphy & R. E. Riggio (Eds.), *The future of leadership development* (pp. 201–222). Mahwah, NJ: Erlbaum.

Baraka-Love, J. N. (1986). Successful women: A racial comparison of variables contributing to socialization and leadership development. (Doctoral dissertation, Western Michigan University, 1986). *ProQuest*, AAT 8714653.

Baruch, Y., & Hall, D. T. (2004a). Preface for the JVB special issue on careers in academia. *Journal of Vocational Behavior, 64*(2), 237–240.

Baruch, Y., & Hall, D. T. (2004b). The academic career: A model for future careers in other sectors? *Journal of Vocational Behavior, 64*(2), 241–262.

Bass, B. M. (1990). *Bass & Stogdill's handbook of leadership: Theory, research, & managerial applications* (3rd ed.). New York: The Free Press.

Bennett, S. M., & Shayner, J. A. (1988). The role of senior administrators in women's leadership development. In M. D. Sagaria (Ed.), *Empowering women: Leadership development strategies on campus.* New Directions for Student Services, No. 44 (pp. 27–38). San Francisco: Jossey-Bass.

Bennis, W. (1989). *On becoming a leader.* Boston: Addison-Wesley.

Bennis, W. G., & Goldsmith, J. (2003). *Learning to lead: A workbook on becoming a leader* (3rd ed.). New York: Basic Books.

Boatwright, K. J., & Egidio, R. K. (2003). Psychological predictors of college women's leadership. *Journal of College Student Development 44*(5), 653–669.

Burke, S., & Collins, K. M. (2001). Gender differences in leadership styles and management skills. *Women in Management Review, 16*(5/6), 244–256.

Caffarella, R. C., & Barnett, B. G. (1997). Psychosocial development of women: Linking this literature to the study of leadership. *Journal of Adult Education, 25*(1), 2–16.

Caffarella, R. S. (1992). *Psychosocial development of women: Linkages to teaching and leadership in adult education.* Columbus, Ohio: ERIC Clearinghouse on Adult, Career, and Vocational Education (Information Series No. 35).

Caffarella, R. S., & Olson, S. K. (1993). Psychosocial development of women: A critical review of the literature. *Adult Education Quarterly, 43*(3), 125–151.

Cantor, D. W. & Bernay, T. (1992). *Women in power.* New York: Houghton Mifflin.

Carlson, D. S., Kacmar, K. M., & Williams, L. J. (2000). Construction and initial validation of a multidimensional measure of work-family conflict. *Journal of Vocational Behavior, 56*(2), 249–276.

Chao, G. T., Walz, P. M., & Gardner, P. D. (1992). Formal and informal mentorships: A comparison on mentoring functions and contrast with nonmentored counterparts. *Personnel Psychology, 45*(3), 619–636.

Cheng, B. D. (1988). *A profile of selected women leaders: Toward a new model of leadership* [Abstract]. (ERIC Document Reproduction Service No. ED303397)

Chrisler, J. C., Herr, L., & Murstein, N. K. (1998). Women as faculty leaders. In L. H. Collins, J. C. Chrisler, & K. Quina (Eds.), *Career strategies for women in academe: Arming Athena* (pp. 189–208). Thousand Oaks, CA: Sage.

Clark M. C., Caffarella, R. S., & Ingram, P. B. (1999). Women in leadership: Living with the constraints of the glass ceiling. *Initiatives, 59*(1), 65–75.

Cohen, J. *et al.* (1996). *Girls in the middle: Working to succeed in school* [Abstract]. Annapolis Junction, MD: AAUW. (ERIC Document Reproduction Service No. ED402005)

Collins, J. (2001). *Good to great: Why some companies make the leap. . .and others don't.* New York: HarperBusiness.

Collins, K. M., & Killough, L. N. (1992). An empirical examination of stress in public accounting. *Accounting, Organizations, and Society, 17*(6), 535–547.

Collins, L. H., Chrisler, J. C., & Quina, K. (Eds.). (1998). *Career strategies for women in academe: Arming Athena.* Thousand Oaks, CA: Sage.

Cooke, L. H. (2004). *Finding the self who leads: From one woman's perspective.* Unpublished doctoral dissertation, University of North Carolina at Greensboro, Greensboro, NC.

Cornwall, D. J. (1993). Women and work. *Harvard Business Review, 71*(5), 184.

Coutu, D. L. (2004). Putting leaders on the couch: A conversation with Manfred F. R. Kets de Vries. *Harvard Business Review, 82*(1), 65–71.

Crosby, F. K. (1991). *Juggling: The unexpected advantages of balancing career and home for women and their families.* New York: Free Press.

Cubillo, L. & Brown, M. (2003). Women into educational leadership and management: International differences? *Journal of Educational Administration, 41*(3), 278–291.

Cullen, D. L., & Luna, G. (1993). Women mentoring in academe: Addressing the gender gap in higher education. *Gender & Education, 5*(2), 125–137.

D'Abate, C. P., Eddy, E. R., & Tannenbaum, S. I. (2003). What's in a name? A literature-based approach to understanding mentoring, coaching, and other constructs that describe developmental interactions. *Human Resource Development Review, 2*(4), 360–384.

Day, D. V., & O'Connor, P. M. G. (2003). Leadership development: Understanding the process. In S. E. Murphy & R. E. Riggio (Eds.), *The future of leadership development* (pp. 11–28). Mahwah, NJ: Erlbaum.

Day, D. V., Schleicher, D. J., Unckless, A. L., & Hiller, N. J. (2002). Self-monitoring personality at work: A meta-analytic investigation of construct validity. *Journal of Applied Psychology, 87*(2), 390–401.

De la Rey, C. & Suffla, S. (2003). Women's leadership programs in South Africa: A strategy for community intervention. *Journal of Prevention & Intervention in the Community, 25*(1), 49–64.

DeNitto, D., Aguilar, M. A., Franklin, C., & Jordan, C. (1995). Over the edge? Women and tenure in today's academic environment. *Affilia: Journal of Women & Social Work, 10*(3), 255–279.

Dickerson, A., & Taylor, M. A. (2000). Self-limiting behavior in women. *Group & Organization Management, 25*(2), 191–210.

Drucker, P. F. (2001). *The essential Drucker.* New York: HarperCollins.

Drucker, P. F. (1988). The coming of the new organization. *Harvard Business Review, 66*(1), 45–54.

Dunlap, D. M., & Schmuck, P. A. (Eds.). (1995). *Women leading in education.* Albany: State University of New York Press.

Ebbers, L. H., Gallisath, G., Rockel, V., & Coyan, M. N. (2000). The leadership institute for a new century: LINCing women and minorities into tomorrow's community college leadership roles. *Community College Journal of Research and Practice, 24*(5), 375–382.

Egan, T. M., & Rosser, M. H. (2004, February). Do formal mentoring programs matter? A longitudinal randomized experimental study of women healthcare workers. Paper presented at the 2004 annual international research conference of the Academy of Human Resource Development, Austin, TX.

Enkelis, L., Olsen, K., Lewenstein, M., & Applegate, J. (1995). *On our own terms: Portraits of women business leaders.* San Francisco: Berrett-Koehler.

Erickson, V. L. (1978). The development of women: An issue of justice. In P. Scarf (Ed.), *Readings in moral education* (pp. 110–122). Minneapolis: Winston Press.

Ernst, R. J. (1982). Women in higher education leadership positions—It doesn't happen by accident. *Journal of the College and University Personnel Association, 33*(2), 19–22.

Farkas, C. M., & Wetlaufer, S. (1996). The ways chief executive officers lead. *Harvard Business Review, 74*(3), 110–121.

Fels, A. (2004). Do women lack ambition? *Harvard Business Review, 82*(4), 50–60.

Fennell, H. (2005). Living leadership in an era of change. *International Journal of Leadership in Education, 8*(2), 145–165.

Fisher, V. D. (1991). Women and leadership: Do sororities help or hinder? *Campus Activities Programming, 24*(4), 64–66.

Galambos, C. M., & Hughes, S. L. (2000). Using political and community activism to develop leadership skills in women. *Race, Gender & Class, 7*(4), 18–36.

Glazer-Raymo, J. (1999). *Shattering the myths: Women in academe.* Baltimore, MD: John Hopkins University Press.

Goldwasser, S. W. (1988). Competency and success: A study of women business leaders. (Doctoral dissertation, Georgia State University, 1988). *ProQuest,* AAT 8910183.

Green, C. E., & King, V. G. (2001). Sisters mentoring sisters: Africentric leadership development for black women in the academy. *Journal of Negro Education, 70*(3), 156–165.

Greenhaus, J. H., & Powell, G. N. (2006). When work and family are allies: A theory of work-family enrichment. *Academy of Management Review, 31*(1), 72–92.

Growe, R., & Montgomery, P. (1999). *Women and the leadership paradigm: Bridging the gender gap.* (ERIC Document Reproduction Service No. ED452614)

Guido-DiBrito, F., & Batchelor, S. W. (1988). Developing leadership potential through student activities and organizations. In M. D. Sagaria (Ed.), *Empowering women: Leadership development strategies on campus.* New Directions for Student Services, No. 44 (pp. 51–62). San Francisco: Jossey-Bass.

Gupton, S. L., & Slick, G. A. (1996). *Highly successful women administrators: The inside stories of how they got there.* Thousand Oaks, CA: Corwin Press.

Gupton, S. L., & Del Rosario, R. M. (1997, March). *An analyses of federal initiatives to support women's upward mobility in educational administration.* Paper presented at the annual meeting of the American Educational Research Association, Chicago, IL.

Hammond, L. A., & Fong, M. L. (1988, August). *Mediator of stress and role satisfaction in multiple role persons.* Paper presented at the annual meeting of the American Psychological Association, Atlanta, GA.

Haring-Hidore, M., Freeman, S. C., Phelps, S. Spann, N. G., & Wooten, H. R. (1990). Women administrators' ways of knowing. *Education and Urban Society, 22*(2), 170–181.

Hartman, M. S. (Ed.). (1999). *Talking leadership: Conversations with powerful women.* New Brunswick, NJ: Rutgers University Press.

Helgesen, S. (1995). *The female advantage: Women's ways of leadership.* New York: Doubleday.

Hennig, M., & Jardim, A. (1977). *The managerial women.* Garden City, NY: Anchor Press/Doubleday.

Hill, M. S., & Ragland, J. C. (1995). *Women as educational leaders: Opening windows, pushing ceilings.* Thousand Oaks, CA: Corwin Press.

Hojaard, L. (2002). Tracing differentiation in gendered leadership: An analysis of differences in gender composition in top management in business, politics and the civil service. *Gender, Work and Organization, 9*(1), 15–38.

Hoy, W. K, & Miskel, C. G. (2005). *Educational administration: Theory, research, and practice* (7th ed.). New York: McGraw-Hill.

Jurgens, J. C., & Dodd, J. L. (2003). Women's institute for leadership development: A W.I.L.D. venture. *College Student Affairs Journal, 22*(2), 195–202.

Kaminski, M. (2003). Teaching leadership to union women: The use of stories. *Labor Studies Journal, 28*(2), 67–77.

Katira, K. (2003). Learning, leading, and teaching for justice: Celebrating Aisha—a friend, colleague and leader [1]. *International Journal of Leadership in Education*, 6(3), 251–260.

Kelinske, B., Mayer, B. W., & Chen, K. (2001). Perceived benefits from participation in sports: A gender study. *Women in Management Review*, 16(2), 75–84.

Kelly, R. M., & Marin, A. J. D. (1998) Position power and women's career advancement. *Women in Management Review*, 13(2), 53–66.

Keown, C. F., & Keown, A. L. (1982). Successful factors for corporate woman executives. *Group & Organization Studies*, 7(4), 446–456.

King, P. M., & Bauer, B. A. (1988). Leadership issues for nontraditional-aged women students. In M. D. Sagaria (Ed.), *Empowering women: Leadership development strategies on campus*. New Directions for Student Services, No. 44 (pp. 77–88). San Francisco: Jossey-Bass.

Klenke, K. (1996). *Women and leadership: A contextual perspective*. New York: Springer.

Kochan, F. K. (2002). Examining the organizational and human dimensions of mentoring: A textual data analysis. In F. K. Kochan (Ed.), *The organizational and human dimensions of successful mentoring programs and relationships* (pp. 259–286). Greenwich, CT: Information Age Publishing.

Koonce, R. (2004, October) Women-only executive development. *T&D*, 58(10), 78–85.

Korabik, K. (1990). Androgyny and leadership style. *Journal of Business Ethics*, 9(4, 5), 283–292.

Kotter, J. P. (1996). *Leading change*. Boston: Harvard Business School Press.

Kram, K. E. (1988). *Mentoring at work: Developmental relationships in organizational life*. Lanham, MD: University Press of America.

Leonard, R. (1981, April). *Managerial styles in academe: Do men and women differ?* Paper presented at the annual meeting of the Southern Speech Communication Association, Austin, TX.

Lewis, A. E., & Fagenson, E. A. (1995). Strategies for developing women managers: How well do they fare? *Journal of Management Development, 14*(2), 39–53.

Loeffler, T. A. (2000). The seasons of competency development for women. *Pathways: The Ontario Journal of Outdoor Education, 12*(4), 4–8.

Lombardo, M. M., & Eichinger, R. W. (2000). High potentials as high learners. *Human Resource Management, 39*(4), 321–329.

Lorenzen, Z. (1996). Female leadership: Some personal and professional reflections. *Leadership & Organization Development Journal, 17*(6), 24–31.

Lyman, L. L. (1995). Connected knowing: A leadership seminar for women. *Journal of School Leadership, 5*(3), 204–219.

Marongiu, S., & Ekehammar, B. (1999). Internal and external influences on women's and men's entry into management. *Journal of Managerial Psychology, 14*(5/6), 421–435.

Mattis, M. C. (2001). Advancing women in business organizations: Key leadership roles and behaviors of senior leaders and middle managers. *Journal of Management Development, 20*(4), 371–388.

Matz, S. I. (2002). *Women leaders: Their styles, confidence, and influences.* Unpublished doctoral dissertation, Claremont Graduate University, Claremont, CA.

McCaffery, P. (2004). *The higher education manager's handbook: Effective leadership and management in colleges and universities.* New York: Routledge.

McCall, M. W., Lombardo, M. M., & Morrison, A. M. (1988). *The lessons of experience: How successful executives develop on the job.* New York: Free Press.

McCauley, C. D., & Young, D. P. (1993). Creating developmental relationship: Roles and strategies. *Human Resource Management Review, 3*(3), 219–230.

McDonald, K. S., & Hite, L. M. (1999). HRD initiatives contributing to women's career progress. *Performance Improvement, 38*(9), 35–41.

Merriam-Webster Online Dictionary. (2006). *Encourager*. Retrieved December 27, 2006 from http://www.m-w.com/.

Micas, S. S. (1991). The WILL program: An undergraduate leadership program for women. *Initiatives, 53*(4), 19–24.

Moore, K. M., & Amey, M. J. (1988). Some faculty leaders are born women. In M. D. Sagaria (Ed.), *Empowering women: Leadership development strategies on campus*. New directions for student services, No. 44 (pp. 39–50). San Francisco: Jossey-Bass.

Morrison, A. M., White, R. P., & Van Velsor, E. (1994). *Breaking the glass ceiling: Can women reach the top of America's largest corporations?* Reading, MA: Addison-Wesley.

Murphy, S. E., & Riggio, R. E. (Eds.). (2003) *The future of leadership development*. Mahwah, NJ: Erlbaum.

Nidiffer, J. (2001). New leadership for a new century. In J. Nidiffer & C. T. Bashaw (Eds.), *Women administrators in higher education: Historical and contemporary perspectives* (pp. 101–131). New York: State University of New York Press.

Nidiffer, J. N., & Bashaw, C. T. (Eds.). (2001). *Women administrators in higher education: Historical and contemporary perspectives*. New York: State University of New York Press.

Noe, R. A., Greenberger, D. B., & Wang, S. (2002). Mentoring: What we know and where we might go. In G. R. Ferris & J. J. Martocchio (Eds.), *Research in personnel and human resources management, Volume 21* (pp. 129–174). Amsterdam, London: JAI, Elsevier Science.

Olsson, S., & Pringle, J. K. (2004). Women executives: Public and private sectors as sites of advancement? *Women in Management Review, 19*(1/2), 29–39.

Olsson, S. (2002). Gendered heroes: Male and female self-representations of executive identity. *Women in Management Review, 17*(3/4), 142–150.

Orenstein, R. L. (2002). Executive coaching: It's not just about the executive. *Journal of Applied Behavioral Science, 38*(3), 355–374.

Pankake, A. M., Schroth, G., & Funk, C. (2000a). Successful women superintendents: Developing as leaders, learning from failure. *ERS Spectrum, 18*(1), 3–13.

Pankake, A., Schroth, G., & Funk, C. (Eds.). (2000b). *Women as school executives: The complete picture.* Austin, TX: Texas Council of Women School Executives.

Park, D. (1997). Androgynous leadership style: An integration rather than a polarization. *Leadership & Organization Development Journal, 18*(3), 166–171.

Pence, L. J. (1995). Learning leadership through mentorships. In D. M. Dunlap & P. A. Schmuck (Eds.), *Women leading in education* (pp. 125–144). Albany: State University of New York Press.

Pini, B., Brown, K., & Ryan, C. (2004). Women-only networks as a strategy for change? A case study from local government. *Women in Management Review, 19*(6), 286–292.

Rayburn, C. A., Goetz, D. J., & Osman, S. L. (2001). The 'game' of leadership: Exercise, games, sports, and leadership. *International Journal of Value-Based management, 14*, 11–26.

Robinson, F. (1996). African American women leaders in the community college: Where they get their strength. *Thresholds in Education, 22*(1), 49–52.

Rotheram, M. J., & Armstrong, M. (1980). Assertiveness training with high school students. *Adolescence, 15*(58), 267–276.

Ruben, B. D. (2003). *Pursuing excellence in higher education: Eight fundamental challenges*. San Francisco: Jossey-Bass.

Ruderman, M. N., Ohlott, P. J., Panzer, K., & King, S. N. (2002). Benefits of multiple roles for managerial women. *Academy of Management Journal*, *45*(2), 369–386.

Sagaria, M. D. (1988). The case for empowering women as leaders in higher education. In M. D. Sagaria (Ed.), *Empowering women: Leadership development strategies on campus*. New Directions for Student Services, No. 44 (pp. 5–11). San Francisco: Jossey-Bass.

Scanlon, K. C. (1997). Mentoring women adminstrators: Breaking through the glass ceiling. *Initiatives*, *58*(2), 39–59.

Schein, E. H. (2004). *Organizational Culture and Leadership* (3rd. ed.). San Francisco: Jossey-Bass.

Shakeshaft, C. (1989). *Women in educational administration*. Newbury Park, CA: Corwin Press.

Shaw-Hardy, S. (1998). Executive women in development: Career paths, life choices, and advancing to the top. In J. C. Conroy (Ed.), *Women as fundraisers*. New Directions for Philanthropic Fundraising, No. 19 (27–52). San Francisco: Jossey-Bass.

Sills, C. K. (1994). Paths to leadership: Building middle school girls' self-esteem. *Feminist Teacher*, *8*(2), 61–66.

Stephens, J. (2003). The rhetoric of women's leadership: Language, memory and imagination. *Journal of Leadership and Organizational Studies*, *9*(3), 45–60.

Stiles, D. A. (1986). Leadership training for high school girls: An intervention at one school. *Journal of Counseling and Development*, *65*, 211–212.

Sullivan, L. (2003). Learning to lead. *Risk Management*, *50*(6), 48–51.

Taylor, V., & Conradie, I. (1997). *"We have been taught by life itself." Empowering women as leaders: The role of development education*. Pretoria 1000, South Africa: Human Sciences Research Council (HSRC) Publishers.

Thompson, J. J., & Marley, M. A. (1999). Women in human services management: Continued issues and concerns. *Administration in Social Work*, 23(2), 17–31.

Twale, D. J., & Shannon, D. M. (1996). Gender differences among faculty in campus governance: Nature of involvement, satisfaction, and power. *Initiatives*, 57(4), 11–19.

Van Velsor, E., & Hughes, M. W. (1990). *Gender differences in the development of managers: How women managers learn from experience* (Report No. 145). Greensboro, NC: Center for Creative Leadership. (ERIC Document Reproduction Service No. ED 334511)

Van Velsor, E., Taylor, S., & Leslie, J. B. (1993). An examination of the relationships among self-perception accuracy, self-awareness, gender, and leader effectiveness. *Human Resource Management (1986–1998)*, 32(2–3), 249–264.

Vinnicombe, S., & Singh, V. (2003). Women-only management training: An essential part of women's leadership development. *Journal of Change Management*, 3(4), 294–306.

Walsh, D. C. (2006). *Trustworthy leadership: Can we be the leaders we need our students to become?* Kalamazoo, MI: Fetzer Institute.

Walton, K. D. (Ed.). (1996). *Against the tide: Career paths of women leaders in American and British higher education*. Bloomington, ID: Phi Delta Kappa Educational Foundation.

Walton, K. D., & McDade, S. A. (2001). At the top of the faculty: Women as chief academic officers. In J. Nidiffer & C. T. Bashaw (Eds.), *Women administrators in higher education: Historical and contemporary perspectives* (pp. 85–100). New York: State University of New York Press.

Waring, A. L. (2003). African-American female college presidents: Self conceptions of leadership. *Journal of Leadership and Organizational Studies*, 9(3), 31–44.

Watson, C. (1988). When a woman is the boss: Dilemmas in taking charge. *Group and Organization Studies*, 13(2), 163–181.

Weick, A. (1983, March). A growth-task model of human development. *Social Casework: The Journal of Contemporary Social Work*, 131–137.

Wells, S. J. (1998). *Women entrepreneurs: Developing leadership for success*. New York: Garland.

Wesson, L. H. (1998). Exploring the dilemmas of leadership: Voices from the field. *Advancing Women in Leadership*, *1*(2). Retrieved November 14, 2005 from http://www.advancingwomen.com/awl/winter98/awlv2_wesson4final.html.

What presidents think about higher education, their jobs, and their lives. (2005, November 4). *Chronicles of Higher Education*, A25–A39.

White, K. (2003). Women and leadership in higher education in Australia. *Tertiary Education and Management*, *9*(1), 45–60.

Wilder, D. H., Hoyt, A. E., Surbeck, B. S., Wilder, J. C., & Carney, P. I. (1986). Greek affliction and attitude change in college students. *Journal of College Student Personnel*, *27*(6), 510–519.

Wisker, G. (1996). *Empowering women in higher education*. Sterling, VA: Kogan Page.

Woo, L. C. (1985). Women administrators: Profiles of success. *Phi Delta Kappan*, *67*(4), 285–288.

Wood, J. T. (2006). *Gendered lives: Communication, gender and culture*. Belmont, CA: Wadsworth.

WorldofQuotes.com (2007). *Historical quotes and proverbs archive*. Retrieved on January 24, 2007 from http://www.worldofquotes.com/author/Anthony-Jay/1/.

Zenger, J. H., & Folkman, J. (2002). *The extraordinary leader: Turning good mangers into great leaders*. New York: McGraw-Hill.

Index